T0387948

DOCTRINE AND DISEASE IN THE BRITISH AND SPANISH COLONIAL WORLD

Doctrine and Disease in the British and Spanish Colonial World

EDITED BY KATHLEEN MILLER

The Pennsylvania State University Press

University Park, Pennsylvania

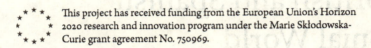
This project has received funding from the European Union's Horizon 2020 research and innovation program under the Marie Skłodowska-Curie grant agreement No. 750969.

Library of Congress Cataloging-in-Publication Data

Names: Miller, Kathleen (Writer on English literature), editor.
Title: Doctrine and disease in the British and Spanish colonial world / edited by Kathleen Miller.
Description: University Park, Pennsylvania : The Pennsylvania State University Press, [2025] | Includes bibliographical references and index.
Summary: "Explores the intersection of religion and medicine in the early modern Atlantic world, reflecting how illness and the body were interpreted within diverse cultural and spiritual contexts"—Provided by publisher.
Identifiers: LCCN 2025004449 | ISBN 9780271099828 (hardback)
Subjects: LCSH: Medicine—Religious aspects. | Medicine—America—History. | America—Religion. | America—History—To 1810. | Great Britain—Colonies—America. | Spain—Colonies—America.
Classification: LCC BL65.M4 .D63 2025 | DDC 201/.661—dc23/eng/20250401
LC record available at https://lccn.loc.gov/2025004449

Copyright © 2025 The Pennsylvania State University
All rights reserved
Printed in the United States of America
Published by The Pennsylvania State University Press,
University Park, PA 16802–1003

The Pennsylvania State University Press is a member of the Association of University Presses.

It is the policy of The Pennsylvania State University Press to use acid-free paper. Publications on uncoated stock satisfy the minimum requirements of American National Standard for Information Sciences—Permanence of Paper for Printed Library Material, ANSI Z39.48–1992.

CONTENTS

List of Illustrations   vi

Acknowledgments   vii

Introduction   1
Kathleen Miller

1   The Secularization of Nature: Jesuit Missionaries and Indigenous
    Healing Knowledge in Early Modern Peru (1590–1710)   16
    Matthew James Crawford

2   Vaccinating in the Name of the Lord: The Catholic Church and
    the Extension of Smallpox Vaccination in the Spanish Empire
    (1803–1810)   40
    Allyson M. Poska

3   John Owen, Plague, and the Meanings of Disaster   56
    Crawford Gribben

4   Maternal Bodies: Religion, Medicine, and Politics in Early America
    and the Atlantic World   74
    Philippa Koch

5   Printing England's Plague Past in New England   100
    Kathleen Miller

6   Contagious Fasts: Occasional Worship and Medical Practice in England
    and Massachusetts Bay Colony   117
    Catherine Reedy

7   Enslaved Bodies and the White Imagination: (Mis)Perceptions of Dirt
    Eating on Jamaican Plantations   150
    Rana A. Hogarth

Afterword   175
Rebecca Totaro

List of Contributors   187

Index   191

ILLUSTRATIONS

4.1. Hans Memling, *Virgin and Child*, ca. 1475–1480   77

4.2. John Singleton Copley, *The Nativity*, ca. 1776   78

4.3. Benjamin West, *The Artist and His Family*, ca. 1772   79

4.4. Plate highlighting the dimensions of the pelvis, from Jean-Louis Baudelocque, *A System of Midwifery*, 1790   86

6.1. Joseph Tompson, *Journal*, "O sorowfull year"   127

6.2. Joseph Tompson's covenant signature, *Journal*   129

6.3. Joseph Tompson, *Journal*   130

ACKNOWLEDGMENTS

My sincere thanks to Matthew James Crawford, Allyson M. Poska, Crawford Gribben, Philippa Koch, Catherine Reedy, and Rana A. Hogarth for their wonderful contributions to this volume and the significant insights their research brought to the subject. Thank you to Rebecca Totaro for composing an afterword that beautifully frames the essays and for her interest in this project.

I greatly appreciate the support I have received from Penn State University Press. Tristan Bates and Josie DiKerby have provided ongoing guidance to see the book through to publication. I am also grateful for Katherine Yahner's early enthusiasm for the project.

I would also like to thank Crawford Gribben and Alan Bewell for their guidance on my Marie Skłodowska-Curie Postdoctoral Fellowship, which included the work toward this collection.

Finally, thank you to my family—Alan, Chloe, Finian, and Savannah—for their support while I worked on this book.

Introduction

KATHLEEN MILLER

As a young adult, Anne Bradstreet traveled across the Atlantic from her birth-place in England and landed in Salem, Massachusetts, in 1630.[1] At sixteen and while still living in England, Bradstreet had suffered a bout of smallpox; throughout her life, and after her arrival in New England, she endured periods of poor health and sickness.[2] Bradstreet's experiences of illness in conjunction with her religious fervor as a Puritan became central subjects in the verse she composed, and Bradstreet would gain a reputation as "the first female poet and the first colonial poet in English."[3] When an edition of Bradstreet's writing was published in 1650 in England, titled *The Tenth Muse Lately Sprung Up in America*, allegedly without the poet's permission and while she resided in New England, it included the poem "A Dialogue Between Old England and New, Concerning Their Present Troubles. Anno 1642." A later version of the collection would be published in Boston by John Foster as *Several Poems Compiled with Great Variety of Wit and Learning, Full of Delight Wherein Especially Is Contained a Compleat Discourse, and Description of the Four Elements, Constitutions, Ages of Man, Seasons of the Year* (1678). In "A Dialogue Between Old England and New," Bradstreet constructs an exchange between the England she left behind and the New England where she settled, describing the numerous afflictions and strug-gles suffered by England. At the heart of the debate is the civil war in England. Bradstreet devises an Atlantic divide represented by Old England as an ailing mother and New England as her daughter. When New England asks, "Alas, deare Mother, fairest Queen, and best, / With honour, wealth, and peace, happy and

2 DOCTRINE AND DISEASE

blest, / What ayles thee hang thy head, and cross thine armes? / And sit i' th
dust, to sigh these sad alarms?" Old England responds by describing her body
and health in decline:

> Art ignorant indeed, of these my woes?
> Or must my forced tongue these griefes disclose?
> And must my selfe dissect my tatter'd state,
> Which 'mazed Christendome stands wondring at?
> And thou a childe, a Limbe, and dost not feele
> My weakned fainting body now to reele?
> This Phisick-purging-potion I have taken,
> Will bring Consumption, or an Ague quaking,
> Unlesse some Cordial thou fetch from high,
> Which present help may ease this malady.
> If I decease, dost think thou shalt survive?
> Or by my wasting state, dost think to thrive?[4]

The mother figure of Old England is afflicted with an illness that leaves her in
a "wasting state." She takes a purging potion, but the source of the illness is
not physiological; instead, her medical strife is occasioned by religious unrest.
When New England asks, "What Medicine shall I seek to cure this woe, / If th'
wound's so dangerous *I* may not know?" Old England responds,

> Before I tell the effect, ile shew the cause,
> Which are my Sins, the breach of sacred Lawes;
> Idolatry, supplanter of a Nation,
> With foolish superstitious adoration;
> And lik'd, and countenanc'd by men of might,
> The Gospel is trod down, and hath no right;
> Church Offices are sold, and bought, for gaine,
> That Pope, had hope, to finde *Rome* here againe;
> For Oathes, and Blasphemies did ever care
> From *Beelzebub* himself, such language heare?
> What scorning of the Saints of the most high,[5]

Bradstreet easily conflates geographical, medical, and religious concerns. She
captures how closely related issues of medicine and religion were for Puritans

INTRODUCTION 3

who had left behind England for a land they believed promised religious freedom. For early New England settlers, medicine and religion were almost indivisible. Often the same men who preached as ministers served as doctors, and as Jean Marie Lutes explains in "Negotiating Theology and Gynecology: Anne Bradstreet's Representations of the Female Body," the lines between medicine and religion were largely porous in Puritan New England: "Medical treatment and religious attitudes affected each other in many concrete ways in Bradstreet's world."[6] Though the physical manifestation of illness in Old England is wide-ranging, many of the symptoms she describes were common features of the illnesses that blighted England and New England in the early modern period. Old England describes her body pestered by sores—"I must confesse, some of those Sores you name, / My beauteous Body at this present mime"—similar to those that might appear during a plague or smallpox outbreak, afflictions that both wrote their symptoms on the body and terrorized England (plague and smallpox) and New England (smallpox).[7] It was not only the arriving settlers in New England who viewed medicine with a religious worldview. Within both Native and colonial populations, some level of spirituality was closely tied to the delivery of medical care in colonial America. While there was a shift toward empiricism in British medicine as the seventeenth century progressed, this was delivered within the context of religious reasoning. In a similar way, the medical practices of the Native Americans, as diverse as they were, often hinged on the understanding that the diseases they were familiar with and health more generally were closely tied to spirits and spiritual matters.[8]

Within the Spanish New World, Sor Juana Inés de La Cruz, who was born in San Miguel Nepantla, Viceroyalty of New Spain (Mexico), was a contemporary of Bradstreet. Sor Juana composed poetry and dramatic works that gained significant popularity in Latin America. Suzanne Shimek notes in her comparative study of Sor Juana's and Bradstreet's verse that the two writers "invite comparison: they were two of the first published poets in the European colonies, they both struggled with religious faith."[9] Sor Juana's writing was both secular and religious in nature, in part reflecting her eventual decision to leave the viceroyalty court and instead take up the vocation as a nun.[10] In "Primero sueño," or "First I Dream" (1692), Sor Juana contrasts the state of the body with that of the soul, describing the descent into a dream state: "the gift of vegetative warmth, the mortal / shell in restful lassitude, cadaver, / yet with a soul imbued, / dead in life, but living still in death."[11] Reflecting on a body that seems suspended between life and death, Sor Juana dissects the bodily vessel into its contingent parts. She settles on the stomach, writing,

4 DOCTRINE AND DISEASE

> That most competent and scientific
> laboratory,
> dispensing warmth to all the body,
> withholding never, ever diligent,
> neither to neighbor showing preference
> nor slighting one remote,
> with nature's instrument is taking note
> of precise measurements
> of chyme it will assign throughout the soma.[12]

Sor Juana's narration of the body is consistent with emerging interpretations of the body and soul in her time. Her writing reflects familiarity with current scientific reasoning and René Descartes's teachings and in particular his *Discourse on Method* (1637).[13] Sor Juana, like Bradstreet, narrates the body in a state of transformation. While Bradstreet refers to Old England's disease-riddled body, Sor Juana's own dissection of the body—heart, lungs, throat, tongue, stomach, brain—and characterization of the stomach as the body's laboratory, "competent and scientific," creates a striking meeting point between concerns of the body and those of the soul.

Both Bradstreet's "A Dialogue Between Old England and New" and Sor Juana's "First I Dream," cast into the literary landscape of the seventeenth-century Atlantic world, show a facility describing corporeal and providential concerns, with each poet depicting the body as a conflicted space. Scholarship has thoroughly addressed the union of medicine and religion in colonial America. Outside of colonial America, however, the subjects of medicine and religion in the Atlantic world have more frequently been treated as discrete areas of inquiry. Religion in the Atlantic world has been the increasing focus of scholarship. Gatherings such as the Catholics and Puritans in the Trans-Atlantic World conference held at Trinity College Dublin in 2013 and book series such as Christianities in the Trans-Atlantic World published by Palgrave Macmillan and edited by Crawford Gribben and Scott Spurlock continue to refine our understanding of how religion shaped the Atlantic world.[14] Meanwhile, a large body of scholarship shows how medicine and science impacted and were impacted by transatlantic movement in the early modern period.[15] This volume insists on a nuanced approach to the intersection of these subjects, building on previous scholarship that has demanded a more accurate view of the cross-currents between medicine and religion in colonial America and reappraising our

INTRODUCTION 5

understanding of the interactions between medicine and religion in the Atlantic world. Each chapter reenters a key moment in the early modern Atlantic world during a period of remarkable upheaval, with the collection applying an interdisciplinary approach to meeting points between medicine and religion that were frequently contingent on location. In addition to addressing the religious belief systems of colonizing forces, as they were understood within the context of medical reasoning, including Puritanism, Protestantism, and Catholicism, this volume also explores spiritual understanding and belief systems within enslaved and Indigenous communities in relation to healing. Within this text, the term "spiritual" is deployed as an adjective to describe beliefs that extend beyond corporeal concerns, and it is used in relation to both colonists and the enslaved or Indigenous peoples described.

The movement of people in the Atlantic world saw diseases taking hold in new locales, creating a frightening moment of medical reckoning foregrounded against an era of unprecedented migration. Care of the body was mediated by and constructed through religious or spiritual belief systems. The religious traditions that accompanied plague outbreaks in early modern England informed devotional customs in the face of smallpox epidemics in New England.[16] Extensive writings by Jesuits on plants and herbs in early modern Peru, derived, in part, from the vast body of knowledge held by Indigenous healers, were stripped of all spiritual meaning, even as Jesuits pursued their own efforts to evangelize Indigenous peoples.[17] The maternal body became contested ground, as all aspects of childbearing and nursing—from the instruments used in childbirth to the subject of male midwives—were interpreted and reinterpreted in moral and providential terms.[18] Illness was framed as an extension of enslaved people's spiritual life on Jamaican plantations.[19] Religious missions led by the Catholic Church were the chosen vehicle for the first vaccine distribution throughout the Spanish Empire.[20] The chapters in this volume demonstrate that, far from being an objective process, the delivery of medical care was contingent on geographical context and the religious and spiritual beliefs of the people who lived there. As such, with the increasingly transatlantic complexion of life in the early modern period, entirely new ways of thinking about the body and its intersection with religious life unfolded.

Travel across the Atlantic revealed the horrific biological potential of humans from different parts of the globe coming together. Bodily health was of eminent concern for both Native populations and colonists; however, the ways in which these bodily concerns were expressed were often strikingly different. The

6 DOCTRINE AND DISEASE

Mohegan people, whose lands are found in the area now known as Connecticut, preserved traditional medical and healing practices despite the devasting effects of colonization.[21] In Siobhan Senier's article "Traditionally, Disability Was Not Seen as Such," she notes that within this culture, while "acute sickness" was readily acknowledged and associated with the destruction that accompanied colonization, "it appears that long-term or permanent bodily impairments and differences were not," with Senier tracing the evolving understanding of disability in Mohegan documents from the mid-eighteenth century into the twenty-first century.[22] Medicine and religion were inextricably connected to much of the colonizing process, and all too often these collisions came at one community's detriment. New illnesses were introduced, leaving people ravaged by disease. The introduction of unfamiliar diseases to new locales, by way of human migration and conquest, decimated populations. While there were clear biological implications that followed the introduction of diseases, their spread was also a consequence of colonizing practices that upended communities.[23] In the past two decades, research has demanded a more nuanced understanding of why these interactions led to such devastating results, most often for Native populations. In "Virgin Soils Revisited," David S. Jones interrogates widespread but reductive ways of interpreting the biological and social phenomena at play during periods of colonization. Jones argues that justifications focused on genetic or biological reasoning risk perpetuating "racial theories of historical development," ignoring "the same forces of poverty, social stress, and environmental vulnerability that cause epidemics in all times and places." He warns, "These new understandings of the mechanisms of depopulation require historians to be extremely careful in their writing about American Indian epidemics."[24] This volume covers a broader geographical area than only colonial America, but the chapters contained feature microhistories, case studies, and literary close readings that attempt to elucidate how religion, in particular, played into the medical landscape of the early modern Atlantic world, often becoming entangled in colonizing practices.

The convergence of medicine and religion in the face of epidemic disease in the Atlantic world was particularly evident. A number of chapters in this volume provide novel approaches to the historical and literary study of epidemics and their corresponding literature, examining how the experience of plague and smallpox were shaped by religious negotiations in a transatlantic context. The devastating effects of plague were well known in England and among early Puritan setters in colonial America. Settlers applied much of their knowledge of pestilence to the more common smallpox outbreaks that terrorized New England. While plague was not a prevalent affliction in New England, smallpox outbreaks ravaged both settlers and Native populations, playing a significant role in how colonization played out. When settlers from England arrived in Massachusetts Bay Colony, they brought with them their knowledge of how disease was dealt with in their birthplace but also the illnesses from that birthplace. As John Duffy explains of smallpox in *From Humors to Medical Science: A History of American Medicine*, "In the same way that it had swept through Central and South America in the sixteenth century, paving the way for the Spanish Conquistadores, so it proved an advance guard for the European occupation of North America."[25] New England settlers addressed smallpox in a manner that closely mirrored responses to plague in early modern England, with a combination of public health and religious measures deemed to have some efficacy against the disease. Furthermore, the spread of disease was essential to the processes of colonial power. In Stephen Greenblatt's "Invisible Bullets: Renaissance Authority and Its Subversion, *Henry IV* and *Henry V*," he describes Thomas Harriot's meticulous reporting on the first colony in Virginia in *A Brief and True Report of the New Found Land of Virginia* (1588) and Harriot's narration not only of the views of the colonizers but also those of the colonized, including their understanding of smallpox as "invisible bullets" shot by colonizers. Greenblatt describes this as part of the colonizing process: "The recording of alien voices, their preservation in Harriot's text, is part of the process whereby Indian culture is constituted as a culture and thus brought into the light for study, discipline, correction, transformation."[26] Smallpox was of eminent concern in the Spanish Empire, as well, with the Catholic Church becoming an essential actor in the first steps toward eradicating the disease through the process of vaccination.[27] Silva Cristobal's *Miraculous Plagues: An Epidemiology of Early New England Narrative*, in which he coins the term "epidemiology of narrative," draws on and critiques epidemiology, noting the limits of epidemiological approaches and seeking to "demonstrate how these discourses are bound up in the cultural assumptions of the communities that produce them—how, for example, their representational practices regulate access to medicine, and define the boundaries of citizenship."[28] This volume contributes significantly to the body of work that is currently being done on both plague and more widely on epidemics, in which the historical and literary role that these diseases and events have played in the early modern world is being explored at an unprecedented pace.[29]

8 DOCTRINE AND DISEASE

This volume marks a robust starting point for further investigations into the intersection of medicine and religion in the Atlantic world. There are limitations to the scope of the volume, however, that cannot be ignored. The essays here focus on British and Spanish colonial interactions, with a particular emphasis on Anglophone contexts; future scholarship could focus on the experiences of Indigenous and enslaved peoples at the intersection point between medicine and religion. Such a project would demand looking critically at how we approach the archive, including information conveyed through the printing press, a technology deeply implicated in imperial actions in the early modern period, as noted in this volume. Mark Alan Mattes traces the important work being done to expand the archive, noting, "Scholars in Native American and Indigenous Studies (NAIS) have long raised important concerns about the equal and equitable treatment of archival media, including the opportunities and limits of expanding the category of writing. Because the particularities of the material forms, affordances, and literacies connected to any archive render any one medium irreducible to another, one must avoid a universalizing conception of any media practice."[30] Within this volume, the limitations of the historical record are perhaps best lamented by Rana Hogarth, who notes how "the tense relationships between Blacks and whites, the lack of written sources from enslaved populations, and the appalling material conditions of slavery" (155) have impacted her own research. The archive of the colonial Atlantic world is full of insufficiencies that reflect these conditions of systemic oppression.

As the organizer of the volume, my research interest in writing that emerged from early modern English plague epidemics, in conjunction with the expertise of the contributors, has resulted in a substantial amount of material that addresses how epidemic disease was understood in religious dialogues that evolved from transatlantic movement between England and colonial America. Placing essays that examine the colonial contexts of medicine and religion in England and early America in dialogue with those describing medical and scientific discovery in the Spanish Empire, however, reveals the extent to which understanding of the body was frequently inseparable from spiritual matters and the surprising parallels that emerge from these interactions. From Jamaican plantations and the construction of the medical conditions that afflicted the enslaved to the first vaccination campaign in the Spanish Empire to the stark categorization of natural knowledge in Peru by missionaries, scientific understanding, medical treatment of the body, and the delivery of bodily care were interpreted and addressed within religious and spiritual belief systems. This

INTRODUCTION 9

volume's interdisciplinary approach proved especially successful at teasing out nuanced research on the intersection of medicine and religion, and a similarly interdisciplinary approach to future research on this point of juncture could take a number of directions: examining other diseases and bodily conditions; focusing on the knowledge and beliefs of different Indigenous communities; or considering how the issues of medicine and religion were entwined in Dutch, French, and Portuguese colonial actions.

CHAPTER DESCRIPTIONS

This volume is organized to underscore the back-and-forth dialogue between people and places guided by conflicting religious and health-related belief systems. Moving broadly between research that focuses on the thought of the colonizer, in contrast to insights into the histories and beliefs tied to Indigenous or enslaved peoples, gives this book space to explore a range of transitions occurring in the early modern Atlantic world. Encompassing a geographical area that includes England, New England, the Spanish New World, and Jamaica, the authors apply interdisciplinary approaches to the subjects of medicine, religion, and transatlantic movement. Drawing together historical, literary, and material culture lines of inquiry, these essays provide novel insights into the collision of medicine and religion in the Atlantic world. From seventeenth-century plague outbreaks in England to the first vaccination campaign in the Spanish Empire, each contribution touches on key moments of conflict and change during a period spanning from 1590 to the early nineteenth century. Arranging the chapters to highlight the tension between divergent religious belief systems and the medical practices tied to those beliefs gives this collection room to scrutinize colonial interactions that shaped medical and scientific discovery.

Matthew James Crawford's "The Secularization of Nature: Jesuit Missionaries and Indigenous Healing Knowledge in Early Modern Peru (1590–1710)" opens the volume, comparing how Indigenous peoples and missionaries used knowledge of herbs native to early modern Peru. Jesuits mined Indigenous healers' understanding of herbs, playing a conflicted role in codifying the medical and scientific value of these plants while in turn promoting an agenda of religious conversion. Crawford problematizes the spread of scientific knowledge within the Spanish Empire, as understanding of the healing potential of plants was divorced from its Indigenous roots by agents of the Catholic Church. Following on from Crawford's deft portrayal of the religious politics underlying the collection and subsequent spread of scientific knowledge, Allyson M. Poska's "Vaccinating in the Name of the Lord: The Catholic Church and the Extension of Smallpox Vaccination in the Spanish Empire (1803–1810)" shows how the Catholic Church played an essential role in the first vaccination campaign and the incredible measures that were taken to both distribute and encourage uptake of the smallpox vaccine via a naval mission to destinations throughout the Spanish Empire. Within the context of the vaccination campaign, the Catholic Church became a central actor in distributing lifesaving medical care and a partner in deploying essential public health measures. While Western religious traditions could be mobilized within colonies to spread positive health outcomes, the Catholic Church's assistance with the distribution of the smallpox vaccine being one example, the relationship between caring for the health of the body and the maintenance of the soul was rarely straightforward in the Atlantic world, as is evident in the erasure of Indigenous healing knowledge when Jesuits rewrote the history of the herbs of early modern Peru.

Within the Western Christian worldview, a sick body often signified moral or spiritual decay, and Crawford Gribben's chapter, "John Owen, Plague, and the Meanings of Disaster," traces the role of dissenters and the state of English nonconformity following the restoration of the monarchy, narrowing in on nonconformist Owen's interpretation of disasters, such as the plague outbreak in 1665 London, as divine judgments. The body and its state of health or ill health could signify one's spiritual well-being, and likewise the maternal body in the Atlantic world was a corporeal space onto which religious beliefs were grafted and interpreted. In "Maternal Bodies: Religion, Medicine, and Politics in Early America and the Atlantic World," Philippa Koch turns, in part, to midwifery manuals that spread through the seventeenth- and eighteenth-century Atlantic world to reveal contentious medical and moral debates over the maternal body and nursing, outlining how Mary, mother of Jesus, signified the redemptive potential of childbirth, a message spread by "American clergy and missionaries of the Atlantic world" (76). Koch narrows in on the divergent ways in which women's bodies, whether that of a colonist or that of an Indigenous or enslaved person, were depicted to meet "the purposes of European colonists" (92). Koch critically examines how value was placed on maternal bodies. If the printing press served to disseminate understanding of the maternal body across the Atlantic world in the form of midwifery manuals, it also allowed medical and religious paradigms to become embedded in new locations and appropriated for local audiences through the spread of print documents. My own essay in this volume,

INTRODUCTION 11

"Printing England's Plague Past in New England," examines how texts about early modern English plague epidemics were recontextualized and reprinted on New England presses; furthermore, I note that the texts favored for reprinting were those that saw plague in divine terms, as a punishment for sin, and, perhaps unsurprisingly, those written by nonconformist ministers. The spread of knowledge about disease made possible through the printing press meant culturally and location-specific approaches to illness could be transferred to occupied lands and to the medical afflictions prevalent in those places. New Englanders facing the threat of smallpox, for example, turned to English religious responses to plague, and Catherine Reedy's "Contagious Fasts: Occasional Worship and Medical Practice in England and Massachusetts Bay Colony" considers occasional worship days and fasting in seventeenth-century Boston in response to the smallpox outbreak from 1677 to 1678. Reedy describes the close ties between the religious responses to smallpox and similar measures enacted during the frequent outbreaks of plague in early modern England. During outbreaks of contagious disease, religious measures were often introduced in tandem with public health directives that addressed the bodily threat of illness, such as quarantine guidelines. In the instances of both plague epidemics in England and smallpox outbreaks in New England, contagious disease was treated as both a spiritual and bodily affliction.

In contrast to contagious disease, which could spread silently among colonists and the colonized alike, the final essay in the volume scrutinizes a bodily condition, dirt eating, that challenged explanation for those who were describing its pathology and that seemingly only afflicted the enslaved. Rana A. Hogarth's "Enslaved Bodies and the White Imagination: (Mis)Perceptions of Dirt Eating on Jamaican Plantations" describes a disease suffered by enslaved people on Jamaican plantations, *Cachexia Africana*, which was widely recorded and endlessly interpreted by white physicians. Turning to accounts of *Cachexia Africana* compiled by plantation physicians and planters, Hogarth interrogates the role this affliction played within enslaved populations and among their spiritual healers, Obeah practitioners. In each of these chapters, the body is a contested space, entangled in colonizing narratives and bending to religious motivations.

Within *Doctrine and Disease in the British and Spanish Colonial World*, unexpected connections become apparent, with ways of thinking within these colonial interactions extending between essays. Crawford states that Jesuits feared Peru's Indigenous healers, whom they called *curanderos*, in part because they viewed these healers "as their direct competitors as spiritual leaders" (26), a sentiment comparable to the phenomenon Hogarth acknowledges on Jamaican plantations, where, in white physicians' accounts, "the Obeah practitioner was more than just a competitor; they became a menace to the health of enslaved bonds people" (161). The overlap between religious and medical practice is evident throughout the volume, as Jesuits collected natural knowledge in early modern Peru, the Catholic Church became a central figure in vaccination efforts in the Spanish Empire, and physician-ministers tended to citizens' physical and spiritual health in early New England. Furthermore, threads of English nonconformity impacted not only how plague was understood in England but also how smallpox would come to be interpreted by New England settlers, with the chapters by Gribben, Reedy, and me exposing porous lines of communication between England and New England that shaped both the printed word and religious thought. Whether illness and the body were addressed by Western religious traditions or within the healing practices of Indigenous or enslaved peoples, such as by Obeah practitioners on Jamaican plantations or by *curanderos* in early modern Peru, poor health was often treated as a natural and magical phenomenon, potentially aided by a combination of magical thinking and natural measures. Much as Crawford notes that *curanderos* treated a range of afflictions, "from those that had natural causes to those that had magical or spiritual causes" (26), New England settlers chose to address smallpox with the spiritual balm of fasting days, fixating over how to best venerate the Lord and identify the moral and spiritual infractions that had caused the divine judgment of bodily devastation by way of disease. As the essays in this volume consistently demonstrate, religious and medical thought bled into each other time and time again in the early modern Atlantic world.

CONCLUSION

With the advent of the COVID-19 pandemic, medical knowledge and language about pandemic disease have become entwined in the public dialogue to a greater extent than at any other moment in history. Despite the remarkable pace at which twenty-first-century medicine has devised effective vaccines to end the pandemic and established vectors of transmission for the virus, the international community has witnessed how easily science and medicine bend to concerns that are geographically, culturally, and religiously contingent, even when these are directly in contradiction of public health measures and

INTRODUCTION 13

evidence-based knowledge. How understanding of disease is mediated by religious belief systems and geographical place has been laid bare before a global audience. Perhaps, then, it is unsurprising that health care in the early modern Atlantic world, as it continues to be today, was frequently indivisible from the religious and cultural meaning that was invested in understanding of the body and its illnesses.

NOTES

1. Keeble, "Bradstreet [née Dudley], Anne."
2. Keeble, "Bradstreet [née Dudley], Anne"; Lutes, "Negotiating Theology and Gynecology," 314; Daly, "Bradstreet, Anne (1612–1672), poet."
3. Keeble, "Bradstreet [née Dudley], Anne."
4. Bradstreet, "Dialogue," 180–81.
5. Bradstreet, "Dialogue," 181, 183–84.
6. Lutes, "Negotiating Theology and Gynecology," 314.
7. Bradstreet, "Dialogue," 182.
8. Duffy, *From Humors to Medical Science*, 1–2.
9. Shimek, "Tenth Muses."
10. Correia and Stavans, "Sor Juana Inés."
11. Cruz, *Poems, Protest, and a Dream*, 89.
12. Cruz, *Poems, Protest, and a Dream*, 91.
13. McKenna, "Rational Thought," 43. For a discussion of other possible influences on Sor Juana's thought in "Primero sueño," see McKenna, "Rational Thought," 40.
14. The Catholics and Puritans in the Trans-Atlantic World, 1500–1800 Conference at Trinity College Dublin in 2013 led to the publication of Gribben and Spurlock's *Puritans and Catholics*; see also Brown and Tackett, *Cambridge History of Christianity*; Mills, "Religion in the Atlantic World"; Kopelson, *Faithful Bodies*; Glasson, *Mastering Christianity*; MacCormack, *Religion in the Andes*.
15. See Duffy, *From Humors to Medical Science*; Breslaw, *Lotions, Potions, Pills, and Magic*; Finch, *Dissenting Bodies*; Jones, "Virgin Soils Revisited"; Brown, *Reaper's Garden*; Crawford, *Andean Wonder Drug*; Cristobal, *Miraculous Plagues*.
16. See Catherine Reedy's chapter in this volume.
17. See Matthew James Crawford's chapter in this volume.
18. See Philippa Koch's chapter in this volume.

19. See Rana A. Hogarth's chapter in this volume.
20. See Allyson M. Poska's chapter in this volume.
21. Senier, "Traditionally, Disability," 214.
22. Senier, "Traditionally, Disability," 219.
23. David S. Jones offers wide-ranging examples of existing research into how the nuanced situations surrounding colonizing practices and those who were being colonized could result in different rates of mortality from encounters with disease. See Jones, "Virgin Soils Revisited," 736–39.
24. Jones, "Virgin Soils Revisited," 705.
25. Duffy, *From Humors to Medical Science*, 5.
26. Greenblatt, "Invisible Bullets," 91.
27. See Allyson M. Poska's chapter in this volume. Smallpox was introduced within the Spanish New World by Spanish colonization. The sixteenth century saw major outbreaks in the Caribbean, Mexico, Peru, and Brazil. Centers for Disease Control and Prevention and World Health Organization, "History of Epidemiology," slide 4.
28. Cristobal, *Miraculous Plagues*, 4, 10.
29. In 2018, two gatherings of scholars brought together new views on plague in the early modern period: The Worlds That Plague Made Conference held at New York University and the London Bills of Mortality Symposium held at the Folger Shakespeare Library in Washington, DC. For early modern plague scholarship, see Gilman, *Plague Writing*; Slack, *Impact of Plague*; Greenberg, "Plague, the Printing Press"; Totaro, *Plague Epic*; Gilman and Totaro, *Representing the Plague*; Totaro, *Suffering in Paradise*; Munkhoff, "Searchers of the Dead."
30. Mattes, "Writing the Indigenous Americas," 1702. See also Ballantyne and Paterson, "Introduction."

BIBLIOGRAPHY

Ballantyne, Tony, and Lachy Paterson. "Introduction: Indigenous Textual Cultures, the Politics of Difference, and the Dynamism of Practice." In *Indigenous Textual Cultures: Reading and Writing in the Age of Global Empire*, edited by Tony Ballantyne, Lachy Paterson, and Angela Wanhalla, 1–28. Durham, NC: Duke University Press, 2020. https://doi.org/10.2307/j.ctv153k5kj.4.

Bradstreet, Anne. "A Dialogue Between Old England and New, Concerning Their Present Troubles. Anno 1642." In *The Tenth Muse Lately Spung Up in America*, 180–90. London, 1650.

———. *Several Poems Compiled with Great Variety of Wit and Learning, Full of Delight Wherein Especially Is Contained a Compleat Discourse, and Description of the Four Elements, Constitutions, Ages of Man, Seasons of the Year*. Boston, 1678.

Breslaw, Elaine G. *Lotions, Potions, Pills, and Magic: Healthcare in Early America*. New York: New York University Press, 2012.

Brown, Stewart J., and Timothy Tackett, eds. *The Cambridge History of Christianity: Enlightenment, Reawakening and Revolution, 1660–1815*. Vol. 7. New York: Cambridge University Press, 2006.

Brown, Vincent. *The Reaper's Garden: Death and Power in the World of Atlantic Slavery*. Cambridge, MA: Harvard University Press, 2008.

Centers for Disease Control and Prevention (US) and World Health Organization. "History of Epidemiology of Global Smallpox Eradication." Module from "Smallpox: Disease, Prevention, and Intervention." 2001. 40 slides. https://stacks.cdc.gov/view/cdc/27929.

Correia, Katharine, and Ilan Stavans. "Sor Juana Inés de la Cruz." In *Oxford Bibliographies Online in Latino Studies*. https://www.doi.org/10.1093/obo/9780199913701-0151.

Crawford, Mathew James. *The Andean Wonder Drug: Cinchona Bark and Imperial Science in the Spanish Atlantic, 1630–1800*. Pittsburgh: University of Pittsburgh Press, 2016.

Cristobal, Silva. *Miraculous Plagues: An Epidemiology of Early New England Narrative*. Oxford: Oxford University Press, 2011.

Cruz, Juana Inés de la. *Poems, Protest, and a Dream: Selected Writings*. Translated by Margaret Sayers Peden. New York: Penguin Books, 1997.

Daly, Robert. "Bradstreet, Anne (1612–1672), Poet." *American National Biography*, February 1, 2000. https://doi.org/10.1093/anb/9780198606697.article.1600169.

Duffy, John. *From Humors to Medical Science: A History of American Medicine*. 2nd ed. Urbana: University of Illinois Press, 1993.

Finch, Martha L. *Dissenting Bodies: Corporealities in Early New England*. New York: Columbia University Press, 2010.

Gilman, Ernest B. *Plague Writing in Early Modern England*. Chicago: University of Chicago Press, 2009.

Gilman, Ernest B., and Rebecca Totaro, eds. *Representing the Plague in Early Modern England*. New York: Routledge, 2011.

Glasson, Travis. *Mastering Christianity: Missionary Anglicanism and Slavery in the Atlantic World*. New York: Oxford University Press, 2012.

Greenberg, Stephen. "Plague, the Printing Press, and Public Health in Seventeenth-Century London." *Huntington Library Quarterly* 67, no. 4 (2004): 508–27.

Greenblatt, Stephen. "Invisible Bullets: Renaissance Authority and Its Subversion, *Henry IV* and *Henry V*." In *New Historicism and Renaissance Drama*, edited by Richard Wilson and Richard Dutton, 82–107. New York: Routledge, 2013.

Gribben, Crawford, and Scott Spurlock, eds. *Puritans and Catholics in the Trans-Atlantic World, 1600–1800*. Basingstoke, UK: Palgrave Macmillan, 2016.

Jones, David S. "Virgin Soils Revisited." *William and Mary Quarterly* 60, no. 4 (2003): 703–42.

Keeble, N. H. "Bradstreet [née Dudley], Anne (1612/13–1672), Poet." *Oxford Dictionary of National Biography*, February 1, 2014. https://doi.org/10.1093/anb/9780198606697.article.1600169. Accessed August 11, 2021.

Kopelson, Heather Miyano. *Faithful Bodies: Performing Religion and Race in the Puritan Atlantic*. New York: New York University Press, 2014.

Lutes, Jean Marie. "Negotiating Theology and Gynecology: Anne Bradstreet's Representations of the Female Body." *Signs* 22, no. 2 (1997): 309–40.

MacCormack, Sabine. *Religion in the Andes: Vision and Imagination in Early Colonial Peru*. Princeton, NJ: Princeton University Press, 1991.

Mattes, Mark Alan. "Writing the Indigenous Americas." *American Literary History* 35, no. 4 (2023): 1702–12. https://doi.org/10.1093/alh/ajad151.

McKenna, Susan M. "Rational Thought and Female Poetics in Sor Juana's 'Primero sueño': The Circumvention of Two Traditions." *Hispanic Review* 68, no. 1 (2000): 37–52.

Mills, Kenneth. "Religion in the Atlantic World." In *Oxford Handbook of the Atlantic World, c. 1450–c. 1850*, edited by Nicholas Canny and Philip Morgan, 433–48. New York: Oxford University Press, 2011.

Munkhoff, Richelle. "Searchers of the Dead: Authority, Marginality, and the Interpretation of Plague in England, 1574–1665." *Gender and History* 11, no. 1 (1999): 1–29.

Senier, Siobhan. "'Traditionally, Disability Was Not Seen as Such': Writing and Healing in the Work of Mohegan Medicine People." *Journal of Literary and Cultural Disability Studies* 7, no. 2 (2013): 213–29.

Shimek, Suzanne. "The Tenth Muses Lately Sprung Up in the Americas: The Borders of the Female Subject in Sor Juana's First Dream and Anne Bradstreet's 'Contemplations.'" *Legacy* 17, no. 1 (2000): 1–17. https://www.proquest.com/scholarly-journals/tenth-muses-lately-sprung-up-americas-borders/docview/223834070/se-2.

Slack, Paul. *The Impact of Plague in Tudor and Stuart England*. Oxford: Oxford University Press, 1985.

Totaro, Rebecca, ed. *The Plague Epic in Early Modern England: Heroic Measures, 1603–1721*. Surrey, UK: Ashgate, 2012.

———. *Suffering in Paradise: The Bubonic Plague in English Literature from More to Milton*. Pittsburgh: Duquesne University Press, 2005.

CHAPTER 1

The Secularization of Nature

Jesuit Missionaries and Indigenous Healing Knowledge in Early Modern Peru (1590–1710)

MATTHEW JAMES CRAWFORD

"The powders of this bark began to be used and to serve as a remedy for men, who were taught by the Indians of that region, according to this true history."[1] This quote comes from a work titled *De pulvere febrifugo Occidentalis Indiae* (On the febrifugal powder of the West Indies), published by the Spanish physician Gaspar Caldera de Heredia in 1663. Here, Caldera credits "Indians" in the province of Quito in South America with discovering some of the medicinal properties of what we now know as cinchona bark. Known as *cascarilla* in Spanish America and as *quina* in Spain, the bark traveled under many names and became one of the most important medicaments in the early modern Atlantic world on account of its utility in treating various intermittent fevers that were prevalent at the time.[2] In spite of Caldera's confident tone, little is known about the origins of the medicinal use of cinchona bark. It is most likely that Indigenous healers in the Andean world were the first to use the bark medicinally. However, due to a lack of archaeological and historical sources, we do not know where, when, how or why Andean *curanderos* made the bark a regular part of their pharmacopoeia.[3]

Even though there is an early, if vague, description of the bark in the late sixteenth-century work of Nicolas Monardes, a Spanish physician based in

Seville, who never traveled to Spanish America, *quina* was not introduced to Europe until the 1630s.[4] Monardes does not identify cinchona by any of the currently recognized names for the bark. The identity of the bark is inferred from his description of its medicinal properties and its geographical origin. As a physician in Seville, Spain's main and only official port city sending ships to Spanish America, Monardes was well positioned to learn about medicaments in the Americas from returning travelers.[5] In the second half of the seventeenth century, many European authors published accounts of this new medicament from Peru and its wondrous medicinal properties.[6] The lack of information on the bark's origins did not stop many of these authors from concocting narratives of discovery that were a heady mixture of fact and hearsay. Many of the details of such narratives are difficult, if not impossible, to confirm with corroborating evidence. As a result, such narratives often tell us more about what their authors thought about the discovery and circulation of healing knowledge in the early modern Atlantic world.[7]

One intriguing feature of many seventeenth-century European narratives of the discovery of *quina* is that they highlight the entanglement of medicine and religion—socially and intellectually—in colonial contexts. To see how, let us revisit Gaspar Caldera de Heredia's "true history" of the discovery of *quina*.[8] His history and the process of discovery can be divided into two parts. In the first part, Caldera explains how the "Indians" commonly used the bark. He notes that in a remote region of the province of Quito near the Amazon River, there were "Indians" who, "spontaneously or for a salary," worked in a gold mine. On their way to and from the mine, these Indigenous miners had to cross a river with freezing-cold water that reached up to their necks. To cross the river, the miners would strip the bark from a tree, reduce it to a powder, and mix it with hot water. Upon ingesting the concoction, the chills and shivers induced by crossing the cold river would end, and they were able to continue on their way.[9]

While the first part of his narrative gives some credit to Indigenous peoples for understanding the bark's medicinal properties, the second part of Caldera's narrative identifies European missionaries as the discoverers of the bark's most important medical use as a treatment for intermittent fevers. According to the narrative, Jesuit missionaries in the region had observed Indigenous people using the bark and asked about its source. Not surprisingly, Caldera's description of such interactions provides a rosy portrait in which the asymmetries of colonial relations are notably absent, if not explicitly overlooked. As noted by Andrés Prieto and Margaret Ewalt, Jesuit missionaries were far from passive observers of Indigenous medicine but took an active role in extracting this knowledge as part of their efforts to further the dual mission of colonization and Christianization.[10] Caldera further explains that the Indigenous people identified the tree as "Quarango" and enthusiastically offered the Jesuits samples of the bark "as a humble gift."[11] The Jesuits also asked members of other missionary orders about the bark and its medicinal use. Through "analogical reasoning," for which they were famous, the Jesuits then deduced that if the bark was effective in treating the chills induced by cold water, it might be effective in treating the chills often experienced by individuals suffering from intermittent fevers.[12] The bark worked. After additional "experiences and observations," the Jesuits shared the bark and their knowledge of its efficacy against intermittent fevers with a pharmacist in Lima named Gabriel de España. From Lima, the new medicament spread to Europe and, eventually, the rest of the world.

While few of the details can be confirmed, Caldera's history of the origins of cinchona bark is useful for what it tells about how people at the time thought about overlap between medicine and religion in the early modern Atlantic world. After all, Caldera published his *De pulvere febrifugo* with the express purpose of establishing the legitimacy and utility of cinchona bark in treating intermittent fevers. And so, it would have been important to provide an origin story that was plausible, especially since Caldera characterizes his account as a "true history." With that in mind, it is notable that the Jesuits play an active role in his narrative of the discovery of the bark's efficacy in the treatment of intermittent fevers not only in developing a rationale for using the bark in this way but also in conducting additional "experiences and observations," a phrase that may refer to some kind of therapeutic test by the Jesuit missionaries, who were known to administer health care to fellow missionaries and Indigenous peoples throughout the Americas.[13] In addition to emphasizing their role in discovering the bark's febrifugal properties, Caldera also highlights the role of the Jesuits in spreading the bark and knowledge of its medicinal properties. In this way, Caldera's account emphasizes both the Jesuits' intellectual and social contributions to the history of this valuable medicament.

In thinking about the history of medicine and religion in the early modern Atlantic world, the role of missionaries should not be overlooked. As various scholars have demonstrated, missionaries—Jesuit or otherwise—served as the leading edge of European colonization in the Americas and acted as intermediaries between Indigenous and European cultures, a role that permitted them not just to extract Indigenous knowledge but also to repurpose such knowledge to serve the ends of Christianization and colonization.[14] More recently, several studies have emphasized the contributions of Jesuit missionaries to knowledge of the natural phenomena of the Americas, from astronomy to natural history.[15] One of the most prominent and well-organized missionary orders, with regard to the circulation of knowledge, was the Society of Jesus. In the past two decades, much scholarship, including key studies by Steven J. Harris and Markus Friedrich, has focused on the ways in which the long-distance networks and bureaucratic techniques of the Jesuits facilitated such activities on a global scale.[16] In addition to studies on the logistics of Jesuit knowledge production, recent work by Prieto, Ewalt, and others has focused specifically on the contributions of Jesuits to the study of nature and natural phenomena in early modern Latin America.[17] In some instances, Jesuits provided some of the earliest natural historical accounts of the flora and fauna of Spanish America, as in the case of José de Acosta's widely read *Historia natural y moral de las Indias*, which was first published in Seville in 1590.

The recent interest in "Jesuit science" emerged in part from ongoing efforts to reevaluate the place of the Catholic Church and Catholic countries in the narratives of early modern science and the Scientific Revolution.[18] The Society of Jesus has received considerable attention in this current of scholarship on account of its emphasis on education and learning. Starting in the late sixteenth century, the Jesuits developed and administered the most extensive network of schools and colleges in western Europe and developed a global network through their missionary efforts around the early modern world. In recent decades, several studies have demonstrated the important contributions that members of the Society of Jesus made to a variety of early modern scientific enterprises.[19] Such studies have contributed significantly to reintegrating the Catholic world into the narrative of the Scientific Revolution.[20]

This chapter builds on this recent scholarship to advance a counterintuitive argument about the consequences of the efforts of Jesuit missionaries to collect and circulate Indigenous knowledge of medicinal plants. By looking more closely at Jesuit efforts to collect, extract and re-present knowledge of medicinal plants from Indigenous peoples in Peru from the sixteenth to the eighteenth centuries, this chapter argues that the writings of Jesuit missionaries about medicinal plants contributed to the broader and longer process of the secularization of nature. In the context of Spanish colonial frontiers, the spiritual meanings attributed to medicinal plants by Indigenous healers were considered erroneous, if not heretical, and, in some contexts, dangerous. As a result, Jesuit

20 DOCTRINE AND DISEASE

missionaries sought to strip knowledge of medicinal plants of the connotations of Indigenous religions and aimed to extract only the most pragmatic and naturalistic knowledge of these plants and their medicinal uses. Focusing on the case of early modern Peru, this chapter calls attention to the apparent paradox that a more naturalistic understanding of medicinal plants—and New World nature more broadly—was, in some contexts, central to Jesuit efforts to Christianize the Indigenous peoples as part of the broader imperial epistemology of Europeans in the Americas, who treated Indigenous knowledge as a resource to be extracted in much the same way that products of the natural world were. At the same time, Indigenous knowledge was vital to the success of European colonial and missionary enterprises and had a significant impact on Jesuit and European understandings of the natural world.

This potential consequence of Jesuit missionary efforts becomes clearer if we look beyond the general natural philosophical statements of Jesuit writings on natural history and materia medica and focus on the specific information that Jesuits reported about indigenous plants and their medicinal uses. To be clear, this chapter is not claiming that medicine and religion were more tightly intertwined in Indigenous cultures than in European culture. Such a statement is not sustainable given all of the scholarship on the integral role that religion played in the healing traditions of early modern Europe.[21] Instead, this chapter argues that missionaries' efforts to extract knowledge of medicinal plants from Indigenous cultures secularized such knowledge and was potentially one factor in weakening the link between medicine and religion in European understandings of the natural world.[22]

JESUIT MISSIONARIES AND NATURE IN THE AMERICAS

Missionaries from the Society of Jesus first arrived in the Spanish Viceroyalty of Peru in 1568 and quickly took an interest in learning about the peoples and places that they encountered. In addition to studying Indigenous languages, which was a crucial part of their efforts to convert Indigenous peoples to Christianity, some Jesuits took an interest in the natural phenomena of the Americas, including medicinal plants and incidents of disease. Some of this knowledge circulated in the regular correspondence that missionaries maintained with their superiors in Lima and in Rome. In a recent article, Elaine Cristina Deckmann Fleck and Roberto Poletto note that Jesuit missionaries in Paraguay throughout the seventeenth century often commented on the illnesses and healing practices

THE SECULARIZATION OF NATURE   21

(or lack thereof) in their regions.[23] For example, in the annual letter of 1613, a missionary observed that "there are a great many sick people, who die for lack of remedies."[24] A few years later, in the annual letter of 1616, another missionary observed, "There was a catarrh sickness to which almost the whole village succumbed and father Juan de Salas made them a syrup with which almost everyone was cured, although some died."[25]

In other instances, Jesuit missionaries wrote natural histories, herbals, and medical handbooks. Of the various kinds of natural phenomena discussed by Jesuit authors, plants received the most attention. Indeed, the sheer numbers of plants described in Jesuit natural histories, herbals, and medical texts provides insight into the scale of Jesuit efforts to know nature in the Americas. One of the earliest and most important Jesuit works on the natural history of the Americas was *Historia natural y oral de las Indias*, written by Acosta and published in Seville in 1590. Acosta was originally from Spain, where he had entered the Society of Jesus in 1552. In 1572, he traveled as a missionary to Peru, where he served briefly as the rector of the Jesuit college in Lima before becoming the Provincial of Peru. While in Peru, Acosta started writing a book with the goal of providing a comprehensive account of the natural history of the Americas as well as a history of Indigenous civilizations. Upon returning to Spain in 1587, after spending a year in New Spain, Acosta published the first two books of his *Historia natural y moral de las Indias* in 1588 as part of a Latin work on evangelization titled *De procuranda Indorum*. In 1590, the entire work was published in Seville in Spanish.[26] In the seven books that made up the final work, Acosta devoted the first four books to all manner of natural phenomena while focusing on the precolonial history of the Indigenous peoples of Mexico and Peru in the final three books. The sections on natural history offered seventeen chapters on plants from the Americas, which discussed in detail more than forty-five different types of trees, bushes, roots, and flowers from all over the Americas, including tobacco, cocoa, and coca.[27] According to the historian Sabine Anagnostou, Acosta mentions more than 150 different plants in the course of his *Historia natural y moral de las Indias*.[28] Of course, as many studies have shown, the knowledge of plants was vital to the Spanish colonial project, as they hoped to exploit plants from the Americas for practical, medicinal, and commercial uses.[29]

Other Jesuit works on the natural history and materia medica of the Americas remained in manuscript and circulated among missions, colleges, and other Jesuit institutions on both sides of the Atlantic. One of the most extensive and comprehensive of the early Jesuit manuscripts was Bernabé Cobo's *Historia del Nuevo Mundo*.[30] Cobo came from a family of minor nobles in Andalusia and originally traveled to the Americas in 1595 as part of an expedition of discovery and conquest. He abandoned this enterprise shortly after arriving in the Caribbean in 1596, and by 1599, he was in Lima studying at the Jesuit College. He became a member of the Society of Jesus in 1601 and was later sent for study and missionary work in Cuzco and other parts of Upper Peru. During his career as a Jesuit, he spent much of his time studying the natural world and history of Peru. Like Acosta, Cobo intended his *Historia del Nuevo Mundo* to be a comprehensive account of the natural history and history of Indigenous civilizations in the Americas, with an emphasis on Peru. He may have started working on the book as early as the late 1630s and did not finish the three volumes until 1651. Unfortunately, the original manuscript is lost, and the only remaining sections are those from the first volume, in which Cobo focused on natural history and the precolonial history of Indigenous civilizations.[31]

Of the extant parts of *Historia del Nuevo Mundo*, three books focus on plants, including herbs (Book IV), shrubs (Book V), and trees (Book VI). Most chapters in each book are devoted to a single type or species of plant.[32] In general, each chapter provides a physical description of the plant, an indication of the geographical origins of the plant, and a discussion of the main uses of the plant, with some identifying how it is used by Indigenous people or Spaniards. While Book IV discusses 108 different kinds of herbs, Cobo only indicates that forty-nine (45.4 percent of the herbs) had medicinal uses. Similarly, of the eighty-seven shrubs described in Book V, only twenty-nine (33.3 percent of the shrubs) had medicinal uses. And finally, in Book VI, Cobo indicates a medicinal use for only thirty-seven (28.7 percent) out of the 129 trees discussed. Overall, roughly a third of the plants discussed had some medical utility, with some plants being used to treat several different ailments.[33]

In addition to the general histories of Acosta and Cobo, a small group of Jesuit texts focused exclusively on medicinal plants. Such texts tended to be produced for and used by missionaries. One notable example of this genre is an early eighteenth-century manuscript now known as "Materia medica misionera," the title that the work was given when it was first published in 1945.[34] The manuscript was written by Pedro Montenegro sometime around 1710. Biographical details on Montenegro are sparse, but we know that he was born in Galicia in 1663 and practiced medicine at the Hospital General in Madrid in 1679. He joined the Society of Jesus in 1691 and took his vows in 1703. At some point,

Montenegro traveled to Spanish America, where he spent much of his career serving in the Guarani missions in Paraguay.[35] The title page of the first book of a manuscript copy of Montenegro's "Materia medica misionera" at the National Library in Madrid notes that the work describes "the medicinal properties of trees and plants of the Missions and provinces of Tucumán with some from Brasil and the East," while the title of the second book notes that the plants described come from the "Missions of Paraguay with some from Brasil and the Province of Chile."[36] The manuscript describes 148 plants with accompanying hand-drawn images. Most of the plants are native to the Americas, and in many cases, Montenegro included the names of the plants in Guarani. However, the text also discusses several medicinal plants from Europe and Asia. Compared to other Jesuit herbals of the time, this number seems low, and Prieto reports that some of the handwritten herbals that circulated among the Jesuit missions of Paraguay described over 300 plants.[37] Similarly, Cobo provides natural historical information on nearly 300 plants in his *Historia del Nuevo Mundo*.

What were the sources of this plant knowledge? It is likely that these authors, like many other Jesuit missionaries, had firsthand experience with some of the plants that they discussed. For example, in Cobo's chapter on quinoa in Book IV of his *Historia del Nuevo Mundo*, he observes, "It has been found by experience, and as I have observed it used myself, the seed of [quinoa], when cooked in water with milk or fat enriched by a mother's breast milk, is beneficial for any type of *caida* [i.e., the sunken fontanel of an infant]."[38] Similarly, in his discussion of *cachun*, a type of cucumber, in chapter 33 of Book IV, Cobo writes, "In the Atrisco Valley (on the northern frontier of Mexico), I saw them in the Convent of El Carmen and, in my experience, they were bland and without the sweetness that they [typically] have in this kingdom [i.e., New Spain]."[39] While such first-person statements of a Jesuit author's experience with a particular plant are rare, even their scarce presence attests to the direct observations of nature and materia medica made by missionaries in the Americas.

In other instances, Jesuit authors learned from other missionaries about the medicinal properties of these plants or, at the very least, healing substances made from plants in the Americas. Once again, Cobo's *Historia del Nuevo Mundo* provides an example. In his chapter on tobacco in Book IV, he provides an example of the ways in which Spanish colonists assimilated and adapted Indigenous plant knowledge and methods for using plants.[40] "Although the Indians, from whom we took this custom of using tobacco, only smoked it," Cobo notes, "the Spanish have invented another method for using it that is more discrete and less offensive which is [to snort it] in powder through the nose."[41] He then reports that he knew a cleric who underwent multiple operations to treat some kind of tumor that the cleric had on his cheek. "A few years later, I saw him and he was healthy and well, although he bore the marks of the previous treatments," Cobo writes. The Jesuit continues that when he asked the cleric "how he had healed so well," the cleric responded that he had done so "only by snorting a little powdered tobacco," when he "felt the blood running in his head."[42]

Of course, the most important source of information and knowledge about nature and medicinal use of plants in the Americas was Indigenous people. As historical, anthropological, and ethnobotanical scholarship has shown, the Indigenous peoples of the Andean world and other regions that made up the Viceroyalty of Peru possessed a long tradition of medicinal knowledge that informed their dynamic theories and practices of healing throughout the colonial period and beyond.[43] Communities of Guarani, Quechua, Aymara, and other Indigenous groups each had a variety of specialists, healing with extensive knowledge of the medicinal uses of local plants, animals, and minerals.

Jesuit sources rarely, if ever, identified individual members of Indigenous communities from whom they learned about the use of materia medica in the Americas. When they do attribute knowledge of materia medica to Indigenous peoples, they tend to attribute the knowledge to "Indians" as a group, rarely identifying a specific tribe or ethnic group. For example, Cobo observes in his discussion of an herb known as *latalata*, "With this crushed herb, the Indians frequently treat broken bones."[44] In another discussion of a medicament made from "molle," a type of tree in Peru, Cobo reports that the "Indians of Ica Valley" used a concoction of molle bark and resin in warm water to treat *mal del valle*, an illness that was "very common" in the Ica Valley.[45] In one instance, Acosta recounts his experience with an individual Indigenous healer but does not identify her by name. In the chapter on vicuñas in his *Historia natural y moral de las Indias*, Acosta describes an episode in which he experienced "terrible pain" in his eyes while staying at a "*tambo*, or inn," in the mountains of Peru. "While I was lying down," Acosta reports, "with so much pain that I almost lost my patience, an Indian woman came in and said, 'Put this over your eyes, father, and you will be well.'" The treatment was "a bit of vicuña meat, recently killed and running with blood," and Acosta notes that the remedy worked.[46] While Acosta shares several details of the treatment, the actual identity of the *curandera* is not one of them.

It is almost certain that the majority of Jesuit knowledge of the medicinal uses of plants in the Americas came from Indigenous peoples more than their own experiences with or observations of these flora. A commitment to studying and learning Indigenous languages, to which Jesuits dedicated themselves as part of their evangelical mission, facilitated missionaries' ability to access this knowledge.[47] In Cobo's time as a Jesuit missionary, for example, he learned both Quechua and Aymara, two of the more prominent Indigenous languages in Peru. In addition, Prieto reports that in *Confesionario breve* (1606), which was a dictionary and grammar of the language of the Mapuche in Chile, Luis de Valdivia, rector of the Jesuit College in Santiago, even instructed Jesuits to ask about healing rituals when taking confession from their Indigenous charges.[48] Yet it is important to recognize that just because missionaries learned languages and asked questions does not mean that Indigenous peoples cooperated with these efforts. As we will see, in some contexts, there could be considerable tension between Indigenous healers and Jesuit missionaries.

JESUIT ACCOUNTS OF INDIGENOUS MATERIA MEDICA

The works of Acosta, Cobo, and Montenegro represent just a small sampling of the kinds of knowledge and information about nature in the Americas that Jesuit missionaries collected and circulated in manuscript and printed works between 1568, when they first arrived in Peru, and 1767, when they were expelled from the Spanish Empire. In light of such evidence, there is no doubt that many Jesuits took great interest in the natural phenomena of the Americas. At the same time, it is important to note that Jesuit missionaries—like all European observers of the wider world—hardly took a passive role in their efforts to collect and circulate such knowledge, especially in the case of the knowledge of medicinal plants learned from Indigenous healers or otherwise extracted from Indigenous communities. Indeed, they actively edited healing knowledge by choosing to record and report some aspects of Indigenous healing while ignoring, if not actively suppressing, other aspects.

To understand how and why Jesuits chose to edit Indigenous healing knowledge, we need to first understand a bit more about Indigenous healers and their role in Indigenous communities. As in most medical traditions, including the medical tradition of early modern Europe, knowledge of local plants and their medicinal use among the Indigenous communities of Peru was rooted in the broader cosmologies and worldviews of those communities.[49] While some healing knowledge was undoubtedly common knowledge in Indigenous communities, these communities also had healers or shaman that specialized in

26 DOCTRINE AND DISEASE

medicine or certain types of healing. Among the Guarani, these healers were known as *paie*; among the Mapuche, they were known as *machis*; and among missionaries and Spanish colonists, Indigenous healers were called a variety of names, from *curandero* (healer) to *hechizero* (sorcerer).[50] As scholarship in modern ethnomedicine and the historical role of Indigenous healers has shown, *curanderos* often practiced many different kinds of healing to address a range of diseases, from those that had natural causes to those that had magical or spiritual causes.[51] Focusing on Indigenous healers in the Andean world, Irene Silverblatt has observed that Andean healers employed a variety of healing practices, including "divination, knowledge of medicinal properties of plants, a sort of confession and ritual cleansing, and the ability to direct rites that accompanied offerings to sacred deities."[52] In turn, many Indigenous communities valued these healers as much for their role as mediators between the spiritual and the physical as for their knowledge of disease and the medicinal uses of plants, animals, and minerals.

Not surprisingly, since Indigenous healers often engaged the spiritual as much as the material, Jesuit missionaries—as well as other Catholic missionaries—in the Americas often viewed Indigenous healers with a mixture of suspicion, disdain, and hostility. For example, in Montenegro's "Prologue to the Reader" from his medical handbook, "Materia medica misionera," he explains that the "curanderos y curanderas" (male and female healers) of the Province of Paraguay, where he was a missionary, "are more deserving of the name quacks rather than surgeons, of the name butchers rather than doctors."[53] Jesuit missionaries had both a social and an intellectual reason for rejecting Indigenous healers. First, the Jesuits often recognized these healers as their direct competitors as spiritual leaders in Indigenous communities.[54] Indeed, many missionaries blamed *curanderos* for the perpetuation of Indigenous religious beliefs—known as "idolatry" from the Jesuit perspective—in the communities that the Jesuits were trying to convert to Christianity.

Another reason why Jesuit missionaries sought to undermine Indigenous healers is that the Jesuits viewed them as agents of the Devil, a characterization that undoubtedly was part of the ways in which European colonists justified the conquest and colonization of Indigenous peoples. In the larger war against the forces of Satan, which formed a key element of the worldview of many Catholics (and Protestants) in the early modern Atlantic world, the Jesuits saw Indigenous shaman as their direct opponents.[55] In a work titled *The Extirpation of Idolatry* published in Lima in 1621, the Jesuit Pablo José de Arriaga groups several different types of Indigenous healers under the heading "Ministers of Idolatry," whether they practiced spiritual healing or not.[56] Similarly, in the book *Corónica moralizada del Orden de San Augustin*, a chronicle of the Augustinian missions in Peru, Antonio de la Calancha characterizes Indigenous healers as "hechizeros" (sorcerers).[57] Since Indigenous healers were the Jesuits' main competitors as spiritual leaders, it is perhaps no surprise that, in Jesuits' efforts to displace Indigenous healers, they increasingly practiced medicine and healing in their missions. Jesuit missionaries understood that, in order to displace Indigenous healers and ensure the spread and success of Christianity in Spanish America, they needed to serve Indigenous communities in similar ways—tending to the physical ailments as well as the spiritual needs of Indigenous peoples.

In spite of Jesuit missionaries' reservations about Indigenous healers, they, nonetheless, recognized the utility, if not necessity, of Indigenous healing knowledge. After all, while evangelization and the "extirpation of idolatry" served as significant motivating factors, many Jesuits also expressed sincere concern about the health of Indigenous communities that, to Jesuit eyes, suffered from outbreaks of disease without any effective remedy.[58] Returning to Arriaga's *Extirpation of Idolatry*, he explains that many of his so-called ministers of idolatry or sorcerers were "ambicayos, or healers."[59] And, while Arriaga notes that many of the "cures" offered by these "ambicayos" involved "superstitions and idolatries," he also explains that "priests" should "examine and instruct" those healers in order to "eliminate what is superstitious and evil and take advantage of what is good: the knowledge and use of some herbs and other simples."[60] In other words, Arriaga and others instructed Jesuit missionaries and other clerics to teach Indigenous healers to strip away any spiritual elements of their healing, which might be rooted in existing Indigenous religions.

Arriaga's text is just one among many that highlight the apparently paradoxical situation in which Jesuits (and other missionaries) found themselves. Even as they suspected Indigenous healers of being purveyors of idolatry, they could not deny the utility of Indigenous knowledge of plants and their medicinal uses. Yet, at the same time, works like Arriaga's *Extirpation of Idolatry* provided the warrant for extracting, filtering, and using the knowledge of Indigenous healers, as long as it was disconnected from the Indigenous worldviews that enriched such healing practices and often made the therapeutic application of plants meaningful and intelligible to Indigenous communities. Arriaga's approach was not just a matter of theology. It was a practical matter. Indeed, the Jesuit extirpator's recommendations seem rooted in a cognizance of the shortage of healers

28 DOCTRINE AND DISEASE

in colonial Spanish America that so many of his coreligionists bemoaned in their annual letters to Rome and other correspondence.[61] Yet Arriaga also seems to recognize that missionaries alone could not meet the health-care needs of Indigenous communities. As a result, his program permits Indigenous healers to continue to practice their craft but only in a more naturalistic way under the watchful eyes of the clergy. In other words, Arriaga's vision is one in which Indigenous healers were expected to become materialists with respect to their craft, even as missionaries pressured them to become Christian in their worldview.

Acosta has much to say in his *Historia natural y moral de las Indias* about the various forms of "idolatry" practiced by the Indigenous peoples of Mexico and Peru.[62] While Acosta describes many different aspects of Indigenous society and culture, he says little about medicine. In spite of that, he takes a moment in his chapter on "liquidambar and other oils and gums and drugs that are brought from the Indies" to make the following observation: "There is such an enormous number in the Indies of other aromatic woods and gums and oils and drugs that it is impossible to list them all." "I will only say," he continues, "that during the time of the Inca kings in Cuzco and the monarchs of Mexico there were famous men who cured with simples and performed excellent cures because they had knowledge of the different virtues and properties of the herbs and roots and woods and plants that grow there, about which the ancients in Europe knew nothing."[63] Notably, at the same time that he recognizes the utility of Indigenous healing knowledge, even suggesting a parallel to the "ancients in Europe," Acosta emphasizes their knowledge of the "virtues and properties" of these plants. In this way, the Jesuit placed the emphasis on the natural characteristics of plants and dispenses with any mention of supernatural healing.

Such approaches to Indigenous healing knowledge by Arriaga and Acosta, which effectively represented a disentanglement of medicine and religion, came to be reflected in the re-presentations of Indigenous healing knowledge in the correspondence and writings of Jesuit missionaries in Peru. Jesuit authors ignored and edited out any sacred meanings of plants or spiritual aspects of healing practices informed by Quechua, Aymara, Guarani, Maphuche, or any other Indigenous religion or cosmology. As a result, Jesuit accounts of medicinal plants from the Americas simply describe the plant's physical characteristics, its medicinal properties (according to the humoral system employed in the works of Galen and Dioscorides), and the physical process for preparing and using these plants therapeutically.[64] Consider Montenegro's account of the medicinal uses of a plant known as "Almaciga." "It greatly helps and cures snake bites and wounds caused by serpents, instruments or stock when it is crushed and cooked with wine; four ounces of a broth, made by cooking one ounce of rosemary leaves and [almaciga] pulp cooked in wine, given as a drink will accelerate childbirth and help to release retained menstrual blood; a powder of the same ingredients drunk with vinegar helps to cure epilepsy, dripping of urine, stomach pains and jaundice; when the juice [of almaciga] is placed at the entrance of the womb, it purges it."[65] Of course, Montenegro, like his fellow Jesuits, understood medicine in an explicitly Christian framework. But, at the same time, such descriptions of individual plants made few, if any, explicit references to a broader Christian natural philosophy.

Montenegro's naturalistic descriptions of plants in the Americas and their medicinal uses in his early eighteenth-century pharmacopoeia echo the naturalistic writing style of Jesuit authors who had preceded him. In chapter 35 of Book V of *Historia del Nuevo Mundo*, Cobo describes a plant from Peru and Hispaniola known as "yerba hedionda" as "a shrub that grows in two stages and produces many branches, whose leaves seem similar to those of the peach tree except they are a clearer green color." "It comes mainly from the farms of the Lima Valley," he continues, "and is useful in medicine because the sap from the leaves heals wounds." Once again, Cobo emphasizes that direct experience was the source of his knowledge of this medicinal plant by observing, "I have seen [this herb] cure the wound of a man who had been bitten by a dog."[66] In describing the medicinal properties or uses of plants, Cobo consistently employs a matter-of-fact tone with an emphasis on naturalistic description. In addition, Cobo and other authors often used the humoral system of the ancient Greek physician Dioscorides to classify plants as to whether they were hot or cold, humid or dry. In discussing "cochayuyu," Cobo notes that the herb was "of a cold and humid temperament" and describes several uses including how "the herb, when crushed, cools down the inflammation in the eyes and the burning heat of gout."[67]

The works of Montenegro and Cobo highlight the ways in which Jesuit authors provided a naturalistic description of plants in the Americas and their medicinal uses with no reference to the spiritual healing practiced by Indigenous healers, even as these Jesuit authors probably incorporated other elements such as the systems for classifying and characterizing the medicinal properties of plants that were a part of Indigenous knowledge systems.[68] As noted earlier, these Jesuit authors understood medicine in general within a broader Christian framework, in which God was the source of all medicine and a kind of divine

30 DOCTRINE AND DISEASE

craftsman who imbued these plants with their medicinal properties. Yet, at the same time, Jesuits rarely referenced this broader Christian framework in their descriptions of individual plants. One important exception was the well-known plant *granadilla* or passionflower, which was found in Peru as well as other regions of Spanish America. In Cobo's *Historia del Nuevo Mundo*, he includes a chapter on the passionflower, which he also called by its Aymara name, "apincoya."[69] His entry begins with a description of the physical characteristics of the plant and includes an explanation of how the "marvelous" flower reflected the "emblems of the passion of Our Savior."[70] He then provides an allegorical reading of how the different parts of the plant signified the stigmata of Jesus. A word search of a digital copy of the nineteenth-century printed edition of Cobo's work reveals only five references to "Christ" or "Jesus Christ," and his description of *granadilla* is the only one where the reference appears as part of a description of a plant.[71] Meanwhile, he makes many explicit references to "Indians" in discussing their names and uses for different plants. And finally, it is interesting to note that Cobo's discussion of *granadilla* appears in a section of his book titled "On the plants found in these Indies of the same species as plants in Spain." In the end, his ability to discuss the Christian symbolism of this plant was premised on being able to claim an equivalency to a plant species from the Mediterranean world.[72]

MISSIONS, MOTIVES, AND INDIGENOUS HEALING KNOWLEDGE

Such descriptions of plants serve as a reminder of the various motivations that prompted Jesuit missionaries to study and write about the natural world. After all, as noted by Prieto and Anagnostou, a variety of motives, from the practical to the philosophical, drove Jesuit missionaries in Spanish America to realize these efforts at encyclopedic knowledge of nature in the Americas.[73] When it came to knowledge of the medicinal uses of these plants, many Jesuits were motivated by the necessity and limits of evangelizing on the frontiers of the Spanish Empire. Many missions in Spanish America were located on the periphery of the empire and, thus, beyond the reach of urban centers and regular trade networks. In such locations, not only was there a lack of medical practitioners, especially those trained in the European healing tradition, but the cost of supplying European materia medica to remote missions was prohibitive. As a result, access to the materia medica from Europe, with which Jesuit missionaries were most familiar, was intermittent at best. Yet illness remained a regular and, at times, pressing feature of missionary life. Evangelization required healthy missionaries. More than that, many Jesuits reported in their annual letters and general histories that Indigenous peoples often suffered various illnesses without any effective remedies.[74]

For other Jesuits, their interest in medicinal plants and knowledge of nature in the Americas had more philosophical or theological motives. For example, in Acosta's letter to the reader that accompanied his *Historia natural y moral de las Indias*, he notes that the goal of his book is to disclose "the natural works that the infinitely wise Author of all Nature has performed, praise and glory may be given to Almighty God who is marvelous in all places."[75] In other words, his descriptions of the various natural phenomena of the New World were a way of glorifying God. Indeed, at several points in the text, Acosta reminds his readers that all natural phenomena were the works of God. For example, in Book IV, which deals directly with the plants, animals, and minerals of the Americas, Acosta urges his readers to "consider the providence and riches of the Creator, who distributed such a variety of trees and fruit trees to such varied parts of the world, all for the service of men who inhabit the earth." "It is a wonderful thing," he continues, "to see so many differences in shape and tastes and properties never before known and heard of in the world before the discovery of the Indies."[76] Furthermore, in his chapter on balsam, Acosta explains that "the Supreme Maker fashioned plants not only to eat but also for recreation and medicine and for man's activities."[77] This sentiment was echoed by Montenegro, a Jesuit missionary in Paraguay, who observes in his early eighteenth-century manuscript medical handbook, "Materia medica misionera," that "the inventor of medicine was the immortal God."[78] Such statements not only reveal the philosophical and theological motivations of glorifying God through the study of the natural world but also illustrate the connection between religion and medicine by showing how Jesuit missionaries used a thoroughly Christian framework to make sense of the indigenous medicinal plants of the Americas. Such assertions were part and parcel of the project of evangelization. After all, as much as the missionary project was about the conversion of Indigenous peoples to the Catholic faith, there was also an epistemological component, especially for missionaries in the Americas, to assimilate this "New World" to the existing Christian cosmology.

Beyond necessity and glorifying God, another motivation was creole patriotism, especially in the later eighteenth century. As described by Jorge Cañizares-Esguerra, creoles in Spanish America, just like their counterparts in

DOCTRINE AND DISEASE

Europe, developed a sense of pride about their home regions as well as a desire to celebrate the natural endowments of those regions. This sensibility gave rise to a "patriotic epistemology" that supported not just an interest in the natural world but a drive to catalog and describe the various natural resources of one's home region. In the eighteenth century, as the numbers of creoles in the Society of Jesus increased, it seems likely that a sense of creole patriotism also played a role in driving efforts to highlight the variety and utility of the natural resources, including medicinal plants, of various regions of Spanish America.[79]

CONCLUSION

The writings and publications of Jesuit missionaries from the seventeenth and eighteenth centuries remain some of the most important sources in the history of science and medicine in early modern Peru. In combination with other early modern sources from the Society of Jesus, they attest to the complexity and scale of Jesuit efforts to collect, record, and circulate knowledge on a global scale. At the same time, these sources provide insight into the dynamics of the flow of information and knowledge in cross-cultural and colonial contexts in the Atlantic world.

Focusing on the case of early modern Peru from the late sixteenth to the early eighteenth centuries, this chapter has argued that Jesuit efforts to collect, record, and report the botanical and healing knowledge of the Indigenous communities of Peru resulted in a secularization of that knowledge. The main evidence for this process comes from Jesuit writings that, for the most part, present naturalistic descriptions of plants and their medicinal use. This chapter has also argued that this process was paradoxically a consequence of Jesuit efforts to Christianize Indigenous communities. Because of their commitment to casting Indigenous beliefs as superstitious and idolatrous as part of the effort to highlight the truth and authority of Christianity, Jesuit missionaries, who wrote about and recorded Indigenous healing knowledge, decontextualized that knowledge by leaving out information on the spiritual aspects of Indigenous healing rituals or any spiritual significance ascribed to plants according to Indigenous belief systems.

At the same time, since many of these plants were new and had no analog in the plant species of the Old World, the Jesuits lacked a tradition for assigning significance to these plants in their Christian worldview. As noted, many Jesuit authors recognized God as the creator of the natural world and the source of any and all medicinal properties found in plants. In turn, many Jesuits emphasized

THE SECULARIZATION OF NATURE 33

the diversity and utility of New World nature as a way to glorify God. Yet, beyond such general references, explicit attempts to make sense of plants in the Americas in terms of a Christian worldview were few and far between in the specific descriptions of plants and their medicinal uses that appeared in Jesuit manuscripts and printed books.

There is another way to make sense of the naturalistic tone in Jesuit accounts of plants and their medicinal properties in the Americas. One of the core values of the Society of Jesus was learning and education. As a result, it is likely that Jesuit missionaries in Peru—like their counterparts in Europe—did their best to be informed about scholarly currents in natural history and in medicine, especially after a series of papal decrees in the seventeenth century made it permissible for Jesuit missionaries to practice medicine under certain conditions.[80] Scholarship on Jesuit libraries shows the regular presence of books on natural history and medicine. Linda Newson notes in her study of pharmacy in colonial Lima that, in the early seventeenth century, the library at the Jesuit College of San Pablo in Lima had forty thousand books, including books on pharmacy, surgery, and medicine printed in Italy, France, and Spain in the sixteenth and seventeenth centuries.[81] Other studies of the libraries of Jesuit pharmacies and Jesuit missions show that medical books were regularly included.[82] As a result, some Jesuit authors may have also been influenced by the emerging rhetorical conventions of European natural historical and medical writing. In the seventeenth and eighteenth centuries, many natural historical and medical texts in Europe jettisoned discussions of the mythical, sacred, or symbolic meanings of plants and animals in favor of strictly materialist or physical descriptions.[83] Jesuit authors, especially those who published their works, may have wanted their writing to follow such emerging conventions of natural historical and medical writing so that readers in Europe would take their works seriously.

While such intellectual motivations may have played a role, the evidence from Jesuit texts on the extirpation of idolatry and from Prieto's recent study on "Jesuit science" in South America shows that the guiding principles of evangelization encouraged Jesuit missionaries to isolate Indigenous healing knowledge from Indigenous belief systems. Moreover, as Rebecca Crocker and others have shown, the practicalities of life in the missions meant that Jesuit missionaries depended on Indigenous healing knowledge to deal with illness, especially since access to physicians and European materia medica was limited, if they had access at all.[84] These various conditions all contributed to a situation in which Jesuit missionaries played an important, if overlooked, role in the secularization of

Indigenous healing and botanical knowledge. Such activities on the part of missionaries matter because they provide further evidence of the complex relationship between religion—in this case, Christianity—and the rise of a more materialist approach to disease, healing, and the natural world in medicine and science. The efforts of Jesuit missionaries to record, edit, and transmit Indigenous healing knowledge in manuscripts and printed books also highlight the importance of considering the colonial and imperial contexts in which knowledge of the natural world was produced. In this case, it almost seems that secular accounts of plant knowledge emerged not necessarily out of a desire to undermine the religious significance of the natural world but out of existing anxieties about the worldviews associated with non-European and non-Christian religious systems that pervaded colonial contexts where Christianity was not just part of the culture of the colonizer but often provided the justification for colonization in the first place, as was the case in Spanish America.

In recent scholarship on the history of science, especially work on the history of science and empire, most studies have focused on the role of naturalists in the decontextualization of flora (and fauna) and the detachment of natural products from their embeddedness in native cultures around the world. It is an important story for understanding the epistemological consequences and violence of European science and European imperialism, working hand in hand to dispossess Indigenous peoples not just of their lands but also of their knowledge. Perhaps the most iconic representation of such decontextualization is the emergence of a visual tradition in European natural history of depicting idealized images of plant and animal specimens on a blank page. Such images not only call attention to the most important parts of the plant for the purposes of identification and classification but also depict the plants and animals as completely separate from the natural worlds and human communities that surrounded them.

At the same time, it is important to recognize that the textual descriptions of plants from outside Europe performed a similar task of ignoring some knowledge about plants and emphasizing other knowledge. As Prieto and others have observed, the Jesuits were largely written out of the history of science for a long time.[85] In part, this situation was a result of a historiographical tradition originating in the Protestant lands of northern Europe that were suspicious of, if not hostile toward, the Catholic Church and its institutions. More recently, scholars working on early modern Europe, colonial Latin America, and the history of science have done much to highlight the importance of the Jesuits to the story of early modern science and to challenge the facile notions of an inherent opposition or conflict between religion and science. The story of the role of Jesuit missionaries in the secularization of Indigenous botanical knowledge from the Americas also shows how missionaries facilitated a modern, secular vision of natural phenomena, with a central irony being that this process took place in the context of an enterprise designed to win converts to the Christian worldview of western Europe.

NOTES

1. Caldera de Heredia, *De pulvere febrifugeo*, 34.

2. On the early modern history of cinchona bark, see Boumediene, *La colonisation du savoir*; Crawford, *Andean Wonder Drug*; Gänger, *Singular Remedy*; Jarcho, *Quinine's Predecessor*.

3. For more on this historical conundrum, see Crawford, *Andean Wonder Drug*, chapter 1.

4. Monardes, *Segunda parte del libro*; Ortiz, "Fragoso, Monardes."

5. In the second part of his treatise on these medicaments, he published a copy of a 1568 letter from Pedro de Osma, a soldier who was based in Lima. See Gänger, *Singular Remedy*, 36–41.

6. For a discussion of early accounts of cinchona, see Jarcho, *Quinine's Predecessor*.

7. On the circulation of healing knowledge in pharmacopoeias, another important genre of the time, see Crawford and Gabriel, *Drugs on the Page*.

8. For Andrés Prieto's take on Gaspar Caldera de Heredia's narrative of *quina's* discovery and other early accounts, see Prieto, *Missionary Scientists*, 1–2.

9. Caldera de Heredia, *De pulvere febrifugeo*, 34.

10. Prieto, *Missionary Scientists*, 40–42, 53–61; Ewalt, *Peripheral Wonders*, 150–55.

11. Caldera de Heredia, *De pulvere febrifugeo*, 34.

12. In malarial fevers, for example, sufferers experience regular bouts of fever interrupted by periods of chills. See Webb, *Humanity's Burden*.

13. Prieto, *Missionary Scientists*; Crocker, "Healing on the Edge."

14. In addition to Prieto and Crocker, there is a vast literature on the Jesuits in the Americas; see Hyland, *Jesuit and the Incas*; Block, *Mission Culture*.

15. Ewalt, *Peripheral Wonders*; Pimentel, "Baroque Natures."

16. Harris, "Confession-Building"; Harris, "Jesuit Scientific Activity"; Friedrich, "Government and Information."

17. Prieto, *Missionary Scientists*; Ewalt, *Peripheral Wonders*; Pimentel, "Baroque Natures."

18. Brooke, *Science and Religion*; Ashworth, "Catholicism and Early Modern Science."

19. Waddell, *Jesuit Science*; Feingold, *Jesuit Science*; Feingold, *New Science and Jesuit Science*.

20. For example, Heilbron, *Sun in the Church*.

21. Berns, *Bible and Natural Philosophy*; Brévart, "Between Medicine, Magic, and Religion"; Brockliss and Jones, *Medical World*; Cunningham and Grell, *Medicine and Religion*; Gentilecore, *Healer and Healing*.

22. Here, I am not making a claim about the effect of the connection between medicine and religion in Indigenous cultures and worldviews.

23. Fleck and Poletto, "Circulation and Production."

24. "Carta ânua de 1613," 3.

25. "Carta ânua de 1616," 3.

26. Anagnostou, "Jesuits in Spanish America," 5–6.

27. These various plants are discussed in chapters 16 to 30 of Book IV. Chapters 31 and 32 also discuss plants but focus on the "plants and fruit trees that have been brought to the Indies from Spain." See Acosta, *Natural and Moral History*, 197–229. An extensive discussion of Indigenous perspectives on such plants is beyond the scope of this chapter; for information on what some of these plants meant in Indigenous cultures and how that knowledge shaped European understanding and usage, see Norton, *Sacred Gifts, Profane Pleasures*.

28. Anagnostou, "Jesuits in Spanish America," 6.

29. Bleichmar, *Visible Empire*; Schiebinger and Swan, *Colonial Botany*.

30. Cobo's work did not appear in print until the nineteenth century, with new editions appearing in the twentieth century. In this chapter, all citations of *Historia del Nuevo Mundo* refer to Cobo, *Obras*, unless otherwise indicated.

31. Prieto, *Missionary Scientists*, 101.

32. Some chapters, such as the chapter on *amancaes*, describe multiple varieties or species of the plant in one chapter. See Cobo, *Historia del Nuevo Mundo*, 179–80.

33. Cobo, *Historia del Nuevo Mundo*, Books IV–VI, 154–284.

34. Anagnostou, "Jesuits in Spanish America," 11.

35. Anagnostou, "Jesuits in Spanish America," 10.

36. Martín, *La farmacia*, 38–39.

37. Prieto, *Missionary Scientists*, 40.

38. Cobo, "Capitulo V. De la quinua," in *Historia del Nuevo Mundo*, 164. Cobo only uses the term *caída* in his description, which is probably a shortening of the phrase *caida de la mollera*, which refers to the sinking of the spaces between the unfused plates of an infant's skull.

39. Cobo, *Historia del Nuevo Mundo*, Book II, 177.

40. For more on this process, see Norton, *Sacred Gifts, Profane Pleasures*.

41. Cobo, "Capitulo LVI. Del Tobaco," in *Historia del Nuevo Mundo*, Book IV, 186.

42. Cobo, "Capitulo LVI. Del Tobaco," in *Historia del Nuevo Mundo*, Book IV, 186.

43. Crawford, *Andean Wonder Drug*, chapter 1; Camino, *Cerros, plantas*; Bastien, *Healers of the Andes*; Pardal, *Medicina aborigen Americana*.

44. Cobo, "Capitulo LXXXVIII. De la latalata," in *Historia del Nuevo Mundo*, Book IV, 194.

45. Cobo, "Capitulo LXXVIII. Del molle," in *Historia del Nuevo Mundo*, Book VI, 268.

46. Acosta, "Chapter 40: Of the Vicuñas and Tarugas of Peru," in *Historia natural y moral*, Book IV, 243.

47. Prieto, *Missionary Scientists*, 29–34.

48. Prieto, *Missionary Scientists*, 58–59.

49. Crawford, *Andean Wonder Drug*, chapter 1.

50. Prieto, *Missionary Scientists*, 40, 64.

51. Bastien, *Healers of the Andes*; Crawford, *Andean Wonder Drug*, 26–30.

52. Silverblatt, "Evolution of Witchcraft," 419.

53. Montenegro, "[Plantas de misiones]," 13. It is interesting that, in his critique of Indigenous healers, he recognizes that both men and women served as healers in Indigenous communities, as indicated by both the masculine and feminine versions of the Spanish term for "healer," *curandero*.

54. For additional examples of competition involving healing knowledge and spiritual beliefs in colonial interactions, see chapter 7 in this volume.

55. Such views were not unique to Jesuit missionaries or even to the Iberian Atlantic, as noted by Cañizares-Esguerra in *Puritan Conquistadors*, 35–82.

56. Arriaga, *Extirpacion*, 17–24. The third chapter of the book is titled "De los ministros de idolatria" (On the ministers of idolatry). On the history of the campaigns to extirpate idolatry in seventeenth-century Peru, see Mills, *Idolatry and Its Enemies*.

57. Calancha, *Corónica moralizada*, 59.

58. Fleck and Poletto note that annual letters from Jesuits in the Paraguay mission in the early seventeenth century make regular references to the prevalence of disease and the lack of effective remedies in the Indigenous communities ("Circulation and Production," 3–5).

59. Arriaga, *Extirpacion*, 74.

60. Arriaga, *Extirpacion*, 74. In the construction of the sentence in the original Spanish, Arriaga implies that Indigenous healers should retain their knowledge of "herbs" and "simples" of Peru with which they are familiar. It is less clear in the English translation.

61. Fleck and Poletto, "Circulation and Production."

62. Idolatry is the main subject of Book V. See Acosta, *Historia natural y moral*, 253–328.

63. Acosta, *Historia natural y moral*, 223.

64. Flachs and Page, "Textos clásicos."

65. Montenegro, "[Plantas de misiones]," 358–59.

66. Cobo, *Historia del Nuevo Mundo*, Book V, 218.

67. Cobo, *Historia del Nuevo Mundo*, Book IV, 179.

68. It is not yet known whether the specific examples of medicinal plants referenced in this chapter were used for spiritual healing by Indigenous healers in early modern Peru. Studies

of the work of Francisco Hernández, a Spanish physician in Mexico, have demonstrated the ways in which the Indigenous taxonomies of plants and animals shaped his work and his understanding of nature. See Chabrán, Varey, and Weiner, *Searching for the Secrets of Nature*.

69. Cobo, *Historia del Nuevo Mundo*, Book V, 207–8.

70. Cobo, *Historia del Nuevo Mundo*, Book V, 208.

71. The digital edition is Cobo, *Historia del Nuevo Mundo* (1890–95).

72. In the future, a more comprehensive survey of Jesuit writings about plants and nature in the Americas would be useful in revealing the extent to which Cobo and other Jesuit missionaries attempted to impart Christian symbolism to any plants native to the Americas that did not have an analogous species in the Old World.

73. Prieto, *Missionary Scientists*, chapter 2; Anagnostou, "Jesuits in Spanish America."

74. Fleck and Poletto provide several examples in "Circulation and Production," 3–5.

75. Acosta, *Historia natural y moral*, 10.

76. Acosta, *Historia natural y moral*, 216.

77. Acosta, *Historia natural y moral*, 220.

78. Montenegro, "[Plantas de misiones]," 4–15.

79. Cañizares-Esguerra, *How to Write*, 206–10.

80. Flachs and Page, "Textos clásicos," 120; Sander, "Medical Topics."

81. Newson, *Making Medicines*, 134–35.

82. Block, *Mission Culture*; Flachs and Page, "Textos clásicos."

83. Ashworth, "Catholicism and Early Modern Science."

84. Crocker, "Healing on the Edge."

85. Prieto, *Missionary Scientists*, 2.

BIBLIOGRAPHY

Acosta, José de. *Historia natural y moral de las Indias*. Seville: Juan de Leon, 1590.

———. *Natural and Moral History of the Indies*. Edited by Jane Mangan. Translated by Frances M. López-Morillas. Durham: Duke University Press, 2002.

Anagnostou, Sabine. "Jesuits in Spanish America: Contributions to the Exploration of American Materia Medica." *History of Pharmacy* 47 (2005): 3–17.

Arriaga, Padro Joseph de. *Extirpacion de la Idolatria del Piru*. Lima: Geronymo de Contreras, 1621.

Ashworth, William B., Jr. "Catholicism and Early Modern Science." In *God and Nature: Historical Essays on the Encounter Between Christianity and Science*, edited by David C. Lindberg and Ronald L. Numbers, 136–66. Berkeley: University of California Press, 1986.

Bastien, Joseph. *Healers of the Andes: Kallawaya Herbalists and Their Plants*. Salt Lake City: University of Utah Press, 1987.

Berns, Andrew. *The Bible and Natural Philosophy in Renaissance Italy: Jewish and Christian Physicians in Search of Truth*. Cambridge: Cambridge University Press, 2015.

Bleichmar, Daniel. *Visible Empire: Botanical Expeditions and Visual Culture in the Hispanic Enlightenment*. Chicago: University of Chicago Press, 2012.

Block, David. *Mission Culture on the Upper Amazon: Native Tradition, Jesuit Enterprise and Secular Policy in Moxos, 1660–1880*. Lincoln: University of Nebraska Press, 1995.

Boumediene, Samir. *La colonisation du savoir: Une histoire des plantes médicinales du "Nouveau Monde" (1492–1750)*. Vaulx-en-Velin: Éditions des Mondes à faire, 2016.

Brévart, Francis B. "Between Medicine, Magic, and Religion: Wonder Drugs in German Medico-Pharmaceutical Treatises Thirteenth to Sixteenth Centuries." *Speculum* 83 (2008): 1–57.

Brockliss, Laurence, and Colin Jones. *The Medical World of Early Modern France*. Oxford: Oxford University Press, 1997.

Brooke, John Hedley. *Science and Religion: Some Historical Perspectives*. Cambridge: Cambridge University Press, 1991.

Calancha, Antonio de la. *Corónica moralizada del Orden de San Augustin en el Peru*. Book 1. Barcelona: Pedro Lacavalleria, 1639.

Caldera de Heredia, Gaspar. *De pulvere febrifugeo Occidentalis Indiae y la introducción de la quina en Europa*. Edited by José María López Piñero and Francisco Calero. Valencia: Instituto de Estudios Documentales e Históricos sobre la Ciencia, 1992.

Camino, Lupe. *Cerros, plantas, y lagunas poderosas: La medicina al norte del Perú.* Piura: CIPCA, 1992.

Cañizares-Esguerra, Jorge. *How to Write the History of the New World: Histories, Epistemologies, and Identities in the Eighteenth-Century Atlantic World.* Stanford: Stanford University Press, 2001.

———. *Puritan Conquistadors: Iberianizing the Atlantic, 1550–1700.* Stanford: Stanford University Press, 2006.

"Carta ânua de 1613." In *Documentos para la historia de Argentina,* vol. 19, 65. Buenos Aires: Jacobo Peuser, 1927.

Chabrán, Rafael, Simon Varey, and Dora B. Weiner, eds. *Searching for the Secrets of Nature: The Life and Works of Francisco Hernández.* Stanford: Stanford University Press, 2002.

Cobo, Bernabé. *Historia del Nuevo Mundo.* Edited by Marcos Jimenez de la Espada. 4 vols. Seville: E. Rasco, 1890–95. https:// archive.org/details/historiadelnuevooco bogoog/page/n5/mode/2up.

———. *Obras.* Edited by P. Francisco Mateos, Biblioteca de Autores Españoles. 2 vols. Madrid: Atlas, 1956.

Crawford, Matthew James. *The Andean Wonder Drug: Cinchona Bark and Imperial Science in the Spanish Atlantic, 1630–1800.* Pittsburgh: University of Pittsburgh Press, 2016.

Crawford, Matthew James, and Joseph M. Gabriel. *Drugs on the Page: Pharmacopoeias and Healing Knowledge in the Early Modern Atlantic World.* Pittsburgh: University of Pittsburgh Press, 2019.

Crocker, Rebecca. "Healing on the Edge: The Construction of Medicine on the Jesuit Frontier of Northern New Spain." *Journal of the Southwest* 56 (2014): 293–318.

Cunningham, Andrew, and Ole Peter Grell, eds. *Medicine and Religion in Enlightenment Europe.* Burlington, VT: Ashgate, 2007.

Ewalt, Margaret. *Peripheral Wonders: Nature, Knowledge, and Enlightenment in the Orinoco.* Lewisburg: Bucknell University Press, 2008.

Feingold, Mordechai, ed. *Jesuit Science and the Republic of Letters.* Cambridge, MA: MIT Press, 2003.

———, ed. *The New Science and Jesuit Science: Seventeenth-Century Perspectives.* Dordrecht: Kluwer Academic, 2003.

Flachs, María Cristina Vera de, and Carlos Page. "Textos clásicos de medicina en la botica Jesuítica del Paraguay." *Cuadernos del Instituto Antonio Nebrija* 13 (2010): 117–35.

Fleck, Elaine Cristina Deckmann, and Roberto Poletto. "Circulation and Production of Knowledge and Scientific Practices in Southern America in the Eighteenth Century: An Analysis of *Materia medica misionera,* a Manuscript by Pedro Montenegro (1710)." *História, Ciências, Saúdo -Manguinhos* 19, no. 4 (2012). http://dx.doi.org/10.1590/S0104 -59702012000400002.

Friedrich, Markus. "Government and Information Management in Early Modern Europe: The Case of the Society of Jesus (1540–1773)." *Journal of Early Modern History* 12 (2008): 539–63.

Gänger, Stefanie. *A Singular Remedy: Cinchona Across the Atlantic World, 1751–1820.* Cambridge: Cambridge University Press, 2021.

Gentilecore, David. *Healer and Healing in Early Modern Italy.* Manchester: University of Manchester Press, 1998.

Harris, Steven J. "Confession-Building, Long-Distance Networks, and the Organization of Jesuit Science." *Early Science and Medicine* 1 (1996): 287–318.

———. "Jesuit Scientific Activity in Overseas, 1540–1773." *Isis* 96 (2005): 71–79.

Heilbron, J. L. *The Sun in the Church: Cathedrals as Solar Observatories.* Cambridge, MA: Harvard University Press, 1999.

Hyland, Sabine. *The Jesuit and the Incas: The Extraordinary Life of Padre Blas Valera, S.J.* Ann Arbor: University of Michigan Press, 2003.

Jarcho, Saul. *Quinine's Predecessor: Francesco Torti and the Early History of Cinchona.* Baltimore: Johns Hopkins University Press, 1993.

Martín, Carmen Martín, and Jose Luis Valverde. *La farmacia en la América colonial: El arte de preparar medicamentos.* Granada: Universidad de Granada, 1996.

Mills, Kenneth. *Idolatry and Its Enemies: Colonial Andean Religion and Extirpation,*

1550–1700. Princeton: Princeton University Press, 1997.

Monardes, Nicolas. *Segunda parte del libro, de las cosas que se traen de nuestras Indias Occidentales, que sirven al uso de medicina*. Seville: Casa de Alonso Escriuano Impressor, 1571.

Montenegro, Pedro. "[Plantas de misiones]." ca. 1710. Manuscript. John Carter Brown Library, Providence, RI. https://archive.org/details/plantasdemisioneoomont/page/2/mode/2up.

Newson, Linda A. *Making Medicines in Early Colonial Lima, Peru: Apothecaries, Science and Society*. Leiden: Brill, 2017.

Norton, Marcy. *Sacred Gifts, Profane Pleasures: A History of Tobacco and Chocolate in the Atlantic World*. Philadelphia: University of Pennsylvania Press, 2004.

Ortiz, Fernando Crespo. "Fragoso, Monardes, and Pre-Cinchona Knowledge of Cinchona." *Archives of Natural History* 95 (1995): 169–81.

Pardal, Ramón. *Medicina aborigen Americana*. 1937. Reprint, Seville: Facsimiles Renacimiento, 1998.

Pimentel, Juan. "Baroque Natures: Juan Nieremberg, American Wonders, and Preterimperial Natural History." In

Science in the Spanish and Portuguese Empires, 1500–1800, edited by Daniela Bleichmar, Paula De Vos, Kristine Huffine, and Kevin Sheehan, 93–114. Stanford: Stanford University Press, 2009.

Prieto, Andrés. *Missionary Scientists: Jesuit Science in Spanish South America, 1570–1810*. Nashville: Vanderbilt University Press, 2011.

Sander, Christoph. "Medical Topics in the *De Anima* Commentary of Coimbra (1598) and the Jesuits' Attitude Towards Medicine in Education and Natural Philosophy." *Early Science and Medicine* 19 (2014): 76–101.

Schiebinger, Londa, and Claudia Swan, eds. *Colonial Botany: Science, Commerce and Politics in the Early Modern World*. Philadelphia: University of Pennsylvania Press, 2007.

Silverblatt, Irene. "The Evolution of Witchcraft and the Meaning of Healing in Colonial Andean Society." *Culture, Medicine and Psychiatry* 7 (1993): 413–27.

Waddell, Mark. *Jesuit Science and the End of Nature's Secrets*. New York: Routledge, 2015.

Webb, James L., Jr. *Humanity's Burden: A Global History of Malaria*. Cambridge: Cambridge University Press, 2008.

CHAPTER 2

Vaccinating in the Name of the Lord

The Catholic Church and the Extension of Smallpox Vaccination in the Spanish Empire (1803–1810)

ALLYSON M. POSKA

During the early modern period, recurring smallpox epidemics stole lives, terrorized the populace, and threatened the very stability of the Spanish Empire. From Madrid to Manila, imperial authorities feared that the next epidemic might provoke violent insurrection, as each outbreak was a painful reminder of the Crown's inability to ensure the health and well-being of its subjects. Those anxieties accelerated in what would be the empire's waning years, when New Spain (Mexico) and Chile experienced horrific epidemics in the 1790s, and again in 1802, with devastating outbreaks in the American viceroyalties of New Granada (now Colombia and Venezuela) and Peru. However, in the midst of these crises, the announcement of the publication of Edward Jenner's *Inquiry into the Causes and Effects of the Variolae Vaccine* (London, 1798), in which he asserted that exposure to cowpox provided immunity from smallpox, appeared in Spain, piquing the interest of medical professionals and King Charles IV (r. 1788–1808).[1] The procedure was quite simple. A small lesion was made in the arm, and the cowpox lymph (the fluid from the pustules that resulted from the disease) was inserted. Over the course of about ten days, the lymph stimulated the body to produce antibodies to the infected matter, leaving the patient immune to smallpox without any accompanying ill effects. When the infection was at its peak, the lymph could be taken from that patient and placed into the arm of another. Thus, the use of cowpox to provide immunity against smallpox became the first vaccine in human history.

Responding to pleas for assistance from colonial administrators, Charles IV authorized the extension of the cowpox vaccine throughout his realms. The vaccination campaign took two forms. First, to bring the cowpox fluid to his overseas territories, he accepted a proposal from Francisco Xavier de Balmis y Berenguer (1753–1819), a physician with experience in Cuba and Mexico, to head what would become known as the Royal Philanthropic Expedition to bring smallpox vaccination to the Spanish Empire. The Royal Philanthropic Expedition consisted of Balmis, another physician, José Salvany y Lleopart (1774–1810), some medical assistants and nurses, and twenty-two boys between the ages of three and nine years old. Conscripted from an orphanage in the port city of La Coruña in northwestern Spain, the boys had not yet been infected with the disease, and Balmis used them to keep the cowpox virus alive during the Atlantic crossing by vaccinating them sequentially. One woman, the rectoress of the orphanage, Doña Isabel, volunteered to care for the children during the journey. The expedition left La Coruña on November 30, 1803, stopping to vaccinate the inhabitants of the Canary Islands. After crossing the Atlantic, they arrived first in Puerto Rico. The doctors then moved the expedition to the Venezuelan coast, where Balmis and Salvany decided to split up. Balmis and Doña Isabel took the vaccine to Cuba and New Spain (Mexico). Six months later, they sailed from Acapulco to the Philippines, using twenty-six Mexican boys to transport the vaccine across the Pacific, where Balmis and other physicians vaccinated thousands of Filipinos. Doña Isabel eventually returned to New Spain, but in 1805, Balmis moved on to China, taking three Filipino boys to Macao and Canton. While Balmis circumnavigated the globe, returning to Europe in 1806, Salvany and his crew carried the vaccine through South America. After Caracas, he vaccinated thousands in the Viceroyalty of New Granada and across Peru, until his death in 1810. At the same time, King Charles promulgated a royal edict requiring the opening of vaccination rooms in hospitals across Spain. With these two mechanisms in place to bring the vaccine to the entire empire, the Spanish Crown initiated the first truly global public health campaign.[2]

THE VACCINE AND THE CATHOLIC CHURCH

From the outset, the Spanish monarchy decided not to make vaccination compulsory and chose to rely instead on persuasion to encourage parents of all races and classes to submit themselves and their children, servants, and enslaved persons to the procedure. To aid them in this daunting task, authorities looked to the Catholic Church as a critical ally in the propagation of the vaccine. The church enthusiastically accepted this responsibility, using the opportunity to assert both its support of monarchical authority and its leadership in the promotion of this new medical technology.

There are two critical issues that undergird any analysis of the Catholic Church's participation in the smallpox vaccination campaign. First, it is important to note that the Vatican never issued a bull either for or against vaccination; thus, clergy were not bound by any papal directive on the issue.[3] Second, since the end of the fifteenth century, the Spanish Crown had acquired extensive control over the clergy both on the peninsula and across the empire. Known as the Real Patronato, the monarchy held the right to appoint most clerical benefices and had access to considerable ecclesiastical income, rights that were extended by the Concordat of 1753 between Ferdinand VI (r. 1746–59) and Pope Benedict XIV (r. 1740–58). Both Charles III (r. 1759–88) and Charles IV further consolidated monarchical power at the expense of the Catholic Church through regalist policies that denied the papacy almost any authority in Spanish lands, including asserting the Crown's right to examine all papal bulls and pontifical letters directed at a Spanish subject or an ecclesiastical official within the Spanish Empire and even to prohibit their publication (known as the *pase regio*).[4] Thus, to a significant degree, the church and its clergy functioned as an arm of the Spanish monarchy, which then employed the church and its resources to advance its own political and social goals.

The realities of governing a worldwide empire forced the Spanish Crown to rely on the church as a central participant in the smallpox vaccination campaign, as even late in the colonial period, royal and ecclesiastical authority were quite diffuse outside of the major urban centers. Thus, all the royal directives on vaccination promoted the engagement of religious as well as secular authorities. In May 1803, the Marquis of Bajamar recommended that the state direct the initial circulars to the archbishops and bishops so that they might exhort the faithful to cooperate in their efforts to extend vaccination.[5] A month later, using similar language, the Council of the Indies called on the zeal of the bishops and missionaries to help with the campaign.[6] The following September, the announcement about the formation of the Royal Philanthropic Expedition was to be sent to all the archbishops and bishops of the overseas territories.[7] And finally, the 1805 royal decree requiring the opening of vaccination rooms insisted that "archbishops, bishops and any other ecclesiastical prelates and the venerable parish priests . . . strive to persuade their parishioners to accept the beneficial practice of vaccination."[8] Although secular officials are also mentioned in these decrees, it is striking the degree to which the Crown placed the responsibility for communicating and promoting the cause of vaccination on the Catholic clergy.

The Crown expected archbishops and bishops, upon receipt of these directives, to animate the clergy over whom they held authority to promote vaccination. In response, in pastoral letters and sermons, bishops explicitly connected the clergy's spiritual responsibilities to the physical benefits of the vaccine. In New Spain, Don Antonio Bergosa y Jordan (1748–1819), the bishop of Antequera (New Spain), reminded his clergy that they could not be good doctors of the soul if they did not maintain the bodily health of their parishioners. According to Bergosa y Jordan, "those who aspire to holy orders" should dedicate themselves to the "benefit of humanity" and "persuade, extend, and execute for themselves this very easy operation."[9] Those who were diligent would be rewarded, and those who were not would be rebuked during parish visitations. Bergosa y Jordan concluded his enthusiastic message with the offer of forty days of indulgence for each person who vaccinated, as well as for those who performed the procedure, explained it, or convinced others to vaccinate.[10] Similarly, in Puebla (New Spain), Bishop Don Manuel Ignacio González del Campillo (1740–1813) noted that "the obligations of our pastoral work . . . require the provision of not only spiritual but also temporal aid." He went on to say, "Curates and our brothers, with you all we principally entrust the establishment and propagation of a procedure so important to the health of the members of our diocese."[11] When Dr. Tomás Romay, the vaccine's key proponent in Cuba, had difficulty getting people to submit to the procedure, he contacted the bishop of Havana and asked him to admonish both his rural and his urban parish priests to "encourage their parishioners during the administration of the sacrament of baptism to vaccinate their children promptly, recommending the simplicity and security of this operation."[12] Bishop José Díaz de Espada y Fernández de Landa (1756–1832) responded by calling the vaccine a "gift from the heavens" and reminding his clergy that although "it seems that we are only destined to seek the spiritual health of men, we must by the same principle (and because we are commissioned by the sovereign, and it is practiced by our brethren) contribute all our energy to enhance that which pertains to the body and diminish the evils that oppose it, both physical but especially moral ones."[13] Clergy were expected to support vaccination because the care of the body and the care of the soul went hand in hand.

44 DOCTRINE AND DISEASE

PARISH PRIESTS AND THE VACCINATION EFFORT

Although the edicts and circulars were sent to members of the episcopal hierarchy, everyone involved clearly understood that it was parish priests, *parrocos* or *curas*, who would be critical to vaccination efforts, as they had the most direct access to the empire's diverse populations and were perceived to have the most influence over mothers, fathers, owners of enslaved people, and other heads of household. Secular officials regularly pointed to parish priests as the first in line for information about the vaccination campaign. In 1805, after Dr. Cosme Argerich presented a proposal to the city council of Buenos Aires to vaccinate the poor for free, the council decided that this offer should be communicated to "the parish priests of the city and its jurisdiction so that they might make it well known to their parishioners and so that the poor might assemble at the house of the said doctor at three in the afternoon to receive this benefit."[14] Similarly, in the Spanish city of Betanzos, parish priests were the first to be provided with the notices and instructions about moving forward with vaccinations in the city.[15] As Salvany traveled through Peru, he requested the assistance of local clergy, asking the bishop of Trujillo to "command the priests of all his diocese to exhort and persuade everyone by example and preaching to quickly enjoy the prodigious benefit [of vaccination]."[16] Thus, the promotion of vaccination became an extension of the clergy's pastoral duties.

Both secular and ecclesiastical authorities recognized that parish priests had direct contact with those who were most vulnerable to smallpox—newborns and Indigenous and enslaved people—through the administration of the sacraments and, in particular, baptism. Thus, as authorities considered protocols for establishing exactly who should receive vaccination, it was often suggested that parish priests collect lists of newborns for local authorities so that they could then work with parents to ensure that they all underwent the procedure.[17] When the Council of the Indies asked Dr. José Flores (1751–1824), a Guatemalan physician, to submit his recommendations for a vaccination campaign, he suggested that when a child was brought to be baptized, the parish priest should take the opportunity to persuade the parents to bring the child back in four to six months to be vaccinated, that the priest keep a separate ledger of vaccinated children, and even that he keep some of the lymph in a separate box in the sacristy along with the holy oils. During bishops' pastoral visitations, they could then ensure that all infants had received the vaccine.[18] In Spain, the captain-general of Extremadura, Juan Carrafa, suggested that once a month, parish priests submit a list of the recently baptized so that "the justices might look for them and make them vaccinate."[19] Although royal authorities liked the idea of the priests submitting the lists, they did not approve of justices tracking down parents and forcing them to vaccinate their children; rather, they reminded Carrafa to encourage the parish priests to persuade parents to partake of the vaccine and never to use coercion.[20] The need to rely on clergy only increased in the next few years. After initial enthusiasm for the vaccine lagged, authorities looked again to parish clergy to encourage the population. In Madrid in 1808, the main hospital was having a difficult time maintaining the vaccine due to the dearth of people coming forward for the procedure. In response, authorities asserted that the lack of interest in the vaccine was due to "ignorance in the common people of Christian charity which reciprocally links men for the common benefit of the human species" and argued, "Nothing is more appropriate than the pastoral zeal of the parish priests to inculcate these principles [common Christian charity] in public and private admonishments to their parishioners."[21] More than anyone else, parish priests had access to the essential mechanisms for finding those who most needed the vaccine and convincing them of its utility.

Parish priests also had a deep personal interest in bringing vaccination to their parishioners. They knew both the afflicted and those who survived the horrible disease intimately. With each epidemic, they buried the very same children whom they had baptized only weeks before. Then, they undertook the painful task of giving comfort to the grieving parents. In La Palma in the Canary Islands, Manuel Díaz reminded his parishioners of the "horror and sadness" of the 1778 epidemic, in which "the grim contagion smallpox snatched a very considerable part of our fellow citizens and in which, not only the mothers saw their tender children pass in an instant from their sweet arms to those of death but also the wives from their husbands and these from those [husbands from their wives]."[22] Having experienced the horrors of the disease, they were duty bound to prevent further death.

In addition to keeping track of those who were most vulnerable to smallpox, the decrees and regulations that promoted and ensured the perpetuation of the vaccination called on archbishops, bishops, parish priests, and cathedral chapters (in addition to secular authorities) to actively promote the vaccine. In the language of the era, the goal was to *entusiasmar*, to enthuse the population. They were directed to "employ all their persuasion and aid" to "announce the greatness and importance of this happy discovery that providence has granted us."[23] Generating enthusiasm for vaccination could be expensive, and with regard

46 DOCTRINE AND DISEASE

to access to resources and experience in orchestrating elaborate spectacles, no early modern institution was better suited than the Catholic Church.

SPECTACLE, SERMONS, AND THE ROYAL PHILANTHROPIC EXPEDITION

In the orchestration of spectacles designed to enthuse the population to vaccinate, ecclesiastical authorities took advantage of the global procession that Balmis engineered, as the Royal Philanthropic Expedition traveled from town to town, organizing events in which the local clergy could effusively demonstrate their enthusiasm for vaccination. In most places, this display began with extravagant entourages composed of both secular and ecclesiastical officials who traveled to ports and city entrances to welcome Balmis and the boys. In the Canary Islands, the captain-general, the Marquis of Casa-Cagigal, had all the clergy as well as the military and civil authorities meet at his home and then process behind a military band to the dock to greet the expedition. Then Bishop Manuel Verdugo magnanimously took three of the boys into his carriage and drove them to the church.[24] When the expedition arrived in New Spain, the clergy also placed themselves at the center of the festivities. The bishop of Puebla used his carriage to transport a vaccinated boy.[25] Along the way, they were cheered by large crowds, military bands played, fireworks lit up the sky, and the church bells rang out. In Zacatecas, a senior cleric sat the two boys who carried the vaccine right next to him, giving them "the best view" of the event and displaying their healthy, vaccinated bodies for all in attendance.[26]

Once the entourage arrived in the city center, the political/religious ceremonies began in earnest. Although the order varied, there was almost always some combination of a solemn mass, a Te Deum, and a sermon. Clearly, the mass sacralized the otherwise secular event and all its participants and implicitly connected the miracle of the Eucharist with the medical miracle of vaccination. The Te Deum, a song of praise and thanksgiving that was recited at the end of Matins, had become central to nearly all public spectacles across Europe and the Iberian world.[27] It was a profoundly uniting moment—although led by a cleric from within the church, the people in attendance sang it in unison, and its boisterous sound spilled out into the plaza beyond the church doors, often accompanied by the ringing of the church bells.[28] The resultant soundscape both excited the people in attendance and drew people to the main plaza, where the authorities could then make the case for vaccination. In Zacatecas (New Spain), the entourage marched from the edge of town to the church, where a local prelate preached a sermon and music played. The service then concluded with a Te Deum.[29] Salvany was also greeted by these spectacles as he wound his way through South America. Ecclesiastical authorities in Cartagena (New Granada) feted him with a solemn mass, followed by the Te Deum, and concluded the festivities with a prayer from cathedral canon Juan Marimón that was "meant to arouse the most vivid recognition of divine providence and generous hand of the monarch for the gift received."[30] Through these spectacles, the church immediately co-opted the vaccination campaign and used its spiritual and temporal resources to assert its primary role in the effort.

Although the edict accompanying the Royal Philanthropic Expedition called for the creation of vaccination rooms, they were not always ready when the expedition arrived. In the interim, in many cities, the bishops provided the episcopal palace as a site for the first vaccinations. Even before the Royal Philanthropic Expedition left Spain, the bishop of Santiago de Compostela, Rafael de Múzquiz y Aldunate (1747–1821), reported to the king that he had allowed vaccinations in his palace as a means to instruct professors of surgery in the procedure.[31] He also had Balmis bring the boys from the orphanage to the episcopal palace "at his expense."[32] On the other side of the Atlantic, the bishop of Puebla (New Spain) provided "comfortable and decent" rooms near the episcopal palace for Balmis to use for the vaccinations.[33] Hosting the initial vaccinations was a public and dramatic demonstration of the church's generosity and offered yet another opportunity for the church to display its support for and authority over the effort.

The church also employed its extensive communication networks to reach as many people as possible about the benefits of vaccination. Sermons, homilies, and other works, both preached and printed, promoted vaccination, excited audiences, and reinforced the relationship between the church and the Crown. In the Canary Islands, the Dominican friar Bernadino de Acosta composed "La vacuna o patriotismo lanzaroteño," a theatrical piece that explicitly linked vaccination to the generosity and benevolence of both the church and the state.[34] A skilled preacher could rouse the crowds and convince them to undergo vaccination. In Zacatecas (New Spain), the senior ecclesiastical judge, Vicente Ramírez, looked to his best preacher to enthuse the populace. With only twenty-four hours' notice, he charged José María Semper with giving the sermon about vaccination. According to the account, when the expedition arrived at the church, Semper ascended the pulpit and praised the king for having propagated this "incalculable benefit" across his kingdoms for the "advancement of the state and the good of religion."[35] The sermon preached by the Mercederian friar Domingo Viana when the expedition arrived in Caracas (New Granada) was so well received that the captain-general, Manuel de Guevara Vasconcelos, reported that this "panegyric gave new value and energy to the feelings and continuous ovations of these inhabitants."[36] Authorities were so impressed that both the city council and some unnamed friends gave this "outstanding preacher" an additional one hundred pesos.[37]

While the solemn masses and Te Deums praised God and his glory, the sermons generally focused much more intensely on the generosity and beneficence of the king. In fact, the documentation regularly refers to the need to fulfill "the pious intentions of the King for the benefit of his beloved vassals."[38] In the Canary Islands, Acosta began "La vacuna o patriotismo lanzaroteño" by praising God but then moved quickly to laud the king and the Marquis of Casa-Cagigal for their greatness in bringing the vaccine to the islands.[39] In Antequera (New Spain), Bishop Bergosa invoked Christ at the beginning of his sermon, wishing "to our beloved priests, vicars and other clerics and to all the faithful of our bishopric health in our lord Jesus Christ," but he then praised the king, whose love for his subjects had brought priests to administer the sacraments, had created schools to teach Castilian, had fomented industry, agriculture, and art, and had now brought the vaccine.[40] The bishop of Puebla (New Spain) attributed the vaccine to their "august" and "wise" sovereign, whose decision to provide the vaccine, despite the current problems and the costs of the last two wars, was "decisive evidence" of the "zeal, enlightenment and love of our Sovereign."[41] Although the rector of the Colegio Mayor del Rosario in Santa Fe de Bogotá (New Granada), Andrés Rosillo y Meruelo, spent much of his sermon in the cathedral describing God's power to both punish with disease and then, through vaccine, remove it, the text also focused on the power of the king, even comparing the monarch to Jesus. "When in his eternal wisdom he resolved the spiritual atonement of the world, he sent his only begotten son, because he alone was capable of sanctifying our souls. Now . . . he has chosen a King according to the measure of his heart, endowed with all the willingness and virtues required to give health to bodies, by conquering the most insuperable obstacles."[42] Each of these clerics reinforced the close relationship between the king and the church, but at the same time, by emphasizing the authority of the king, they also underscored how vaccination reinforced the relationship between the monarch and his subjects. Charles IV had provided the gift of vaccination as a sign of his royal beneficence toward his subjects, and in return, his subjects of all races and classes were expected to reciprocate his generosity by submitting themselves or their charges to the vaccine.

Some of the sermons and pastoral letters also convey what Yves-Marie Bercé has called a "theology of hygiene," combining spiritual and medical information and assuring their audiences that the vaccine and its ability to ensure bodily health were as much the gift of God as was the disease.[43] Rosillo y Meruelo reminded his audience, "The Lord not only gives us health, but has also given us the preventative against a deadly disease."[44] Bishop González del Campillo in Puebla (New Spain) went further, including in his sermon discussions of the safety of the lymph and detailed explanations of the procedure.[45]

THE ECONOMICS AND LOGISTICS OF VACCINATION

Bishops also played a critical role in providing financial support for the vaccination campaign. Although in the edict that accompanied the Royal Philanthropic Expedition, the Crown accepted responsibility for the costs of the expedition and the vaccinations, local authorities had to cover, among other expenses, the festivities, hosting the entourage, and the creation of vaccination rooms. In Cuba, the bishop offered to pay the cost of bringing the vaccine to the towns that did not yet have access to it.[46] When the inhabitants of Guadalajara (New Spain) proved reluctant to provide their sons to transport the vaccine to the Philippines, the bishop paid the parents of the six boys 150 pesos each in compensation for allowing them to travel with Balmis.[47] Once all the boys brought from Spain had been vaccinated, Balmis and the Crown had to arrange for their futures in the Americas, and the archbishop of Mexico saw to and paid for their care and education.[48] Some bishops did their best to comply with the royal decree despite their ostensible poverty. In Spain, Andrés Aguiar Caamaño, the bishop of Mondoñedo, complained that he could barely support himself in the manner appropriate to a bishop, but nevertheless, he was able to provide a vaccination room and some other assistance.[49] Similarly, although the bishop of Lugo expressed a desire to aid in the vaccination efforts, he was hampered by a lack of funds.[50]

One of the most interesting clerical interventions in the Royal Philanthropic Expedition was the role of bishops in providing the boys who had not yet had smallpox to carry the vaccine to the next stop. The church was involved in this part of the process from the beginning, as Balmis had to petition the bishop of Santiago de Compostela (Spain) to ask permission to remove the boys from the orphanage in La Coruña.[51] In the Canary Islands, Bishop Verdugo y Albiturría paid the costs of taking seven additional boys accompanied by their parents from Tenerife to Santa Cruz to carry the vaccine.[52] As we have already seen, in Guadalajara (New Spain), the bishop personally compensated parents who would allow their sons to transport the vaccine with the expedition.

Finally, in many places, authorities understood the importance of having a cleric present during the procedure both to alleviate parental anxiety and to reinforce the church's authority throughout the vaccination process. In major cities, bishops supervised at least the initial vaccinations, while in rural areas, that task fell to parish priests. In Guatemala, the regulations concerning vaccination required that "in [towns] without a hospital, a vaccinator will conduct vaccinations in parish buildings with the priest and someone from the provincial junta present."[53] Although Flores had mentioned the possibility of priests performing the procedure, Balmis questioned the desirability of nonmedical practitioners vaccinating. Nevertheless, texts circulated describing the procedure, and particularly in rural areas, priests took it upon themselves to learn how to insert the lymph into the arms of their parishioners.[54] Don Francisco Sánchez de León, the parish priest, provincial vicar, and ecclesiastical judge in Antigua Guatemala, was certified to do the procedure.[55] Salvany found support and assistance from Bethlemite brother Lorenzo Justiniano de los Desamparados, to whom he entrusted the vaccine when he moved down the coast of Peru.[56] In Panamá, Lorenzo Manuel de Amaya, a friar Hospitaller of the Order of San Juan de Dios who had been trained as a surgeon in Cartagena, vaccinated 138 children and adults in his cell in the monastery.[57] Although Balmis's opposition led the bishop of Antequera (New Spain) to urge his clergy to stop vaccinating and leave the procedure to secular officials and professors, a note at the end of the same document indicates that the Crown had affirmed the ability of the clerics to administer the procedure.[58] This kind of hands-on support for vaccination was important everywhere, but it was particularly important in the Americas. The population could choose between a remarkable array of Indigenous *curanderos*, certified doctors, barber surgeons, and wise women, all of whom were believed able to provide healing and care even during the most devastating smallpox epidemics. Priests, by administering the vaccine themselves, not only could persuade otherwise-distrustful people of the efficacy of vaccination but also became trusted participants in the medical marketplace.[59]

CONCLUSION

The prominent role of the church in the vaccination campaign continued long after these initial interventions, as Balmis's instructions required that Juntas de Vacuna (Vaccination Boards) be established across the empire. The Juntas were to include the most prominent men in the community, both secular and ecclesiastical, to help preserve the fluid, educate, ensure no "false" vaccine, and act as "protectors" of the vaccine.[60] In major cities, bishops were expected to serve on the boards, and in smaller towns, parish priests served on the Juntas Subalternas.[61] Unfortunately, the ability of the clergy to influence these Juntas was significantly compromised by unforeseen changes in the political situation: the Napoleonic invasion of the peninsula and the subsequent wars of independence in the Americas. The promotion of vaccination was sidelined by the collapse of the Spanish Empire.

Faced with the potential deaths of thousands of subjects and anxious about the possibility of violence or even revolt, the Spanish monarchy embarked on a campaign to bring smallpox vaccination to its subjects. From the outset, the monarchy realized that this global effort would require it to rely intensely on the Catholic Church, which had both the personnel and the resources to persuade the empire's diverse populations to submit to the procedure. Most of the ecclesiastical hierarchy, from bishops to parish priests to missionary friars, eagerly complied. Bishops enjoined their clergy to extoll the virtues of vaccination and encouraged their parishioners to submit themselves and their charges to the procedure. They put on spectacles, gave sermons, opened their coffers, and used their influence to gently persuade parents about the efficacy of the vaccine. At a critical moment, the church's participation fulfilled an array of political, social, and spiritual goals. Promoting vaccination reinforced the church's relationship with the Crown, provided a new way to fulfill pastoral responsibilities, and reasserted its authority over the bodies and souls of parishioners throughout the Spanish Empire.

NOTES

1. The notice appeared in March 1799: *Semanario de Agricultura y Artes Dirigido a los Parrocos* no. 116 (21 March 1799). On the introduction of the vaccine to Spain, see Riera Palmero, "La introducción"; and Olagüe de Ros and Astrain Gallart, "¡Salvad a los niños!"

2. For a discussion of religious responses to smallpox outbreaks in the Massachusetts Bay Colony, see chapter 6 in this volume.

3. Bercé and Otteni, "Pratique de la vaccination."

4. Paquette, *Enlightenment, Governance, and Reform*, 71–72. For more on the Bourbon monarchy's regalist policies, see Callahan, *Church,*

Politics, and Society. On the *pase regio*, see Morales Payán, "El pase regio"; and Paquette, *Enlightenment, Governance, and Reform*, 68.

5. Archivo General de Indias (hereafter AGI), Indiferente General, legajo 1558ᵃ fol. 18v.

6. AGI, Indiferente General, legajo 1558ᵃ, fol. 19r–v.

7. "Circular de 1º de septiembre de 1803 sobre la expedición de la vacuna," AGI, Indiferente General, legajo 1558ᵃ, fol. 64, expediente no. 10.

8. *Real cedula de S.M.*

9. AGI, Indiferente General, legajo 1558ᵃ, fols. 820v–821v.

10. AGI, Indiferente General, legajo 1558ᵃ, fol. 822r.

11. González del Campillo, *Exhortación*, 4, 23–24.

12. Romay, "Informe," 30.

13. Díaz de Espada y Fernández de Landa, "Exhortación," 202.

14. Santos and Lalouf, "La construcción de las viruelas," 9.

15. Archivo Histórico Nacional (hereafter AHN), Estado, legajo 3215, no. 103, fol. 5v.

16. AGI, Indiferente General, legajo 1558ᵃ, fol. 1342r.

17. For example, AGI, Indiferente General, legajo 1558ᵃ, fol. 74v.

18. Few, "Circulating Smallpox Knowledge." Flores's text is transcribed in Yraola, *La vuelta al mundo*, 209–19 (here 218).

19. AGI, Indiferente General, legajo 3163, fol. 91v.

20. AGI, Indiferente General, legajo 3163, fol. 92v.

21. AHN, Estado, legajo 3215, expediente 241, no. 88.

22. "D. Exhorto," in García Nieto, *El barco*, 112.

23. "Reglamento por S.M. para que se propague," AGI, Indiferente General, legajo 1558ᵃ, fol. 1421v.

24. AGI, Indiferente General, legajo 1558ᵇ, fol. 17v. On the expedition in the Canary Islands, see García Nieto and Hernández, "La Real Expedición Filantrópica"; and Anes y Álvarez de Castrillón, "La Real Expedición Filantrópica."

25. AGI, Indiferente General, legajo 1558ᵃ, fol. 695r.

26. Archivo General de la Nación, México (hereafter AGN), Gobierno Virreinal, Epidemias 9, expediente 4, fols. 54r and 54v.

27. On Te Deums in Mexico, see Russell, *From Serra to Sancho*, 134–35. In Buenos Aires, see Ortemberg, "El tedeum." For examples on both sides of the Iberian Atlantic, see Torre Molina, *Música y ceremonial*. On festival culture in the Spanish Empire more broadly, see Checa Cremades and Fernández-González, *Festival Culture*; and Mínguez, González Tornel, and Rodríguez Moya, *Triunfos Barrocos*.

28. Fisher, *Music, Piety, and Propaganda*, 170.

29. AGN, Gobierno Virreinal, Epidemias 9, expediente 4, fols. 54r and 54v.

30. AGI, Indiferente General, legajo 1558ᵃ, fol. 1285v.

31. AGI, Indiferente General, legajo 3163, fol. 337v.

32. AGI, Indiferente General, legajo 3163, fol. 354r.

33. AGI, Indiferente General, legajo 1558ᵃ, fol. 696r.

34. For the text of "La vacuna o patriotismo lanzaroteño," see García Nieto, *El barco*, appendix C.

35. AGN, Gobierno Virreinal, Epidemias 9, expediente 4, fol. 52r.

36. AGI, Indiferente General, legajo 1558ᵃ, fol. 499r–v.

37. AGI, Indiferente General, legajo 1558ᵃ, fol. 499v.

38. The phrase occurs frequently in AGI, Indiferente General, legajo 1558ᵃ. For a discussion of politics and sermons in eighteenth-century Spain, see Eastman, *Preaching Spanish Nationalism*, 25–30.

39. García Nieto, *El barco*, appendix C

40. AGI, Indiferente General, legajo 1558ᵃ, fol. 816r.

41. Gonzalez del Campillo, *Exhortación*, 17–18.

42. Rosillo y Meruelo, *Sermón predicado*, 5.

43. Bercé, *Le chaudron*, 124–32.

44. Rosillo y Meruelo, *Sermón predicado*, 21.

45. González del Campillo, *Exhortación*, 5–6.

46. AGI, Indiferente General, legajo 1558ᵃ, fol. 123r.

47. AGI, Indiferente General, legajo 1558ᵃ, fol. 1036r.

48. AGI, Indiferente General, legajo 1558ᵃ, fol. 1090r.

49. AGI, Indiferente General, legajo 3163, fol. 330r.

50. AGI, Indiferente General, legajo 3163, fol. 405r.

51. Duro-Torrijos, "Los inicios de la lucha."
52. Béthancourt Massieu, "Inoculación," 290.
53. *Reglamento para la propagación*, 18.
54. For example, Gatti, *Breve instrucción*.
55. AGI, Indiferente General, legajo 1558ª, fol. 1282r.
56. AGI, Indiferente General, legajo 1558ª, fol. 1328r.
57. Renán Silva, *Las epidemias de la viruela*, 140.
58. AGI, Indiferente General, legajo 1558ª, fol. 811r.
59. On parish priests vaccinating in Argentina, see Stefano, *El púlpito y la plaza*, 84. For more on smallpox and the diverse medical marketplace in Spanish America, see Few, *For All Humanity*; and Ramírez, *Enlightened Immunity*.
60. "Reglamento de S.M. para perpetuar en Indias la Vacuna," AGI, Indiferente General 1558ª, fol. 1422r.
61. On the Juntas de Vacuna, see Ramírez Martín, *La salud del imperio*, 179–203.

BIBLIOGRAPHY

Archives

Archivo General de Indias (AGI). Seville, Spain.
Archivo General de la Nación, México (AGN). Mexico City, Mexico.
Archivo Histórico Nacional (AHN). Madrid, Spain.

Published Sources

Anes y Álvarez de Castrillón, Gonzalo. "La Real Expedición Filantrópica de la Vacuna en las islas Canarias." *Anuario de Estudios Atlánticos* 54, no. 1 (2008): 53–144.
Bercé, Yves-Marie. *Le chaudron et la lancette: Croyances populares et médecine préventive 1798–1830*. Paris: Presses de la Renaissance, 1984.
Bercé, Yves-Marie, and Jean-Claude Otteni. "Pratique de la vaccination antivariolique dans les provinces de l'État pontifical au 19e s.: Remarques sur le supposé interdit vaccinal de Léon XII." *Revue d'Histoire Ecclésiastique* 103, no. 2 (2008): 448–66.
Béthencourt Massieu, Antonio de. "Inoculación y vacuna antivariólica en Canarias 1760–1830." In *Actas del V Coloquio de Historia Canario-Americana* , edited by Francisco Morales Padrón, 2:280–307. Madrid: Ediciones del Cabildo Insular de Gran Canaria, 1982.
Callahan, William J. *Church, Politics, and Society in Spain, 1750–1874*. Cambridge, MA: Harvard University Press, 1984.
Checa Cremades, Fernando, and Laura Fernández-González, eds. *Festival Culture in the World of Spanish Habsburgs*. New York: Routledge, 2015.
Díaz de Espada y Fernández de Landa, José. "Exhortación al uso general de la vacuna (Havana 27 de enero de 1806)." In *Obispo de Espada: Papeles Biblioteca de Clásicos Cubanos*, 201–5. Havana: Ediciones Imagen Contemporánea, 1999.
Duro-Torrijos, José Luis. "Los inicios de la lucha contra la viruela en España: Técnica e ideología durante la transición de la inoculación a la vacuna (1750–1808)." PhD diss., Universidad de Alicante, España, 2014. http://rua.ua.es/dspace/handle/10045/45825.
Eastman, Scott. *Preaching Spanish Nationalism Across the Hispanic Atlantic, 1759–1823*. Baton Rouge: Louisiana State University Press, 2012.
Few, Martha. "Circulating Smallpox Knowledge: Guatemalan Doctors, Maya Indians and Designing Spain's Smallpox Vaccination Expedition, 1780–1803." *British Journal for the History of Science* 43, no. 4 (2010): 519–37.
———. *For All Humanity: Mesoamerican and Colonial Medicine in Enlightenment Guatemala*. Tucson: University of Arizona Press, 2015.
Fisher, Alexander J. *Music, Piety, and Propaganda: The Soundscapes of Counter-Reformation Bavaria*. Oxford: Oxford University Press, 2014.
García Nieto, Víctor Manuel. *El barco de la viruela: La escala de Balmis en Tenerife*. Santa Cruz de Tenerife: Ediciones Idea, 2004.
García Nieto, Víctor Manuel, and Justo Hernández. "La Real Expedición Filantrópica de la Vacuna en Canarias (9 de diciembre de 1803–6 de enero de 1804)." *Asclepio* 57, no. 2 (2005): 151–72.
Gatti, Juan Bandini. *Breve instrucción para los que se dedican a vacunar en los campos donde*

no hay profesor revalidado. Las Palmas de Gran Canarias: Imprenta de la Real Sociedad, 1804. https://bvpb.mcu.es/es /consulta/registro.do?id=447696.

González del Campillo, Manuel Ignacio. *Exhortación que el ilustrísimo Señor Don Miguel Ignacio Gonzalez del Campillo, obispo electo de la Puebla, hace á sus diocesanos para que se presten con docilidad á la importante práctica de la vacuna*. Mexico: Don Mariano Joseph de Zúñiga y Ontiveros, 1804. https://wellcomecollection .org/works/x8hd4w5f.

Mínguez, Victor, Pablo González Tornel, and Immaculada Rodríguez Moya, eds. *Triunfos barrocos: La fiesta barroca*. 3 vols. Castelló de la Plana: Universitat Jaume I; Las Palmas: Universidad de Las Palmas de Gran Canaria, 2010–14.

Morales Payán, Miguel Angel. "El pase regio y las bulas de jubileo universal: 1769–1829." *Anuario de Historia del Derecho Español 75* (2005): 919–42.

Olagüe de Ros, Guillermo, and Mikel Astrain Gallart. "¡Salvad a los niños! Los primeros pasos de la vacunación antivariólica en España (1799–1805)." *Asclepio 56*, no. 1 (2004): 7–32.

Ortemberg, Pablo. "El tedeum en el ritual político: Usos y sentidos de un dispositivo de pactos en la América española y en la revolución de Mayo." *Anuario del Instituto de Historia Argentina 10* (2010): 199–226. http://www.anuarioiha.fahce .unlp.edu.ar/article/view/AHn10a08 /html.

Paquette, Gabriel B. *Enlightenment, Governance, and Reform in Spain and Its Empire, 1759–1808*. Basingstoke, UK: Palgrave Macmillan, 2008.

Ramírez, Paul. *Enlightened Immunity: Mexico's Experiments with Disease Prevention in the Age of Reason*. Stanford: Stanford University Press, 2018.

Ramírez Martín, Susana María. *La salud del imperio: La Real Expedición Filantrópica de la Vacuna*. Madrid: Ediciones Dos Calles, 2002.

Real cedula de S.M. y señores del Consejo por lo qual se manda que en todos los hospitales de las Capitales de España se destine una sala para conservar el fluido vacuno, y comunicarlo á quantos concurran á disfrutar de este beneficio, y gratuitamente á los pobres, baxo la inspección y reglas que se expresan. Madrid: Imprenta Real, 1805.

Reglamento para la propagación y estabilidad de la vacuna en el Reyno de Guatemala. Nueva Guatemala: D. Ignacio Beteta, 1805.

Riera Palmero, Juan. "La introducción de la vacuna Jenneriana en España." *Anales de la Real Academia de Medicina y Cirugía de Valladolid 52* (2015): 191–213.

Romay, Tomás. "Informe presentado en juntas generales celebradas por la Real Sociedad Económica de la Habana, el 12 de diciembre 1804 por el Dr. D. Tomás Romay." In *Obras escogidas del Dr. D. Tomás Romay precedidas de una noticia histórico-biográfica de su vida y escritos por Ramon Francisco Valdes*, 3:29–35. Havana: Imprenta del Gobierno y Capitanía General por S.M., 1858.

Rosillo y Meruelo, D. don Andrés. *Sermón predicado en la iglesia catedral de la ciudad de Santa Fe de Bogotá el dia 24 de febrero de 1805 . . .* Santa Fe de Bogotá: Imprenta Real, 1805.

Russell, Craig H. *From Serra to Sancho: Music and Pageantry in the California Missions*. New York: Oxford University Press, 2009.

Santos, Guillermo, and Alberto Lalouf. "La construcción de las viruelas como artefactos médico-sanitarios: Análisis sociotécnico de la inoculación y la variolización en el Río de la Plata (1796–1805)." *XII Jornadas Interescuelas / Departamentos de Historia*. San Carlos de Bariloche: Universidad Nacional del Comahue, 2009. http:// www.aacademica.org/000-008/572.

Silva, Renán. *Las epidemias de la viruela de 1782 y 1802 en la Nueva Granada*. Cali: Centro Editorial Universidad del Valle, 1992.

Stefano, Roberto di. *El púlpito y la plaza: Clero, sociedad y política de la monarquía católica a la república rosista*. Buenos Aires: Siglo Veintiuno Editores Argentina, 2004.

Torre Molina, María José de la. *Música y ceremonial en las fiestas reales de proclamación de España e Hispanoamérica (1746–1814)*.

Granada: Editorial Universidad de Granada, 2004.

Yraola, Gonzalo Díaz de. *La vuelta al mundo de la expedición de la vacuna (1803–1810)*.

Facsimile edition and English version translated and edited by Catherine Mark. Madrid: Consejo Superior de Investigaciones Científicas, 2003.

CHAPTER 3

John Owen, Plague, and the Meanings of Disaster

CRAWFORD GRIBBEN

In 1670, as English dissenters came to terms with the long-term effects of the Great Plague of London, the Fire of London, and military defeat at the end of the Second Dutch War, one of their leading theologians found himself subject to an anonymous attack.[1] *A Letter to a Friend Concerning Some of Dr Owens Principles and Practices* complained that John Owen, the former vice chancellor of the University of Oxford and architect of the Cromwellian religious settlement, was undermining the institutional and theological credibility of the Church of England by encouraging dissenters to understand England's plight in providential terms. There was plenty of evidence to support this charge. In the 1660s, England had experienced a sequence of terrible calamities. Owen offered explanations for these horrific displays of God's wrath, including the claim that God had been offended by the faith and order of the established church. In *A Brief Instruction in the Worship of God* (1667), he had argued that the "cause of all the plagues and destructions" that had come upon England was the "corrupting and contaminating of the ordinances of . . . worship, or the introduction of false worship, joined with the persecution of those who refused to submit thereunto."[2] In other words, God had sent plague, fire, and humiliation because of the introduction of liturgical worship into the Church of England and because of the persecution of those dissenters who opposed it. The Great Plague was a great punishment for the sins of the godly and for the sins of the established church by which the godly were being persecuted.

For the author of *A Letter to a Friend*, the interpretations of providence that were being offered by England's leading Independent divine were encouraging the spread of an "Enthusiastick Owenistical Spirit" across the communities of dissent.[3] After all, the anonymous author argued, Owen was not qualified to offer interpretations of current events. As in so many other disputes between conformists and dissenters, the anonymous author disputed Owen's arguments by referring to questions of authority and power. Had any recognized institution "made Dr Owen a Judge of Gods proceedings against England," he asked, "or informated him that the Liturgy of our Church in which we pray to be delivered from Plagues and Famines, Battels and Murthers, should be the procuring Cause of all such Calamities? It seems the Divine Judgements are not so great a deep but the Doctor can fathome them."[4] Of course, Owen was not alone in connecting with the effects of divine punishment the spread of the bacterium *Yersinia pestis* and the consequent epidemic of bubonic plague. Neither were his claims especially novel, given the long history of providential interpretations of similar outbreaks.[5] Nevertheless, his move was risky. While Owen's letters show him counseling the bereaved, the tendency in his preaching and writing in this period to blame, rather than pity, the victims of plague raised obvious issues with regard to pastoral care.[6] Owen was responding to England's troubles in a prophetic rather than a pastoral mode, but the claim in *A Letter to a Friend* that he was suffering from an "Enthusiastick Owenistical Spirit" suggested that he might be the one in need of medical attention.

In the years after the Restoration, plague and the meanings of disaster framed some of the key debates in religious politics. Puritans on both sides of the Atlantic were offering providential interpretations of plague and other providential reversals, and Owen's writing was sometimes central to those discussions. After all, Owen was well-known in New England. He had important contacts in the region, including Edward Whalley and William Goffe, his close associates in the republican cause, and was sufficiently admired by the godly to be invited to replace John Norton as pastor of the church in Boston, Massachusetts.[7] But Owen's work could send out mixed messages in the colonies: royalist propagandists found that some of his more ambivalent responses to the restoration of monarchy played directly into their hands.[8] Owen's interpretation of the meaning of disaster was widely shared and sometimes qualified. In 1674, Increase Mather, a leading Congregationalist divine in Boston, remembered that "pestilences" had been listed among the signs of the end of the age. While

58 DOCTRINE AND DISEASE

elsewhere he was happy to draw on Owen's arguments, he dismissed the idea that there was a necessary link between illness and moral standing: "Some have made a question of it, Whether a godly man may be sick of the Plague? A needless question.... We should be very uncharitable, did we conclude, that all those that died of the Plague . . . perished eternally."[9] The controversy highlighted the extent to which, by the later 1660s, health and medical issues were marking out the differences that continued to exist between established churchmen and the leaders of persecuted dissent as they debated the environmental and political effects of the Little Ice Age.[10] But, as this chapter argues, these public health crises also marked out the tensions that existed within the communities of dissent and the growing suspicion among some of the leaders of dissent that providence could not be so easily understood. Even Owen, the "Atlas of the Independents," who had built much of his ministry around interpretations of providence, became less confident that he could properly understand the meaning of plague and the discouraging situation of the godly.[11] In the years after the Restoration, sick bodies became contested signifiers as religious leaders debated the cause and consequence of disaster.[12]

RELIGIOUS NONCONFORMITY IN RESTORATION ENGLAND

In the years that followed upon the Restoration, a significant number of religious leaders found themselves defined by law as dissenters—that is, as clergy who were unable to take up posts in the established church and forbidden from exercising their ministry outside it. Under an expanding body of penal law, those who could not conform to the new Church of England were subject to a raft of measures that were known collectively as the Clarendon Code. This body of legislation, enacted in stages from 1661 to 1665, pushed dissenters into religious and sometimes physical quarantine. The Corporation Act (1661) prohibited dissenters from exercising any public office. The Act of Uniformity (1662) prohibited any divine worship that did not follow the Book of Common Prayer. The Conventicle Act (1664) prohibited religious meetings of groups of more than five individuals who were not of the same household. And the Five Mile Act (1665) prohibited those who had worked as dissenting ministers from coming within five miles of their former livings. For the good of wider society, the godly were to self-isolate. Of course, the rhetorical link between disease and religious heterodoxy was well established, even among those who found themselves suddenly shut out of the Church of England and other English

JOHN OWEN, PLAGUE, AND THE MEANINGS OF DISASTER 59

institutions. Almost twenty years earlier, the title of the English Presbyterian minister Thomas Edwards's *Gangreana* (1646) had alluded to 2 Timothy 2:17 in worrying that the unorthodox ideas of religious radicals would spread "as doth a canker" (King James Version). But now the tables were turned. In the early 1660s, anyone—including Presbyterians—who would not conform to the expectations of the restored Church of England was identified as a vector of spiritual contagion and had to be put in quarantine.

Given these circumstances, it is hardly surprising that many of those who could not conform to the worship of the Church of England sought out alternative careers or that many of those who might otherwise have worked as dissenting preachers took up careers in medicine. Whatever the individual significance of these career moves, they illustrate, even as they qualify, the broader links that are understood to exist between "puritanism"—always a contested term—and the rise of science.[13] Although most recent scholarship on the English Revolution and its aftermath has tended to overlook medical and scientific discourses in favor of focusing on cultural, literary, or economic questions, pioneering work in this field by Charles Webster and Peter Elmer has been qualified in recent work, which has highlighted the development of medical and scientific interest among what might be described as the Puritan elite.[14] But the transition into medical careers that was made by many radical religious leaders after the failure of the revolution suggests that the domain of health and healing could be understood to offer the continuation of religious and political contest by other means. In the mid-seventeenth century, Nigel Smith has argued, "the meaning of the body became a matter of inter-sectarian dispute," but much of this dispute has still to be uncovered.[15]

In the work of medical men who concealed their republican past by taking up positions in out-of-the-way locations, as well as among the high-flying theorists who attended the meetings of the Royal Society, the organization promoted by Charles II that brought together the small circles of natural philosophers into a major scientific institution, writing about health and healing became an important, if relatively understudied, part of the "literary culture of nonconformity" and sustained important interests in the scientific cultures of the North American colonies.[16] Of course, there was a great deal of variety among those dissenters who took up opportunities in health and healing after the failure of the revolution. Some of these individuals were returning to medical careers in which they were already distinguished. In some cases, these individuals were able to retain their private religious opinions while being given positions of significant responsibility within the new regime. Peter Chamberlen, for example, had been physician to Charles I, but the seventh-day Baptist convictions that he adopted and promoted during the revolution did not prevent his also being appointed as physician to Charles II.[17] Henry Stubbe, who during his stint in Oxford in the 1650s had been an occasional research assistant for Owen as well as a friend and supporter of Thomas Hobbes, acquired enough medical knowledge to be appointed as His Majesty's Physician for Jamaica in 1662.[18] But these examples were exceptional. More often, preachers-turned-doctors sought out less conspicuous livelihoods in more obscure locations, which explains why it is so often difficult to reconstruct the details of their later careers or in many cases even to establish their dates of death. Some religious radicals expanded the practice of medicine that they had taken up during the 1650s.[19] William Walwyn, the Leveller leader, transferred his political and religious optimism into the medical career that he began sometime during the years of the republic and continued until his death in 1681.[20] John Rogers, formerly a leader of the Fifth Monarchists, took his MD from Utrecht in 1662, the same year in which he published *Disputatio medica inauguralis* as a rather unexpected postscript to his several works of religious polemic, but we do not know how long his new career—or, indeed, his life—continued.[21] Some religious radicals moved more slowly into new careers in medicine. Abiezer Coppe, the Baptist preacher who became notorious as a Ranter, was licensed to practice medicine and surgery in 1667, but his achievements as a doctor, like his date of death, are unknown.[22]

Some of those erstwhile revolutionaries who took up an interest in health and healing did not pursue any medical qualifications or make any attempt to practice medicine in conventional ways—perhaps, in doing so, staying truer to the antiformal principles of the previous decades. During the 1640s, John Pordage, a Church of England clergyman, practiced medicine without qualifications, becoming a leader of the group that emerged after the Restoration to be known as the Philadelphian Society.[23] Roger Crab, who would become a member of the Philadelphian Society, promoted his dietary ideas in such publications as *The English Hermite, or, Wonder of This Age: Being a Relation of the Life of Roger Crab . . . Shewing His Strange Reserved and Unparallel'd Kind of Life, Who Counteth It a Sin Against His Body and Soule to Eate Any Sort of Flesh, Fish, or Living Creature, or to Drinke Any Wine, Ale, or Beere* (1655). Crab understood that the consumption of meat led immediately to plague, citing biblical texts to that effect: "the Lord granted them flesh . . . and his wrath and plague came with it, as you may see in *Numb.* 11.33. & *Psal.* 78.31. *While the flesh was yet between their teeth, before it was chewed, even then the wrath of the Lord was kindled against the people, and the Lord smote the people with an exceeding great plague.*"[24] In this and similar texts, herbalism and vegetarianism were identified as means by which individuals could recover something of the experience of life in an unfallen world—and as means to avoid plague.[25] Others with more esoteric interests promoted the possibility of miraculous cures or even of achieving immortality.[26] After the Restoration, the repetition of these kinds of claims was often inherently political. Valentine Greatrakes, the so-called Irish stroker, was celebrated for his abilities as a faith healer, but his cures were thought to be especially effective among former republicans, a fact that added a significant political edge to his work by challenging assumptions that the king alone had power to cure scrofula, thus contributing to the desacralization of monarchy.[27] Many of those who faced the end of their clerical career after being forced into dissent regarded medicine as a viable and not especially demanding source of alternative employment. Owen himself, writing to a friend in July 1661, suggested, somewhat with tongue in cheek, that he might support himself in the changing circumstances of the Restoration by taking up the "study of physick and arithmetick, surgery, etc.".: "so I may bee capable in some country towne or other to get a Livelyhood, as I perceive some as ignorant dunces as I doe, and grow rich too, who have yet only a few english bookes and receipts."[28] Thus, while Rogers pursued a formal medical qualification and sought in publishing his *Disputatio medica inauguralis* to contribute to scientific knowledge, other dissenters believed that their new careers in health and healing would require no more than some familiarity with "a few english bookes and receipts" or even an awakening of their own thaumaturgical power. For many of these individuals, a career in health and healing could make up for the losses incurred by ejection—and, in some cases, an opportunity to continue by other means the religious politics of the revolution.

ENGLISH DISSENTERS AND DISASTER

If the practice of healing was represented in religious terms, so too religious explanations were invoked to frame the experience of sickness and death. In the aftermath of the Great Plague in 1665, these interpretations of health and healing were rapidly politicized. By the mid-1660s, English dissenters were interpreting England's calamities in terms of their own experience of defeat.[29] After all, the first years of the new government had been traumatic for the newly created dissenting community. From 1660 to 1662, thirteen of those who had been most

62   DOCTRINE AND DISEASE

closely associated with the republican regime were executed, all but one of them being hung, drawn, and quartered, after which what remained of their corpses was put on public display around London. It was in this period that Whalley and Goffe fled as fugitives to New England. In August 1662, up to two thousand teachers, academics, and minsters who would not submit to episcopal reordination and support the use of the Book of Common Prayer in parish worship were ejected from their positions, as repressive measures began to restrict dissenters' movements. These horrors were followed by strange wonders. From November 1664 until August 1665, dramatic appearances of unknown comets caused public comment and alarm—not least in the first issues of the *Philosophical Transactions*.[30] In March 1665, the beginning of a naval war against the Dutch republic raised questions as to the whether the English Crown and Parliament had become entangled in the affairs of Catholic states on the Continent. And then the pestilence began. In the weeks that followed, the first cases were reported of what would become the worst outbreak of bubonic plague in the history of early modern England—and the beginnings of the struggle to establish its providential meanings.

After 1660, as many religious radicals considered new careers in medicine, theologians and medical men debated whether the outbreak of plague was best understood in material or spiritual terms. Even if Owen did not follow his colleagues into a medical career, he took an active interest in public health and thought carefully about the religious meaning of plague and other forms of disaster. He had a long-standing, if critical, interest in medicine and other scientific disciplines.[31] In the early 1650s, Webster has noticed, Owen's calls for education reforms in Ireland were followed by the establishment of a committee that was dominated by members of the Hartlib circle.[32] Much of his interest in medicine and science was personal. He had, after all, experienced the deaths in difficult circumstances of most of his ten children. His first child, John, had been born in 1644. By 1649, when this son died, he had already witnessed the deaths of two sisters and a brother, in circumstances of death and disease that were vividly described by Ralph Josselin, a family friend and minister of the neighboring parish.[33] Two more sons died in 1656, when rumors circulated that Owen had died along with them.[34] The death of these boys was followed by that of a daughter, Judith, in May 1664, and a son, Matthew, in April 1665.[35] While there is no evidence either way, it is possible that Matthew's death may have come as a consequence of an early outbreak of plague. In the absence of any significant body of life writing, other than the small number of letters in which

JOHN OWEN, PLAGUE, AND THE MEANINGS OF DISASTER   63

these bereavements are not mentioned, we do not know how Owen responded to the loss of his children.[36] His letters illustrate his own long experience of sickness: "I have been a while under physic for my eye and tis now I blesse God very welle. I have found I think the certaine and proper remedy at last, viz. the millegides," he explained to John Thornton in the spring of 1663.[37] If he did not comment on the health of his family members, Owen wrote a great deal about his own well-being.

This reference to "millegides"—a now-unknown medicine, which Peter Toon, who edited Owen's letters, connected with melicrate—suggests that throughout much of his career, Owen paid attention to scientific discovery, even if he contested the ways in which scientific discourses could be used to undercut theological claims.[38] He made frequent, if only ever occasional, scientific references: he discussed Lucretian atomism, for example, in a sermon that he preached to members of Parliament in April 1646, in his treatise *Of Schism* (1657), and again in his discussion of the integrity of biblical manuscripts (1658).[39] Owen's view of the Royal Society could be scathing.[40] He took a critical attitude toward the professionalization of this kind of empirical inquiry and to the institution that historians of science have often identified as a crucial vector in their explanation of the relationship between "puritanism," the Scientific Revolution, and early Enlightenment. In correspondence from the early 1660s, he satirized the Royal Society's members' preoccupation with empirical rather than ethical concerns: "I hope they are upon some serious consultations for the benefit of mankind, how a hen may sit on her eggs and addle none, how oysters may be so geometrically layd that in stead of 200 or 300, an oyster wench may lay 8 or 900 in her basket at once and sell them all without tearing her throat or tyring her head, how his majestys bears may be taught to bite none but fanatickes and that without hurting their teeth."[41] But for all that Owen poked fun at science and scientists, he was certainly serious about the need to interpret crises in public health.

These crises were acute in the mid-1660s. We do not know where Owen was living during the dreadful months in which the capital was ravaged by plague and fire.[42] By the early 1660s, he had divided his family, with some of his children staying in a safe house in Hanslope, Buckinghamshire, while he, his wife, Mary, and his son Matthew lived with Charles Fleetwood's family in Stoke Newington. By the mid-1660s, Mary (1651–1682), Judith (d. 1664), and Matthew (d. 1665) were Owen's only known surviving children. Peter Toon suggests that Owen's children—presumably Mary and Judith—were residing in Hanslope with Sir

64 DOCTRINE AND DISEASE

Thomas Tyrrell, but this must be unlikely, given Tyrrell's role in the trial and execution of the regicides.[43] Owen was living in Charterhouse, London, when Mary, his first wife, died in 1677, after which he moved to new accommodation in Leadenhall Street, London, to be closer to the premises used by the congregation that he led after 1673.[44] Owen may have favored the latter location because it provided him with easy access to London, where, despite the restrictions of the Clarendon Code, dissenters continued to gather, and Owen occasionally preached in these clandestine meetings.[45] As the crisis of the mid-1660s deepened, dissenters began to move into the open. After all, many of the London churches were empty, some having been destroyed by fire, and a large number of conformist clergy had been among those who had fled into the surrounding country. Plague and fire created opportunities for pastoral ministry that many dissenting preachers were keen to take up. Richard Baxter listed in his memoirs the names of a number of dissenting preachers who during the mid-1660s began in the capital city the kind of public ministry that the Clarendon Code had been designed to prevent, including Thomas Manton, Thomas Dolittle, Samuel Annesley, James Janeway, and Thomas Vincent.[46] Baxter clearly admired these men. He was less enthusiastic about Owen's failure to take similar risks. Baxter noted that Owen "kept far off" from London until the fire subsided.[47] He did not explain that Owen had no real reason to enter London during the dangerous months between spring 1665 and late summer 1666. Unlike other ministers whom Baxter named, Owen had never led any of the city's congregations and had, in fact, already taken up pastoral responsibilities elsewhere. After leaving Oxford, in 1659, Owen had returned to Stadhampton, Oxfordshire, "where he was possess'd of a good estate: Here he liv'd privately for some time, 'till the persecution grew so hot, that he was oblig'd to remove from place to place."[48] Owen continued occasionally to preach for this congregation, but his principal pastoral responsibility related to the tiny congregation that he had gathered in London, in Wallingford House, in 1658, which by 1662 had moved from the city to regather in the home of Charles Fleetwood, in Stoke Newington (where Matthew Owen was buried in April 1665).[49] In any case, Owen had turned his mind to the possibility of emigration. Throughout much of 1664, he was involved in conveyancing for the purchase of land in New England—a deal that was never completed—close to where Whalley and Goffe had taken refuge.[50]

It is difficult to know how seriously to take Baxter's description of Owen's movements—and the implied criticism of his lack of pastoral courage. Baxter had been censuring Owen since the late 1640s and had not himself attempted to minister within the plague-stricken city, limiting his exhortatory and evangelistic work to the writing of a handbill, *Short Instructions for the Sick* (1665), copies of which were pasted around London for the benefit of those who could not leave.[51] Even though it is striking how little even the early and admiring Owen biographies speak about this period of his life, Baxter may not have been the most reliable guide to the experiences of his middle career.

But whatever the men's personal differences, Baxter shared with Owen a conviction that he understood why London had been hit by so many calamities. "And now after all the Breaches on the Churches, the Ejection of the Ministers, and Impenitancy under all," he observed,

> Wars and Plague and danger of Famine began all at once upon us. War with the Hollanders, which yet continueth: And the driest Winter, Spring and Summer that ever Man alive knew . . . so that the Grounds were burnt like the High-ways, where the Cattle should have fed. . . . Every Man is a terrour to his Neighbour and himself: for God for our Sins is a Terrour to us all. O how is London, the place which God hath honoured with his Gospel above all Places of the Earth, laid low in Horrours, and wasted almost to Desolation, by the Wrath of God . . . and a God-hating Generation are consumed in their Sins.[52]

As the crises deepened, Owen, Baxter, and other leaders of dissent agreed that the punishment of the establishment and the vindication of the godly were among the meanings of disaster.

OWEN AND DIVINE PROVIDENCE

Owen's high Calvinist theology allowed him to understand history as a theater of divine activity and therefore as something that could be understood, for, as he put it in 1681, God "expounds his works by his word" and "expounds his word by his works."[53] In his early years of ministry, as he had witnessed the success of the cause of Parliament against the king and then the success of the army against Parliament, Owen had been confident that providence could be easily understood. Throughout the late 1640s and the 1650s, he had repeatedly suggested that Parliament's victory in the civil wars and the establishment of a commonwealth that provided religious liberty to the godly had occurred as a consequence of divine intervention.[54] This interpretation of history fit neatly

66 DOCTRINE AND DISEASE

with Owen's eschatological expectations, in which, in his early career, he assumed that the godly would achieve increasing influence until the global population as a whole embraced Protestant Christianity.[55] His preaching gave this expectation an explicitly English focus. Preaching at the relief of the siege of Colchester in September 1648, for example, he had insisted that the "God of Naseby"—who had supported the forces of Parliament in their civil war against the king—had propelled his people into power in order that they might advance God's purposes on Earth (8:88, 102). During the 1650s, Owen became increasingly disenchanted with the Cromwellian regime, which he feared was backsliding from its earlier achievements. This concern led Owen, during his very short tenure as a member of the first Protectoral Parliament (1654), to identify with a group of republican critics of the Cromwellian regime and to provide practical assistance to the group of army officers who warned Cromwell off accepting the offer of the crown (1657). After Oliver's death and the installation of Richard Cromwell as Lord Protector, Owen and the members of a small faction of army republicans who met at Wallingford House intervened dramatically to collapse the government in the hope of renewing the "good old cause." In fact, their actions created the political vacuum, attended by chaos, violence, and the prospect of renewed civil war, that led directly to the conspiracy of moderates that facilitated the return of the king.[56] In the immediate aftermath of the Restoration, Owen struggled to make sense of the new world. In the early 1660s, his publications vacillated between acceptance of the new political realities and clandestine attempts to evade them. Like other dissenters, his concern in the early years of Restoration was to understand why, if God had backed the revolution, he had also allowed it to fail. Owen recovered from this crisis in his providential interpretation of history in the mid-1660s, when a series of catastrophes seemed to suggest that God had not in fact abandoned the "good old cause." The outbreak of plague and other disasters provided Owen with the tools for an effective theodicy and renewed his commitment to providential interpretations of history.

In the middle and later 1660s, after the ambiguity of defeat, Owen was again confident that God's activity in providence could be understood. In these "latter days," he noted in *A Brief Instruction in the Worship of God*, which he published anonymously in 1667, "all the plagues and destructions that . . . are to be brought upon the world" were coming as a consequence of the "righteous judgement of God" (15:477). In July 1673, he reminded his listeners of God's warnings in the "plague, fire, sword" and suggested that further judgments would follow upon the state's continuing persecution of the godly (16:464, 466). Owen returned to this theme in March 1674, when he warned his congregation that terrible events would come upon England because of the "violence they have done to God's portion" (9:295). But, he recognized, members of dissenting churches would also experience these judgments, not because they had persecuted others of the godly but on account of their own "neglect of duty" (9:295). Even dissenters deserved the judgments that were coming their way. Owen intensified these warnings as the wider population turned from the moral and spiritual achievements of the revolution and as the community of dissenters was torn apart by disputes about justification by faith alone and other doctrines that had been central to the Protestant Reformation. In January 1676, Owen warned, "All the contests God hath had with this nation, by poverty, by that dreadful judgement of fire, and the like, threaten us every day. If these be not calls to mourning, we can have none from the word of God nor from conjunctions of providence" (16:525). In May 1677, he warned his congregation that God would have to intervene in a dramatic way because his "warnings are despised," his "patience is abused," and the people of England believed themselves to be secure (9:394–95). In October 1677, he warned of "men so Skillfull at Numbering and Mensuration, as they will tell you, How many feet there are to the Center of the Earth, or to the moone; and how many Inches will compass the Earth." But these were the men who found it so difficult to "number their days" or to understand the course of providence: "All the Warnings that God ever gave to a People, have been upon us, Ordinary, Extraordinary; and the Voice of all of them is, Consider the Power of Gods Anger; But who takes notice of them?"[57] In April 1679, Owen preached on "national sins and national judgements": "London is ruined and England fallen," he lamented, because of the prevalence of "atheism and profaneness, blood and murder, adultery and uncleanness, and pride.... The plague, the fire, the sword, great distresses and poverty" should have been "enough to make the hearts of men to tremble," but they would not repent (16:481–82). Owen continued to develop this theme, preaching to his congregation in December 1681, as his public ministry was coming to an end and as he extended his warning to the dissenting community as a whole. The "churches in this nation are not guilty of those sins whereby God is provoked against the nation to bring on national judgments," he explained, "but I do say, that churches and professors in this nation are guilty of those sins for which Christ will bring correcting judgments upon churches and professors." England and the community of dissenters that it continued to persecute were "all in the same way and bottom, though not all upon the same account" (9:10–11). Looking at the succession of disasters,

68 DOCTRINE AND DISEASE

Owen believed that England deserved its judgment and that dissenters did too: "Will you say the time of the public plague was not perilous, because you are alive? No. Was the fire not dreadful, because your houses were not burned? No you will, notwithstanding, say it was a dreadful plague, and a dreadful fire. And pray consider, is not this a perilous season, when multitudes have an inclination to depart from the truth, and God, in just judgment, hath permitted Satan to stir up seducers to draw them into pernicious ways, and their poor souls perish for ever?" (9:327). Preaching in 1681, he remembered how "prodigious appearances in heaven"—the comets that provoked such alarm in the mid-1660s—had been warnings of the "wasting, desolating plague," the "raging fire," and the "bloody war that ensued thereon" (9:10–11). "Brethren, you know my mind full well in this matter," he continued, reminding his listeners that he had been insisting on this interpretation of providence for the previous three years (9:10–11). For, in the skies above London, strange comets had returned.

And so Owen, at the end of his career, understood that further judgments were coming upon England and its dissenting churches. He recognized that his warnings were not being heeded. Preaching on an unknown date on "the furnace of divine wrath" (Ezekiel 22:17–22), he applied the text to his own congregation: "It is my judgement we are all going into the same furnace . . . with all the brass, and tin, and lead, and iron, in the nation,—going into the same furnace. . . . I have been speaking of it to this congregation for some years, that we are all going into the same furnace. . . . Things are so stated in the rule, so stated in providence, that it is your duty and mine to prepare for the furnace, a fiery furnace, a smoking furnace, that I am afraid God will cast this whole nation into" (16:428). Owen feared that God's providential judgments had not persuaded the godly to separate from the world: "the plague, the fire, have not done it; signs in the heaven above and in the earth beneath have not done it; the sincere preaching of the gospel, though in weakness, hath not done it; entreaties, beggings, exhortations, have not done it; our prayers have not done it; we cleave unto the world still" (16:428). In April 1680, he reminded his listeners, "For many years . . . I have been warning of you continually of an approaching calamitous time. . . . In all these things I have foretold you of perilous, distressing, calamitous times; and in all men's apprehensions they now lie at the door, and are entering in upon us" (9:491). He insisted on the point: "I must repeat it again and again; I have been warning you for some years, and telling you it would be so" (9:499). With the openly Catholic James, the duke of York, almost certain to succeed to the throne, the English Reformation was coming to an end, and England should brace itself for new experiences of disaster (9:505).

CONCLUSION

Owen died fearing for the prospects of English Protestantism and realizing that the providential narratives he had promoted throughout much of his career could not always explain the circumstances in which the dissenting churches found themselves. Plague, fire, and other forms of disaster could have many meanings, it appeared, and not all of them were clear. For all that Owen's providentialism could explain England's calamities, it did not necessarily explain why dissenters were suffering too. "Our Father hath spit in our face," he advised his listeners on July 1, 1681, echoing Fleetwood's comment about the failure of the revolution one generation before (16:492).[58] "I do not know that he hath given me a greater rebuke, in the whole course of my ministry, than that have been labouring in fire to discover the causes of God's withdrawing from us without any success" (16:492). Just before the end of the year, he addressed a congregation in a day of public fasting and admitted, quite frankly, "no man hath less of faith than I,—no man doth more despond" for the future prospects of the English church (9:6). For two decades, God had been sending warnings. These warnings had appeared in the "wasting, desolating plague," the "consuming, raging fire," and the "bloody war that ensued thereon." He had sent warnings in "prodigious appearances in heaven above," a warning that was being repeated in the comet "which at present hangs over us, as an ensign of God's supernal host" (9:11).[59] And no one, he feared, was paying any attention. England appeared to be coming to terms with the prospect of a Catholic monarchy. And the dissenting churches were turning their backs on the achievements of the Reformation. The comets were a warning that plague, fire, and disaster were coming again.

Owen's own health was failing. By August 1683, it was obvious that he was in serious decline. But in death, as in life, he could not escape the impact of the Scientific Revolution. In his last weeks, in his home in Ealing, Owen was attended by Sir Edmund King, a physician to Charles II, ironically, as well as a fellow of the Royal Society and a frequent contributor to the *Philosophical Transactions*.[60] After Owen's death, one of his younger congregants, John Asty, wrote up notes for his first extensive biography (1721), in a notebook that contained detailed commentary on the first issue of the *Philosophical Transactions* (1665–66), which narrated the study of comets in scientific rather than providential terms.[61] It was a telling juxtaposition of content. Asty, who in the early eighteenth century did more than anyone else to preserve Owen's reputation, was studying arguments that made the motion of comets a matter of mathematical rather than providential significance. The "Enthusiastick Owenistical Spirit" that was feared by

70   DOCTRINE AND DISEASE

the anonymous author of *A Letter to a Friend* may have been less contagious than expected.[62] For even those who listened to Owen's preaching, with all of its hesitations about the institutions that were driving forward the Scientific Revolution, were engaging with the new discourses of science. In death, as in life, Owen could not help but be involved in the changing meanings of disaster.

NOTES

1. For a survey of this these disasters, see Hutton, *Restoration*. For recent discussions of plague and its cultural consequences, see Slack, *Impact of Plague*; Munkhoff, "Searchers of the Dead"; Moote and Moote, *Great Plague*; Greenberg, "Plague, the Printing Press, and Public Health"; Gilman, *Plague Writing*; and Miller, *Literary Culture of Plague*. For Owen's circumstances in the 1660s, see Gribben, *John Owen and English Puritanism*. I am grateful to Ariel Hessayon for his comments on an earlier draft of this chapter.

2. Owen, *Works of John Owen*, 15:477. On Owen's congregations in the 1660s and early 1670s, see Gribben, "John Owen, Lucy Hutchinson, and the Experience of Defeat"; Gribben, "Experience of Dissent."

3. *Letter to a Friend*, 60. For a discussion of providentialism in this period, see Worden, "Providence and Politics," in *God's Instruments*, 33–62. For a discussion of the ways in which the "enthusiasm" was politicized in this period, see West, *Dryden and Enthusiasm*, 54–93.

4. *Letter to a Friend*, 41.

5. Rolfe, "Fatal and Memorable."

6. Owen to Lady Elizabeth Hartopp, ca. May 1674, in *Correspondence of John Owen*, 157.

7. Weimer, *Constitutional Culture*, 14–15, 84–85.

8. Weimer, *Constitutional Culture*, 246.

9. Mather, *Day of Trouble*, 6, 21. For Mather's use of Owen, see Mather, *Call from Heaven*, 57, 84.

10. The links between political crisis and global cooling are described in Parker, *Global Crisis*.

11. Owen was described as the "Atlas of the Independents" in Wood, *Athenae Oxoniensis*, 4:98.

12. For a recent discussion of dissenters' responses to plague, see Miller, *Literary Culture of Plague*, 95–130.

13. On the definition of "puritanism," see Collinson, "Antipuritanism."

14. Rattansi, "Helmontian-Galenist Controversy"; Webster, *Great Instauration*; Elmer,

"Medicine, Religion, and the Puritan Revolution"; Calloway, *Natural Theology*. Links between radical politics and medical careers have been noted in McDowell, *English Radical Imagination*, 186.

15. Smith, *Perfection Proclaimed*, 15.

16. On the contours of dissenting print, see, most influentially, Keeble, *Literary Culture of Nonconformity*. For an early example of North American material in the *Philosophical Transactions*, see "Of the Way of Killing Ratle-Snakes, Used in Virginia."

17. King, "Chamberlen, Peter."

18. Jacob, *Henry Stubbe*, 163–64.

19. Hill, *World Turned Upside Down*, 297–301.

20. Taft, "Walwyn, William."

21. Gribben, *Puritan Millennium*, 55–78.

22. Hessayon, "Coppe, Abiezer."

23. Hessayon, "Pordage, John."

24. Crab, *English Hermite*, 9.

25. Rudrum, "Ethical Vegetarianism"; Bowers, "Roger Crab."

26. Leng, *Benjamin Worsley*, 116, 128–29. See also the discussion of the pursuit of immortality in Webster, *Great Instauration*, 246–323; and Haycock, *Mortal Coil*.

27. Gribben, "Angels and Demons."

28. Oxford, Bodleian Library, MS Rawl lett 109 fol. 83. I owe this reference to Jenny-Lyn de Klerk.

29. Hill, *Experience of Defeat*.

30. On the discussion of comets in the Royal Society, see, for example, Auzout, "Motion of the Late Comet"; "Extract of a Letter."

31. Calloway, *Natural Theology*, 24; Calloway, "John Owen and Scientific Reform."

32. Webster, *Great Instauration*, 225–26.

33. Josselin recorded the impact of rising food prices and an epidemic of smallpox in the winter of 1648–49; Josselin, *Diary of Ralph Josselin*, 140, 161.

34. Gribben, *John Owen and English Puritanism*, 166.

35. Gribben, *John Owen and English Puritanism*, 225–27.

36. John Owen to John Thornton, ca. 1664, in *Correspondence of John Owen*, 135.

37. John Owen to John Thornton, 1663, in *Correspondence of John Owen*, 131.

38. Owen, *Correspondence of John Owen*, 131n5.

39. Owen, *Works of John Owen*, 8:12, 13:165, 16:386.

40. For additional discussion of the Royal Society, see chapter 4.

41. John Owen to John Thornton, ca. 1664, in *Correspondence of John Owen*, 132. Owen's satirical comments may be compared with content in the *Philosophical Transactions*, such as "Way of Preserving Birds"; Auzout, "Observations About Shining Worms in Oysters."

42. The biography that was included in Owen, *Seventeen Sermons*, passes over Owen's movements in the 1660s in a single sentence (xxiv).

43. Owen, *Correspondence of John Owen*, 131n3; Handley, "Tyrrell, Sir Thomas."

44. Owen, *Seventeen Sermons*, xxxiv; Gribben, *John Owen and English Puritanism*, 255.

45. Baxter, *Reliquiae Baxterianae*, 2:341n158.

46. Baxter, *Reliquiae Baxterianae*, 2:341. For Vincent's career during the plague, see Miller, *Literary Culture of Plague*, 95–130; for further discussion of Vincent's writing on plague, see chapter 5.

47. Baxter, *Reliquiae Baxterianae*, 2:341; Toon, *God's Statesman*, 131; Gribben, *John Owen and English Puritanism*, 227.

48. Asty, *Memoirs of the Life*, xxii.

49. Gribben, *John Owen and English Puritanism*, 227.

50. Owen was closely associated with Whalley and Goffe in 1659–60; see Gribben, *John Owen and English Puritanism*, 205, 223. On the later careers of Whalley and Goffe, see Jenkinson, *Charles I's Killers*.

51. Baxter, *Reliquiae Baxterianae*, 1:492. For the difficult relationship between Owen and Baxter, see Cooper, *John Owen, Richard Baxter*.

52. Baxter, *Reliquiae Baxterianae*, 2:289–90.

53. Owen, *Works of John Owen*, 16:488. In-text parenthetical citations in the following sections refer to this edition.

54. Gribben, *John Owen and English Puritanism*, 104–23.

55. Gribben, "John Owen's Eschatology."

56. Hutton, *Restoration*, 38.

57. Owen's fast sermon on Psalm 90:11 (Thursday, 18 October 1677), Doctor Williams's Library, London, MS L6/3, fol. 2r–19v.

58. For Fleetwood's use of the same expression in December 1659, see document xxxii.f.205b, Firth, *Clarke Papers*, 4:220. For more on the use of this expression, see Worden, *God's Instruments*, 56.

59. This was an appearance of Halley's Comet.

60. Owen, *Seventeen Sermons*, xxxvi; Martensen, "King, Sir Edmund."

61. Edinburgh, New College MS Comm 2, fols. 338–48; Auzout, "Motion of the Late Comet," 3–8.

62. For a discussion of the ways in which the "enthusiasm" was politicized in this period, see West, *Dryden and Enthusiasm*, 54–93.

BIBLIOGRAPHY

Asty, John. *Memoirs of the Life of John Owen*. London: John Clark, 1721.

Auzout, Adrian. "The Motion of the Late Comet Predicted." *Philosophical Transactions* 1 (1665): 3–8.

———. "Observations About Shining Worms in Oysters." *Philosophical Transactions* 1 (1666): 203–6.

Baxter, Richard. *Reliquiae Baxterianae*. Edited by N. H. Keeble, John Coffee, Tim Cooper, and Tom Charlton. 5 vols. Oxford: Oxford University Press, 2020.

Bowers, Rick. "Roger Crab: Opposition Hunger Artist in 1650s England." *Seventeenth Century* 18, no. 1 (2003): 93–112.

Calloway, Katherine. *Natural Theology in the Scientific Revolution: God's Scientists*. London: Pickering and Chatto, 2014.

———. "Owen and Scientific Reform." In *The T&T Clark Handbook of John Owen*, edited by Crawford Gribben and John Tweeddale, 223–50. London: T&T Clark, 2022.

Collinson, Patrick. "Antipuritanism." In *The Cambridge Companion to Puritanism*, edited by John Coffey and Paul C. H. Lim, 19–33. Cambridge: Cambridge University Press, 2008.

Cooper, Tim. *John Owen, Richard Baxter and the Formation of Nonconformity*. Aldershot, UK: Ashgate, 2011.

Crab, Roger. *The English Hermite, or, Wonder of This Age: Being a Relation of the Life of Roger Crab*. London, 1655.

Elmer, Peter. "Medicine, Religion, and the Puritan Revolution." In *The Medical Revolution of the Seventeenth Century*, edited by Roger French and Andrew Wear, 10–45. Cambridge: Cambridge University Press, 1989.

"Extract of a Letter, Lately Written from Rome, Touching the Late Comet, and a New One." *Philosophical Transactions* 1 (1665): 17–18.

Firth, C. H., ed. *The Clarke Papers: Selections from the Papers of William Clarke.* 4 vols. London: Camden Society, 1891–1901.

Gilman, Ernest B. *Plague Writing in Early Modern England.* Chicago: University of Chicago Press, 2009.

Greenberg, Stephen. "Plague, the Printing Press, and Public Health in Seventeenth-Century London." *Huntington Library Quarterly* 67, no. 4 (2004): 508–27.

Gribben, Crawford. "Angels and Demons in Cromwellian and Restoration Ireland: Heresy and the Supernatural." *Huntington Library Quarterly* 76, no. 3 (2013): 377–92.

———. "The Experience of Dissent: John Owen and Congregational Life in Revolutionary and Restoration London." In *Church Life in Seventeenth-Century England: Pastors, Congregations, and the Experience of Dissent*, edited by Michael Davies, Anne Dunan-Page, and Joel Halcombe, 119–35. Oxford: Oxford University Press, 2019.

———. *John Owen and English Puritanism: Experiences of Defeat.* Oxford: Oxford University Press, 2016.

———. "John Owen, Lucy Hutchinson, and the Experience of Defeat." *Seventeenth Century* 30 (2015): 179–90.

———. "John Owen's Eschatology." In *The Power of God for Salvation: Papers Read at the 2015 Westminster Conference*, 31–50. London: Tentmaker, 2016.

———. *The Puritan Millennium: Literature and Theology, 1550–1682.* Dublin: Four Courts, 2000.

Handley, Stuart. "Tyrrell, Sir Thomas (1593/94–1672)." In *Oxford Dictionary of National Biography.* Oxford: Oxford University Press, 2004; online ed., 2008. https://doi.org/10.1093/ref:odnb/27955.

Haycock, David Boyd. *Mortal Coil: A Short History of Living Longer.* New Haven: Yale University Press, 2010.

Hessayon, Ariel. "Coppe, Abiezer (1619–1672?)." In *Oxford Dictionary of National Biography.* Oxford: Oxford University Press, 2004; online ed., 2008. https://doi.org/10.1093/ref:odnb/6275.

———. "Pordage, John (bap. 1607, d. 1681)." In *Oxford Dictionary of National Biography.* Oxford: Oxford University Press, 2004; online ed., 2008. https://doi.org/10.1093/ref:odnb/22546.

Hill, Christopher. *The Experience of Defeat: Milton and Some Contemporaries.* London: Faber, 1984.

———. *The World Turned Upside Down: Radical Ideas During the English Revolution.* 1972. Reprint, London: Penguin, 1991.

Hutton, Ron. *The Restoration: A Political and Religious History of England and Wales, 1658–1667.* Oxford: Oxford University Press, 1985.

Jacob, James R. *Henry Stubbe, Radical Protestantism and the Early Enlightenment.* Cambridge: Cambridge University Press, 1983.

Jenkinson, Matthew. *Charles I's Killers in America.* Oxford: Oxford University Press, 2019.

Josselin, Ralph. *The Diary of Ralph Josselin, 1616–1683.* Edited by Alan Macfarlane. London: British Academy, 1976.

Keeble, N. H. *The Literary Culture of Nonconformity.* Leicester: Leicester University Press, 1987.

King, Helen. "Chamberlen, Peter (1601–1683)." In *Oxford Dictionary of National Biography.* Oxford: Oxford University Press, 2004; online ed., 2008. https://doi.org/10.1093/ref:odnb/5067.

Leng, Thomas. *Benjamin Worsley (1618–1677): Trade, Interest and the Spirit in Revolutionary England.* Woodbridge, UK: Boydell, 2008.

Letter to a Friend Concerning Some of Dr Owens Principles and Practices with a Postscript to the Author of the Late Ecclesiastical Polity, and an Independent Catechism, A. London: Spencer Hickman, 1670.

Martensen, Robert L. "King, Sir Edmund (bap. 1630, d. 1709)." In *Oxford Dictionary of*

National Biography. Oxford: Oxford University Press, 2004; online ed., 2008. https://doi.org/10.1093/ref:odnb/15557.

Mather, Increase. *A Call from Heaven to the Present and Succeeding Generations*. Boston: John Ratcliff, 1679.

———. *The Day of Trouble Is Near*. Cambridge, MA: Marmaduke Johnson, 1674.

McDowell, Nicholas. *The English Radical Imagination: Culture, Religion, and Revolution, 1630–1660*. Oxford, UK: Clarendon Press, 2003.

Miller, Kathleen. *The Literary Culture of Plague in Early Modern England*. New York: Palgrave Macmillan, 2016.

Moote, A. Lloyd, and Dorothy C. Moote. *The Great Plague: The Story of London's Most Deadly Year*. Baltimore: Johns Hopkins University Press, 2004.

Munkhoff, Richelle. "Searchers of the Dead: Authority, Marginality, and the Interpretation of Plague in England, 1574–1665." *Gender and History* 11, no. 1 (1999): 1–29.

"Of the Way of Killing Ratle-Snakes, Used in Virginia." *Philosophical Transactions* 1 (1665): 43–44.

Owen, John. *The Correspondence of John Owen (1616–1683)*. Edited by Peter Toon. Cambridge, UK: James Clarke, 1970.

———. *Seventeen Sermons Preach'd by ... John Owen*. London: William and Joseph Marshall, 1720.

———. *The Works of John Owen*. 24 vols. Edited by W. H. Goold. Edinburgh: Johnstone and Hunter, 1850–55.

Parker, Geoffrey. *Global Crisis: War, Climate Change and Catastrophe in the Seventeenth Century*. New Haven: Yale University Press, 2013.

Rattansi, P. M. "The Helmontian-Galenist Controversy in Restoration England." *Ambix* 12 (1964): 1–23.

Rolfe, Kirsty. "Fatal and Memorable: Plague, Providence and War in English Texts,

1625–6." *Seventeenth Century* 35, no. 3 (2020): 293–314.

Rudrum, Alan. "Ethical Vegetarianism in Seventeenth-Century Britain: Its Roots in Sixteenth-Century European Theological Debate." *Seventeenth Century* 18, no. 1 (2003): 76–92.

Slack, Paul. *The Impact of Plague in Tudor and Stuart England*. Oxford: Oxford University Press, 1985.

Smith, Nigel. *Perfection Proclaimed: Language and Literature in English Radical Religion, 1640–1660*. Oxford, UK: Clarendon Press, 1989.

Taft, Barbara. "Walwyn, William (bap. 1600, d. 1681)." In *Oxford Dictionary of National Biography*. Oxford: Oxford University Press, 2004; online ed., 2008. https://doi.org/10.1093/ref:odnb/28661.

Toon, Peter. 1971. *God's Statesman: The Life and Work of John Owen, Pastor, Educator, Theologian*. Exeter, UK: Paternoster Press.

"Way of Preserving Birds Taken out of the Egge, and Other Small Fætus's, A; Communicated by Mr. Boyle." *Philosophical Transactions* 1 (1666): 199–201.

Webster, Charles. *The Great Instauration: Science, Medicine and Reform, 1626–1660*. London: Duckworth, 1975.

Weimer, Adrian Chastain. *A Constitutional Culture: New England and the Struggle against Arbitrary Rule in the Restoration Empire*. Philadelphia: University of Pennsylvania Press, 2023.

West, John. *Dryden and Enthusiasm: Literature, Religion, and Politics in Restoration England*. Oxford: Oxford University Press, 2018.

Wood, Anthony. *Athenae Oxoniensis*. 4 vols. Oxford: Oxford University Press, 1813.

Worden, Blair. *God's Instruments: Political Conduct in the England of Oliver Cromwell*. Oxford: Oxford University Press, 2012.

CHAPTER 4

Maternal Bodies

Religion, Medicine, and Politics in Early
America and the Atlantic World

PHILIPPA KOCH

Women's bodies in eighteenth-century America and the Atlantic world were key sites for emerging medical and political discourses of nature, virtue, and civilization. It is my argument that long-standing Christian visions of motherhood, and in particular childbirth and lactation, fundamentally informed new medical and political ideas of maternity. I consider here a variety of theological tracts, artwork, midwifery literature, and mission and reform reports, in order to highlight how Christian emphases on the providential and redemptive significance of maternity imbued medical and political concepts of nature, design, and duty. These texts occurred in an Atlantic world of colonial and missionary expansion, one that was eagerly concerned with charting and documenting this expansion as the work of God, reaching not only into the lives of family and the health of women but also across oceans. The global nature of missionary and reform movements and their concern for the most intimate matters of human bodies, including gestation and infant care, was further proof, for many, of God's providence. The movement and conversation across the waters of the Atlantic world—and even, in some cases, beyond—demanded (and left behind) a rich variety of sources.

The story of maternity in the eighteenth-century Atlantic world reveals in crucial ways the intersection of religion and medicine. Many scholars have shown the important place of motherhood in philosophical, political, and medical discourse of the eighteenth-century Atlantic world. Nourished by Enlightenment thought, these discourses presented the nursing mother as central to the cultivation of natural sentiment and morality. Other scholars have emphasized the colonial and economic transformations of maternity, showing how new ideals of motherhood delineated gender and class norms and defined notions of racial difference—all central to the political projects of the colonial world and early American republic. European and European-American mothers, then, were to bear and rear future citizens.[1]

The figure of the ideal mother that developed in the eighteenth-century Atlantic world, according to western European and Christian thought, was a way of defining womanhood, the domestic sphere, medical knowledge and practice, and civilization. Undergirding these ideals, however, were physical toil, economic shifts, and racialized exclusion. While seventeenth-century families of means had often hired in the work of nursing and child care, new recommendations on maternal nursing and nurture meant that motherhood and the corresponding labor it entailed became increasingly essential—and uncompensated—women's work. At the same time, domestic ideals of motherhood required ignoring, undermining, or caricaturing the maternal identities of enslaved women and colonized women in positions of servitude or indenture, except insofar as their maternity affected their ability to provide commodities like labor, infants, and breast milk.[2]

Both the ideals and day-to-day realities of maternity deeply affected the lived experiences of early modern women of the Atlantic world, shaping their families, livelihoods, and bodies. The attention here, however, is the transatlantic religious and medical construction of womanhood in relation to childbirth and care. In Christian thought, as represented here by ministers, artists, and reformers, motherhood was imagined as providentially ordained by God and with redemptive significance. These religious ideas, in conversation with emerging medical ideas of mechanism, merged to create a vision of motherhood—including childbirth, lactation, and care—as an essential part of a woman's "design" or "nature." Medical practitioners observed maternity with a moral lens, with advice frequently touching on factors like piety, constitution, class, and race. Women's choices and actions as mothers were understood to reflect and affect their larger spiritual and political worlds. Religion and medicine, together, created the virtuous, republican mother, who, by design and through redemptive sacrifice, shaped the nation.

CHRISTIANITY, MATERNITY, AND REDEMPTION

Within Christianity, maternity has long played a key role in the story of redemption and faith. This is exemplified most keenly with the story of Mary, the mother of Jesus, who willingly accepted God's challenging call to bear the redeemer of humankind. Other scriptural mothers, like Sarah and Hannah, likewise offered models of faithfulness: though they struggled to bear children, they were, eventually, rewarded for their piety in the conception of their children. Mary's maternity was venerated in Christian communities; even after the Protestant Reformation, when this veneration was questioned as a Catholic corruption, Mary remained for Protestants a touchstone for imagining the spiritual significance of childbirth and child care.[3]

Mary's continuing resonance would have important implications for seventeenth- and eighteenth-century Protestant British, German, and (eventually) American clergy and missionaries of the Atlantic world. The prolific author and Puritan minister Cotton Mather, for example, turned to Mary to describe the "dignity" God offered women through childbirth.[4] Christians had generally attributed the pains of childbirth to women's inheritance of Eve's original sin; Mary, however, gave birth to the savior of humankind, an act that—according to Mather—gave childbirth and its suffering a sacred and redemptive significance for all believing women. The German Pietist Johann Arndt, a key spiritual writer for the wide-reaching Pietist movement, which collaborated with the British in missions throughout the Atlantic world as well as in India, likewise highlighted Mary, along with Hannah, as a role model of a joyful faith formed through complete dependence on God; they were rewarded through their experiences of motherhood.[5]

Mary's breastfeeding of Jesus, with its evocative imagery and symbolism, was also the subject of much artwork and theological commentary. Through her breast milk, Mary's maternal love and sacrifice represented and prefigured Jesus's love of humankind. For centuries, breast milk had been understood to be, in fact, redirected menstrual blood. Jesus, in his death, fed and redeemed humanity through his sacrifice and blood; likewise, a nursing mother fed an infant her own blood, transformed into milk. As Caroline Walker Bynum has shown, late medieval artwork of Mary breastfeeding the infant Jesus not only highlighted spiritual themes of Christ's sacrifice but also shaped views of maternal love and sacrifice more broadly in late medieval society (fig. 4.1).[6]

FIG. 4.1 Hans Memling, *Virgin and Child*, ca. 1475–80. Metropolitan Museum of Art, New York. The Friedsam Collection, Bequest of Michael Friedsam, 1931. Photograph: Metropolitan Museum of Art.

Mary and the image of Christ's nativity remained important in Protestant art in England and North America, even in not explicitly religious contexts, as it shaped views of domesticity and civilization. In British and American art, the nativity scene was often transformed to represent themes of individual family members, reunion, and tranquility, rather than the exemplary relationship of the future redeemer of humankind and his mother, chosen by God. John Singleton Copley, an eighteenth-century American artist, depicted Mary and Jesus in *The Nativity*, painted around 1776 (fig. 4.2). Copley used his own wife and child as the models for Mary and Jesus. This painting is said to have been influenced by the American Quaker Benjamin West's family portrait, *The Artist and His Family*, which one curator has described as a kind of "secular" nativity, perhaps nodding to the replacement of the holy family with a contemporary one (fig. 4.3). It depicts West's family reunited in London before the revolution. His wife and new baby represent the Madonna and child, his father and brother are filling the spot of the magi, and the artist himself is painted into the background, as a sort of Joseph.[7] The painting is, however, far from secular but rather shows a Quaker family imagining maternal and domestic experiences through Mary and the nativity. Quakers, as Janet Moore Lindman has argued, "shared a cultural script similar to that of other Protestants regarding the performance of

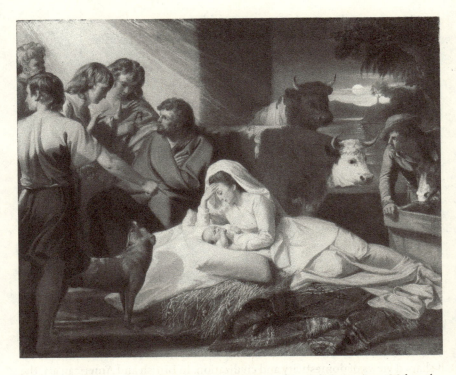

FIG. 4.2   John Singleton Copley, *The Nativity*, ca. 1776. Museum of Fine Arts, Boston. Ernest Wadsworth Longfellow Fund, 1972.981. Photograph © 2025 Museum of Fine Arts, Boston.

maternity."[8] While Mary lost her place as an intercessor in Protestant thought, Protestants continued to revere and uphold the themes of faith, love, humility, and selflessness evoked by her story.

The image of Mary as exemplar of motherhood, particularly in her nursing, played an important role in the popular theological and devotional treatise *The Great Exemplar of Sanctity and Holy Life According to the Christian Institution*, first published in 1649 by the Anglican Jeremy Taylor. Taylor was an early product of the English Reformation; the first edition was published while he was chaplain to Charles I, shortly before the monarch's execution, though Taylor was able to maintain his standing within the church through subsequent editions. Given the time frame and political context in which he wrote, it is unsurprising that Mary appeared in Taylor's spiritual writings. Yet his writings on the life of Christ—including his reflections on Mary's childbirth and lactation—continued to be published in multiple editions and formats into the nineteenth century

FIG. 4.3 Benjamin West, *The Artist and His Family*, ca. 1772. Yale Center for British Art, Paul Mellon Collection, B1981.25.674. Photograph: Yale Center for British Art.

in both Great Britain and North America. Some of the late eighteenth- and early nineteenth-century editions in the United States were much abridged, appearing in a smaller and more accessible format but maintaining the discussion of the nativity. Throughout Taylor's meditations, he sought to provide both spiritual and practical advice for readers. In his discussion "Of Nursing Children in Imitation of the Blessed Virgin Mother," for example, he outlined the ways in which a mother's milk was natural, transformative for her child's life of piety and virtue, and critical for society and the political order. His explanation of the interlocking nature of religion, maternity, and politics offers an early glimpse of how religious leaders sought to make connections between the individual and the social world, through the bodies of mothers. Such connections, as they developed throughout the Protestant Atlantic world, were crucial to eighteenth-century interpretations of maternity.[9]

Taylor's focus on Mary was part of a larger project of "Theologie which is wholly practical." Writing in the midst of the English Civil War, he sought to engage and guide Christians in their "daily office" and devotions, even—and especially—in an era of Christian fracture and disagreement. Thus, in each section of his history of the life of Jesus, Taylor offered not only narrative but also a short reflection, a prayer, and, finally, a discourse, in which he applied scripture's practical lessons to believers' everyday life. In his narrative of the nativity, for example, Taylor explained how Mary's childbirth was atypical, because she—alone among all women—avoided the pain that had accompanied birth since the punishment of Eve. As a sign of the painlessness of her birth and of her humble chosenness, Mary's only attendants in birth were angels. Following prophecy, further, Mary's body remained pure in both conception and parturition. Although Mary was unique among women, Taylor nonetheless drew "considerations" from the story of the nativity by focusing particularly on her care for her newborn. He reflected on how she swaddled her baby, rocked him, and "from this deportment she read a lecture of Piety and maternal care, which Mothers should perform toward their children when they are born, not to neglect any of that duty which nature and maternal piety requires."[10]

For Taylor, the nativity was both a story of patience and humanity and a story of God's plan and direction. Jesus was not "hasty" in his arrival; he did not try to "prevent the period of Nature" or to "break the laws of the Womb," established by "his own sanctions." His birth story was one of humility; he was surrounded by beasts and provided with the bare "necessities" of the human body: a "course Robe" and "a little breast-milk." Jesus's birth was a reminder to put off worldly pleasures and affluence and to consider that the savior "suck'd the paps of a Woman."[11] Mary's role in Taylor's recounting, to that point, seemed somewhat ambiguous. She was chosen, but she was also a sign—in her "paps" and alongside the beasts—of the material and earthy start of the incarnation story.

In the discourse that followed, however, Taylor made Mary a model for his extensive and practical advice on nursing for Christian women. Through his discourse, he examined Christian understandings of duty and law, studies of the natural world, medical ideas of the relationship between body and soul, and historical writings on ancient civilizations. Starting with Mary's maternal care for Jesus, Taylor expanded on nursing as a human act with transcendent significance. He argued that nursing was both a natural instinct and a higher obligation or law, "exalted by grace." While humans, like all beasts, were designed by God to nurse their offspring through instinct, human inclination raised above mere "nature" and this "impulsive force." Humans, in short, had reason and knowledge concerning the act of breastfeeding, making it not simply an instinct but a duty. With reason, humans could see that women were gifted by nature with "two exuberant Fontinels," which served both for nursing and "cradl[ing] in the entertainments of love and maternal embraces." History had shown that nurses could not love a child as a mother did, nor could they "endure the inconveniences, the tediousnesses and unhandsomnesses of a nursery" as a mother, with her "natural affection."[12]

Maternal nursing, further, entered the realm of law—beyond duty—because it was a matter of justice and charity. "With all their powers which God to that purpose gave them," mothers owed it to their children to "promote their capacities and improve their faculties." Offspring could not thrive with the nourishment of another mother. Taylor turned to "naturalists" to remind the reader that animals that nursed from other animals changed in their physical properties, as, Taylor claimed, fleece became hair when a lamb nursed from a goat. Through such observation, humans could plainly see how the "Instrument"—the body—was liable to change depending on nutrition and care. Such transformation posed a major problem, he explained, as the body should be "apt and organical to the faculty"; the soul suffered without "its proper Instruments"—that is, when its body was altered by foreign, external factors. In order to promote the child in a "virtuous life," Taylor therefore argued, mothers must "secure [the child's] first seasonings; because, whatever it sucks in first, it swallows and believes infinitely, and practices easily, and continues longest." While hired nurses may be able—at the most mechanical level—to deliver milk, they tended to limit their sense of duty to basic nourishment and cleanliness. A mother, however, "cannot think herself so easily discharged." She must provide the "spiritual milk" necessary for her child's development in piety and virtue.[13]

Taylor's views on nursing highlight the religious language surrounding motherhood and nursing that would persist in the medical advice and discourses of "nature" and civilization that emerged in the following centuries. An ideal "moral motherhood," as the historian Ruth Bloch has shown, emerged by the end of the eighteenth century from two trajectories—one evangelical and one Enlightenment. Taylor's treatise suggests how these two trajectories developed together in the early modern era. Ideas of nature, virtue, and civilization were a central part of Christian views of maternity as early as the sixteenth century and would join with the philosophical writings on child rearing by men like John Locke and, later, Jean-Jacques Rousseau in shaping white Anglo-American conceptions of the ideal mother.[14]

Taylor's description of nature's role in the design and function of maternal bodies, in fact, points to a long-standing intersection of medicine and religion. Many of Taylor's contemporaries remained shaped by the Galenic idea of "a provident nature," including in the scientific community. The Royal Society of London for Improving Natural Knowledge, founded thirteen years after Taylor's writings on nursing first appeared, described as its explicit goal "to illustrate the providential glory of God manifested in the works of His Creation." Early Society fellows "grappled" with how to relate "the providential deity of Christianity" with a natural world increasingly understood in mechanical ways—including a human body imagined as a predictable and observable "machine."[15] While Taylor's writings were theological, moving from Christian exegesis to practical piety, they were not far removed from contemporary medical and scientific discussions and debates over women's bodies, childbirth, and lactation. And, just as study of the natural world shaped Taylor's practical theology, the long tradition of Christian interest in a humble, natural, and dutiful maternity was critical to how midwifery manuals imagined women's bodies, childbirth, and lactation in the eighteenth century.

MATERNAL BODIES: NATURE, REASON, AND MORALITY

Into the eighteenth century, the complex relationship between the machine of the human body, on the one hand, and God's providence, on the other, remained a key question. Medical debates over intervention in childbirth focused on the design of the maternal body, the role of practitioners, the profession of male midwifery, and the appropriateness of instruments like forceps or fillets. These debates reflected concerns about the moral and social implications of such interventions. Questions surrounding maternity reflected, at heart, the early and prevailing concerns of the Royal Society: the relationship between design—of providence, "Nature," or a "Creator"—and a mechanical physical world, which was the site of human experimentation, knowledge, and social change.[16]

The early modern synthesis of providential design and mechanism affected advice on the practitioner's role in childbirth in midwifery manuals. This is clear in Hendrik van Deventer's *Art of Midwifery Improv'd*, a book that drew practitioners' attention to the importance of bone structure in childbirth and that was published in dozens of editions and at least five languages between 1701 and 1746. Deventer's work was known throughout the Atlantic world, both in his own volume and also in discussions of his ideas and methods in other works on midwifery.[17] The role of providence in Deventer's understanding was made clear in a preface to an edition published in London in 1728. The author of the preface, an "eminent physician," explained that childbirth was a matter of mechanism, designed by providence and requiring little intervention. The "great Providence" of the "Creator" had "contriv[ed] the most necessary Machines" of the human body to be "least liable to Accidents and Error." Medical practitioners nonetheless still played a critical role; humans remained mortal and subject to "decay." The "various Machines" within the human required constant or frequent attention (such as the sustenance of food or the evacuation of the blood) to stave off decay and mortality. The machines of "Generation," for their part, required the attention of a midwife. Through "her *Knowledge* and *Practice*," a midwife ensured "a Child's Passage into the World." While "Almighty God has ordered this Passage the most Safe," there were instances when the "preter-natural *Bulk*, or *Shape* of a *Child*; the wrong *Posture* of the *Womb*, or of the Child in it; and an ill Make of the *Os Sacrum*, or some other of these Bones, prove a great Obstacle to its being brought with Ease or Safety into the World." In these cases, a midwife is necessary. In all other instances, "matters are so wisely ordered" that safe passage can be assured by a mother "or any Woman who had once brought a Child herself." With Deventer's understanding of maternal design, he questioned the recent rise in male midwifery and the use of "dilating instruments," which he viewed as more likely to harm or kill an infant than to help. His work was thus a call to the "Humanity wherewith Midwifery ought to be practised" and a "Vindication of divine Providence."[18]

In the popular *Synopsis Medicinæ*, first published in 1719, John Allen likewise emphasized the mechanical design of the "Creator" in order to argue against aggressive intervention from a practitioner. Allen offered a mechanical study of the female human skeleton in comparison to the male. He observed that "in a Female . . . the lower Parts of the Sedentary Bones are generally further distant from each other, and don't bend down so much towards the *Os Coccygis* as in a Male one." This basic anatomical difference, Allen wrote, was by design: "the most wise and beneficent Creator thus contrived to obviate the many Difficulties of Childbirth." There were, nonetheless, cases in which assistance was necessary, and Allen outlined how a midwife could touch or use a hand—not instruments—to assist humanely with childbirth.[19]

By the mid-eighteenth century, an aggressive new emphasis on mechanism and human intervention in childbirth emerged with William Smellie, a British male midwife who sought to reform midwifery from its feminine roots and, in

84 DOCTRINE AND DISEASE

so doing, save the lives of women and children who, under earlier approaches, would have been lost to the superstitions and "ridiculous prejudices" of the "fair sex." In this pursuit, Smellie advocated strongly for scientific education, direct experience, and the use of male practitioners and medical instruments. His provocative work, *A Treatise on the Theory and Practice of Midwifery*, was first published in three volumes between 1752 and 1764. Smellie was outspoken in his promotion of male knowledge, hands-on investigation, and methodological progress. He based his work on extensive experience in practice, particularly among "poor women," and in teaching. For his courses, Smellie had even devised and constructed a "machine" to mimic a woman's body with a doll for a fetus that could be positioned in various ways. In his publications, he included detailed anatomical plates. He told a history of midwifery in which women were almost entirely absent, in part, as he argued, because "none of their writings are extant."[20] But he also had little use for female knowledge; he decried what he described as the secret knowledge that had long defined the work of childbirth, particularly when the practice was limited to women. He wanted a story of progress and of the expansion of knowledge through experiment and publication.

Midwifery, by Smellie's account, was about the public good and the preservation of life, which required a redeemed human knowledge, one that was not limited to superstition but expanded through hands-on investigation and mechanical intervention. An entire section of his treatise is titled "Of Touching." It begins, "Touching is performed by introducing the fore-finger lubricated with pomatum into the *Vagina*." Smellie detailed the use of instruments such as fillets, forceps, and scissors, and he offered cases detailing, for example, how to cut apart conjoined twins in the womb, how to drain the head of a fetus suffering from dropsy in order to deliver it and save the mother, and how to perform a Caesarian operation after the mother's death (always in the presence of a witness who could first confirm the state of death). Smellie's work was incredibly mechanical in its description of the condition of the pregnant and laboring woman and of the work of the midwife. He described women—for example, the impoverished Parisian women at the Hotel Dieu—as "opportunities" for surgeons to improve their knowledge. Despite his scientific and mechanical language, Smellie claimed an ethical goal. After losing "several children, and sometimes, the mother," in his early practice, Smellie had set off to create a "better method of practice," always with "a view of saving" women and children, "honour[ing] . . . the profession," and promoting "the good of society."[21]

Smellie's work provoked both extreme criticism and support. On both sides, practitioners published responses that turned to long-standing ideas of providence and nature as they outlined appropriate forms of human intervention. The debates over male midwives and instruments raised questions about midwives' character, motivations, and knowledge, patients' purity, and, at base, the potential effects of maternity care on human morality and civilization. One of Smellie's detractors questioned the naturalness of male midwives, finding them effeminate and foreign in origin. Beginning in France and spreading elsewhere, male midwives stifled the work of "Goody Nature." They sought "haste," celebrity, and money, and, more sinisterly, they worked to steal the virtue of unsuspecting wives, whom they unnecessarily touched in examination. They pursued unwarranted procedures with "iron instruments," perhaps leaving "the woman's person less *agreeable*, and often loathsome to her husband," and thus undermining domestic life and stability—the foundation of any successful civilization. Smellie's critics argued that nature had been sufficient for "many generations" and that, indeed, "Nature left to herself scarce ever errs." Providence was careful in the preservation of even "brute creation" in the process of gestation and parturition. How could one doubt the care of providence for "the noblest part of her production?"[22]

Smellie's anonymous critic here not only blamed the male midwives but also the larger community that had been seduced by the "fashion" of male midwifery, blind to its unnaturalness and threat to family and civilization. Male midwifery had developed in France and had therefore appealed to "my Lady Betty Modish" and her followers among the middling class. This "fashion" and appeal of male midwifery, for some, gave lie to its "naturalness" and honor. Male midwives were not natural; they were "mongrels" and "amphibious." They were like the male stay-makers and hairdressers of Italy, a place of questionable civilization: not only were honorable men and virtuous women scarce, but so also were key commodities of the civilized world, like wood and fish. Male midwives were imagined as mysterious and dangerous; they seduced women, they touched women, and they destroyed women both in body and in marital fidelity—all with the consent of the unsuspecting husband.[23]

While this anonymous critique was rather hyperbolic, defenses of Smellie's work suggest that there were widespread concerns regarding nature, human knowledge, and the morality of male midwifery. Jean-Louis Baudelocque, a French obstetrician, was influenced by Smellie and helped popularize his

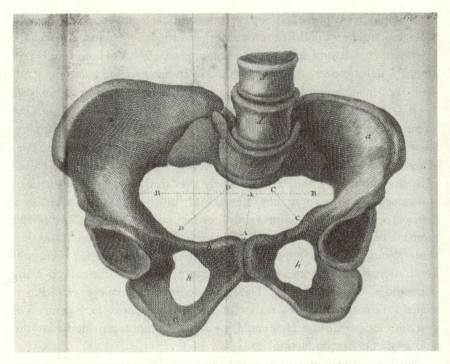

FIG. 4.4   Plate highlighting the dimensions of the pelvis, from Jean-Louis Baudelocque, *A System of Midwifery*, trans. John Heath (London: Parkinson, 1790). Source: Wellcome Collection.

writings and techniques. In an advertisement introducing the English edition of Baudelocque's *A System of Midwifery* (1790), the surgeon John Heath responded to recent publications, which he felt upheld nature and design to the detriment of scientific study and learning. He criticized books in which "the powers of Nature are so magnified that a young student might be led to believe the whole art may be reduced to this single precept, *do nothing*: and that in this particular instance man is dispensed from the exercise of that reason with which the Creator has endued him." At issue here was the very meaning of "Nature" and design. Christians had long accepted that God's providence—or design—did not limit human intervention in the realm of medicine. Rather, God had given humans reason to explore the natural world, to learn, and to heal. In the debate over obstetrical instruments and male midwives, Heath relied on a similar logic: a commitment to Nature and design required likewise a commitment to full use of the reason bestowed on humans by "the Creator." A practitioner, with "a real and accurate knowledge of the parts concerned in delivery, and of the mechanism by which it is performed, is absolutely necessary to enable the operator to assist Nature when she [Nature] is at fault."[24] Baudelocque claimed a place for Nature and design in both the woman's body and the male practitioner's knowledge, reason, and intervention (fig. 4.4).

Those who supported male midwifery further argued that human reason, even as endowed by the Creator, required specific, formal instruction on the machine and workings of the human body in order to investigate and improve the natural world. This form of knowledge was not a given. Supporters of male midwifery argued that women midwives had no claim to a particular natural knowledge of childbirth or to a reasoned understanding; their alleged skill and practice had advanced merely by "accident" through personal and familial experiences. Faced with the continuing practice of female midwifery—and widespread resistance to male midwives—in the late eighteenth century, the New York surgeon Valentine Seaman decided to offer a course on midwifery for female practitioners. If society remained prejudiced by a "false delicacy" against male practitioners, he wrote, "it is our duty to instruct females how to give them the necessary aid." Seaman, who was "Physician Extraordinary to the Lying-In Ward in the Alms House," had a very low opinion of women's knowledge in general and skill as midwives in particular. He emphasized midwives' ignorance in terms of their lack of formal medical education and corresponding ignorance of the inner workings of the human body: "I much doubt whether one out of twenty of them have ever seen the bones that support and protect the womb: indeed I cannot but suspect whether some even know, that, in being born, a child has to pass through a bony passage." Although he was willing to work with those women who availed themselves of his teaching, Seaman consigned the rest to "indolence" and "to grope on in their original darkness."[25]

Seaman perceived scientific learning to be a Christian response to the corrupting forces of fashion and luxury and their deleterious effects on not only society but also the female anatomy. The scientific practice of midwifery became necessary, he explained, when civilization decayed from an earlier state of humility, nature, and order. "Probably in the early ages," he wrote, "before the pampering stews of luxury had taken the place of the salutary calls of nature in diet, and before the warping trammels of fashion had taken the lead of comfort and convenience in dress, seldom, very seldom, was there any disease in childbearing, or difficulty in travail." Luxury and fashion had distorted society and the female body itself. Seaman grounded his scientifically based practice in Christian principles of benevolence and the social order it promoted. He ended

88 DOCTRINE AND DISEASE

his tract with reference to Proverbs 28:27, "He that giveth unto the poor shall not lack." He urged his readers not to pursue the profession of midwifery from the "sordid motive" of riches but rather from the "desire of doing good": to pursue industry, enlightenment, and order through "the judicious establishment of regularly instructed midwives." Male or female mattered little in the end; important was education, mechanical practice, and a calling "to relieve the major part of the community."[26]

Eighteenth-century medical discussions of childbirth reveal a world in motion. Mechanical views of the human body and medical intervention permeated depictions of the maternal body as well as the debates over male practitioners and the use of instruments. And yet, these debates took place within a larger framework of design—be it providential, natural, or both. Some of the resistance to male midwives and instruments could almost be grounded in Taylor's idealized depiction of the nativity: Jesus's patient gestation and humble birth were a far cry from the "haste," ego, profit, "fashion," and seduction of male midwifery. On the other hand, those who defended male practitioners emphasized human reason—provided by the Creator—and, like Taylor, a human duty to utilize reason toward the ends of charity. Through knowledge and practice, appropriate intervention in childbirth was an opportunity to "do good" and to redeem humankind from the excesses of luxury that could corrupt the maternal body, the domestic family, and civilization itself.

MATERNAL NURSING: DUTY AND CIVILIZATION

As with childbirth, eighteenth-century medical discourse surrounding nursing was shaped by mechanical questions of design and related social and moral concerns. The religious overtones in medical discussions of nursing were, if anything, even stronger. Midwifery manuals, medical correspondence, and clerical writings highlighted a prevailing attitude that for a mother to nurse her own infant was a chance to avoid potential vices, to fulfill a maternal instinct and religious duty, and to offer a key service to society. These views on nursing and infant care also shaped—and were shaped by—how missionaries, reformers, and colonists imagined race and civilization.

Central to Taylor's discourse on Jesus's nativity had been a religious vision of the nursing mother and her contribution to social stability and progress. In sketching the practical implications of Mary's maternity, Taylor found an obvious application in her nursing; while Mary had not suffered the pains of childbirth, no one doubted her full human experience in the work of infant care. Mary could thus serve as the epitome of moral, charitable, economical, and sincere motherhood. Taylor expanded quickly from this ideal with other examples from scripture and antiquity to make an argument about the role of motherhood and the domestic family in the stability of civilizations. To nurse your own child was to ensure familial loyalty and social stability, and history offered countless cases in which vain and careless mothers had been grim portents of coming decline. In ancient Rome, Taylor argued, a woman's refusal to nurse her own child—to instead dry up her milk "with artificial applications" like a puppy—was a sure omen of social and political disintegration. At one point in his text, Taylor further graphically describes "that many tyrants have killed their mothers, but never did violence to [their] nurse; as if they were desirous to suck the blood of their mother raw, which she refused to give to them digested into milk." With gendered and racialized language, Taylor decried the "softness" of his own age, "above the effeminacy of *Asian* Princes." He was appalled that people rejected their children in favor of "custom and fashion" and against the "Laws and prescriptions of Nature." Such actions were foreign and corrupting to Taylor's Christian society: they undermined order and nature.[27]

Within the field of medicine, meanwhile, the laws of nature concerning the suckling of an infant had been under increasing, if inconclusive, investigation. The mid-seventeenth century saw new scientific inquiry into the nature of milk, blood, and nursing. For example, *The Compleat Midwife* (1698), a popular late seventeenth-century midwifery manual, offered detailed scientific discussion of conception and the development of blood vessels and major internal organs, complete with reference to the medical work of well-known physicians such as William Harvey and Isbrand de Diemerbrock. There remained, nonetheless, questions of how exactly nourishment was delivered to the fetus in the womb and to the infant after birth; it is one of the few places in the manual where the authors appealed, finally, to divine knowledge. Faced with the conundrum of how the "nutritious juice" would know "after the Child is born, and instead of going down to the womb, rise up to the breasts," the authors concluded that, like "many other things in nature," the reason was "only known to Almighty God, the maker of all things."[28]

Many aspects of lactation remained mysterious for seventeenth- and eighteenth-century writers, including how infants and mothers knew how to nurse. *The Compleat Midwife* posited that the infant must have learned to suck in the womb; a century later, Baudelocque rejected the "ancient" idea that the fetus "sucked certain *tubercles* of the *uterus*" and recognized that the source of nutrition was the umbilical cord, arguing that the "proof of it is so clear, that no one would dare to contest it." He nonetheless still remarked on the "inclination of a newborn to suck" and offered no explanation for this "great aptitude." In the early eighteenth century, the New England Puritan Mather, who wrote extensively on the topic of medicine, had likewise turned to the language of "instinct" to understand the infant's ability to suck. For Mather, such instinct was an operation of the human's lower soul, implanted by God with the express purpose of protecting creation. While, unlike Taylor, Mather did not consider instinct to be within the higher realm of reason, he still viewed nursing with "astonishment": as a manifestation of a soul imprinted by God and integrated into the human body for the purposes of its material survival. He urged women to follow "*Nature*" and "*Suckle your infant your Self if you can.*" For those who wanted to avoid the practice, Mather remarked that, it was "*Unnatural*" to "complain of a State, whereinto the *Laws of Nature* established by God, have brought you."[29]

While Mather, as a minister, was forthright in his view of the spiritual significance of breastfeeding, his views of the naturalness, rightness, and obligation of maternal nursing were widely shared among medical writers of the eighteenth century. Breast milk was purgative, healing, and transformative. "No aliment is fitter for a child than its mother's milk," Baudelocque wrote. "There is nothing equal to their mother's milk," Seaman argued. When mothers "suckle their own children," Smellie explained, they avoided further medical problems and interventions. "Superfluous fluids" like lochia are "drained off" without need of evacuation. Mothers who nursed avoided "milk fever." Breast milk itself was purgative for the newborn, "carry[ing] off the black matter contained in its bowles," preempting the need for "gentle" medicinal purges recommended for clearing meconium. Breast milk could also help in the treatment of thrush, and, according to some, the stimulation of lactation in a barren woman could even promote fertility.[30] Nursing was not only an instinct and design; it was also salutary in its effects of restoring and preserving the balance and function of maternal and infant bodies and health.

The medical interest in nursing was part of a larger discussion of the "intentions of nature" in newborn care, including questions over human interventions in head shape and clothing. While in the mid-eighteenth century, for example, Smellie argued that male midwives could use their hands to "reduce" the newborn's head "into its pristine shape," Baudelocque later cautioned against the use of such pressure, "for the head soon recovers its natural form of itself." Medical writers also began to emphasize nature and simplicity in newborn care when warning against luxury in clothing and food. The physician William Cadogan, a mid-eighteenth-century reformer and director of the foundling hospital in London, argued against the dangers of "a load of Finery" and "Dainties," by which overly fond mothers might inadvertently smother their infants. Physicians like Cadogan applied to infant care the lessons of a medical world increasingly attentive to diseases of excess, which came with corresponding moral judgments against fashion and flesh. He and Mather both admonished women to breast-feed, even though they must sacrifice their vanity and life of "ease." By following nature, women and children could avoid the diseases and problems that beset the well-off. Cadogan pointed to the "lower Class of Mankind," who, despite hardships, had healthy infants: "The Mother who has only a few Rags to cover her Child loosely, and little more than her own Breast to feed it, sees it healthy and strong, and very soon able to shift for itself." By following nature and by avoiding the seduction of fashion, poor women and their children, according to Cadogan, thrived.[31] For women and children living in poverty, however, this was less a matter of choice and more so a matter of circumstances.

Cadogan's romanticized image of "nature" here, captured in the impoverished but robust mother and newborn, points to an emerging economic and racialized discourse of motherhood and civilization in the colonial Atlantic world. Cadogan's work was both republished in North America and cited by North American authors.[32] Medical writers of this time found in poor women, with their supposed proximity to nature, the best demonstration of nursing's salutary effects. It is important to note, though, that poor women were a test case, an extreme. They were not, actually, perceived as the ideal, but they rather served as examples of the strength afforded by measures of simplicity and humility. Prowess in motherhood could, in fact, be dehumanizing. As Jennifer Morgan has shown, African women's bodies were considered—or made—savage in part through depictions of their natural ability as mothers who conceived easily, who labored "painlessly," and whose breasts were so grotesquely large that they could nurse their infants over their shoulders. If they did not suffer the maternal pains associated with Eve, as Morgan argues, it was easier to consider African women as animals or a different species—and easier to enslave them.[33]

The image of the infant reaching over the shoulder to nurse also worked to separate African women from the ideal vision of the nursing mother within Christianity. The African child was not nestled like Jesus at Mary's bosom—or, as Taylor wrote, "to the breast where naturally . . . the child is cradled in the entertainments of love and maternal embraces."[34] When useful to the purposes of European colonists, nonetheless, colonized women could be portrayed in such a maternal pose. In Benjamin West's painting *Penn's Treaty with the Indians*, for example, he depicted a nursing Native American woman in the lower right-hand corner, a scene of domesticity balancing the political and economic negotiation occurring at the painting's center. The nursing Native woman here, however, was not an ideal but again a mere prop to West's story of America and its place as a setting for peaceful encounter.[35]

Concerns over wet nursing further highlight how discussions of nursing operated at the complex intersection of not only medicine and religion but also economics, race, class, and colonialism. While maternal nursing was recommended, midwifery manuals almost always offered advice on the selection of a wet nurse, advice that reflected concerns of nature or design, affection, and the potential for the corruption of the infant. A midwife should be chosen based on a variety of factors, including complexion, hair color, age, and other indicators of the nurse's humoral constitution, which ideally should be in sympathy with the birth mother and the child. Manuals also urged attention to "the qualities of the mind." Causes for special concern were obvious external characteristics such as bad breath, decayed or false teeth, and crooked noses. Many manuals also warned of negative consequences should the nurse engage in sexual activity. The general assumption was that the child would suck in the bad or "disorderly" qualities of the nurse—be it the mother or someone else—with lasting consequences for the child's health and temper. In some cases, a "good wholesome nurse" could correct for the "ill complexion of the Mother," although the mother was almost universally preferable. Regardless, the stakes were high; children often died or became diseased, and writers claimed that "the chief cause is the Nurses milk." Such tragedies (and logic) were explained by recourse to scripture, as Jane Sharpe's 1671 *Midwives Book* explained: "If a nurse be well complexioned her milk cannot be ill; for a Fig-Tree bears not Thistles: a good Tree will bring forth good Fruit."[36]

Personal correspondence and missionary accounts of the eighteenth century reveal widespread and serious consideration of these recommended characteristics of nurses—with their far-from-implicit racial and class overtones—and related fears over the corruption of infants. Concerns over nurses could be intense. Parents, relatives, friends, and missionaries fixated on a nurse's appearance, including her age, heartiness, potential "disorders," level of "common sense," offspring, "contentedness," morality, and sexual activity.[37] There is one particularly telling example from colonial India. While India was not a part of the geographic Atlantic world, the missionaries who worked and lived in India were deeply connected to the larger missionary endeavors of the Atlantic world through extensive correspondence networks.[38] In this instance, lengthy letters between German missionaries in India and physicians at the center of their missionary enterprises, in Halle, Germany, described anxieties over Tamil wet nurses, concerns that had come to light due to instances of syphilis, adultery, and abortion. When the local missionary investigated, he learned that Tamil women, who often worked as wet nurses, sought to avoid sex with their husbands and to prevent pregnancy because they feared harming the nursing child—and losing their employment. Whether these fears stemmed from local tradition or were caused by warnings and threats from their masters is not disclosed. The women and their families depended on the income from this work; indeed, one woman was reportedly "rented" from her "heathen" husband as a wet nurse. Another woman was described as a "bonded servant." In any case, when Johann Juncker, a physician in Germany, replied to the missionaries, he argued that sexual relationships and pregnancy were not, in fact, harmful to a nursing child. Sounding remarkably like Cadogan, Juncker pointed to the poor: impoverished people the world over, he explained, could not afford wet nurses, often nursed while pregnant, and had some of the healthiest infants. Nonetheless, he continued, women should not use wet nurses, whose "vices flow into the child through the milk."[39] The physician's advice here is, in ways, general; it is not singling out unconverted Tamil women. Yet missionary reports from India had expressed alarm over an apparent lack of maternal feeling among the local women, and that perception, along with the reports over sexual misconduct, may have contributed to apprehensions about Indian mothers and the practice of wet nursing.[40]

When a mother nursed her own infant, she avoided the transfer of potential vices, she fulfilled a role for which nature had designed her, she acted on religious duty, and, finally, she offered a key service to her political community. As in Taylor's writings, late seventeenth-century popular midwifery manuals, like Sharpe's *Midwives Book* and Nicholas Culpeper's *Directory for Midwives*, turned to scriptural and classical examples of maternal care in producing dutiful children: the strength of the Germans and the Spartans came through nursing mothers; maternal nursing—not birth order—likewise determined succession among the Lacedemonians. Nonetheless, Sharpe and Culpeper still offered advice for the selection of wet nurses, recognizing that women needed and continued to use nurses for various reasons.[41]

94 DOCTRINE AND DISEASE

Many writers on midwifery and infant care nonetheless still echoed Taylor, as they continued to locate in maternal care—and in nursing, in particular—a natural good and duty, a means to escape corruption, and a key to the success of the political order. The symbolic weight of nursing was evident, on the one hand, in the heart of the domestic home, where some women reported feeling great joy in nursing or were disappointed by an inability to do so.[42] And it was evident, on the other hand, in medical and political discourse. In Cadogan's revolutionary 1748 *Essay on Nursing,* he stressed the importance of nursing as a natural and necessary means to promote infant health and survival, crucial for the future welfare and security of the nation. The mortality rates in England for children under the age of five were abysmal: "Half the People that come into the World, go out of it again before they become of the least Use to it." Cadogan insisted that the wholesome milk of a loving mother could prevent corruption and death, and, after all, a "Multitude of Inhabitants is the greatest Strength and best Support of a Commonwealth."[43] Cadogan's language was not rife with religion, but his concern with nature and maternal duty and their implications for society echoed Taylor's language of the previous century. Taylor had ended his discussion on nursing by applying it to the example of the two mothers arguing over a babe before King Solomon: the "true mother" was she who would not see her child divided. According to Taylor, she kept her child whole and completed her duty by both bearing *and* nursing her child. An unwilling mother was a sign of political decline and danger. Society rested on maternal sacrifice in the nourishment and education of its virtuous citizens. These ideas, heavy with both religious and medical significance, contributed in crucial ways to the figuration of womanhood in the early American republic, the Atlantic world, and colonial sites throughout the larger British Empire.[44]

CONCLUSION

Early modern theological treatises, eighteenth-century midwifery manuals, and personal and missionary correspondence on childbirth and nursing reveal the critical merging of religion and medicine in political understandings of motherhood, with implications, more broadly, for the construction of womanhood in the colonial Atlantic world and the early American republic. While scholars have argued for the important role of "motherhood" in shaping ideals of womanhood in the early American nation, they have often overlooked the significant ways in which a transatlantic conversation between Christianity and medical discourse underpinned this role. With recourse to Christian language of humility, love, and duty, and alongside mechanical visions of the woman's body, design, and intervention, eighteenth-century ministers, medical practitioners, and missionaries cemented ideas of nature, civilization, and virtue in the lives and work of Atlantic mothers.

NOTES

Parts of this chapter were previously published in the fifth chapter of Philippa Koch, *The Course of God's Providence: Religion, Health, and the Body in Early America* (New York: New York University Press, 2021).

1. On motherhood and Enlightenment thought, the literature is extensive. See, for example, Garrett, "Self-Made Son"; Rousseau, *Emile*, 11–18; Bloch, *Gender and Morality*, 57–77; Kerber, *Women of the Republic*, 7–32; Fermon, "Domesticating Women."

2. On motherhood, economics, and colonialism, see Perry, "Colonizing the Breast"; Klepp, "Revolutionary Bodies"; Doyle, *Maternal Bodies*; Morgan, *Laboring Women*. On medicine and maternity, see Fissell, *Vernacular Bodies*, 1–13; and the excellent collection of essays and articles in Wilson, *Midwifery Theory and Practice*.

3. Fissell, *Vernacular Bodies*, 14–52; Stevens, "Mary's Magnificat."

4. For discussion of Cotton Mather in relation to smallpox, see chapter 6.

5. Mather, *Elizabeth*, 4–7, 16, 19–20; Arndt, *Paradis-Gärtlein*, 10–11. This edition was bound together with *Wahres Christentum*.

6. Bynum, *Jesus as Mother*, 131–34. Cf. Juster, "Mystical Pregnancy and Holy Bleeding," 257.

7. Prown, *Art as Evidence*, 127–28; Kamensky, *Revolution in Color*, 270–74; Albinson, catalog entry for Benjamin West, *The Artist and His Family*.

8. Lindman, "To Have a Gradual Weaning," 501. According to Lindman, Quakers shared in widespread Protestant understandings of resignation and communal support in sickness, pain, and maternity, although they often stressed humility to a greater extent, particularly as they eschewed customs such as churching. Quaker women who pursued ministry were also more likely to challenge widespread notions of domesticity. See also Larson, *Daughters of Light*.

9. Taylor, *Great Exemplar*. I viewed a copy of the first edition available at the Library of Congress, Washington, DC, as well as two much-abbreviated American editions there: Taylor, *Life of Our Blessed Saviour* (1796); and Taylor, *Life of Our Blessed Saviour* (1818). In 1829, Charles Francis Adams, the grandson of John Adams, records reading Taylor on the subject of nursing and finding the discourse displeasing. See Adams, diary entry, December 20, 1829, in *Diary of Charles Francis Adams*, vol. 3.

10. Taylor, *Great Exemplar*, epistle dedicatory (n.p.), 14–15.

11. Taylor, *Great Exemplar*, 14–15. Even in the much-abridged editions that were printed in the late eighteenth and early nineteenth centuries in the United States, there is an emphasis on this theme of humility and a God who drank "a little breastmilk" at "Mary's knees thy table." See Taylor, *Life of Our Blessed Saviour* (1796), 22–23; Taylor, *Life of Our Blessed Saviour* (1818), 28–30.

12. Taylor, *Great Exemplar*, 34, 36, 37, 39.

13. Taylor, *Great Exemplar*, 37–38. "Spiritual milk" is a clear reference to 1 Corinthians 3:2: "I have fed you with milk, and not with meat: for hitherto ye were not able to bear it, neither yet now are ye able" (cf. 1 Peter 2:2). The phrase also was commonly used in early modern catechisms. See, for example, Cotton, *Milk for Babes*; Münchhausen, *Geistliche Kinder-Milch*. On Cotton's catechism, see Royster, abstract to *Milk for Babes*. Note: Cotton's catechism also appeared under the title *Spiritual Milk for Boston Babes*.

14. Bloch, *Gender and Morality*, 66. For a wonderful discussion of the variety of Christian discourse on female piety and nursing among sixteenth- and seventeenth-century Catholics and Protestants, see McManus, "Carefull Nourse."

15. Flemming, "Pathology of Pregnancy"; Force, "Hume and the Relation"; Clark,

96 DOCTRINE AND DISEASE

"Providence, Predestination and Progress."
For an example of this kind of work of relating
providence and mechanism and its relationship to
maternity, see Arbuthnott, "Argument for Divine
Providence."

16. On the diffuse ways in which the word
"Nature" or phrases like "laws of nature" were
meant and interpreted in seventeenth- and eigh-
teenth-century England, see Clark, "Providence,
Predestination and Progress," 569; Jager, *Book of
God*, 2–4, 12–14.

17. For a brief background of Deventer, see
Hatoum, "Art of Midwifery Improv'd"; for
examples of Deventer's ideas mentioned in North
American publications on midwifery, see, for
example, Smellie, *Abridgement of the Practice*, 42;
Denman, *Introduction*, xlvi, 399.

18. Deventer, *Art of Midwifery Improv'd*, preface.
Note that Deventer is misspelled ("Daventer") on
the title page.

19. Allen, *Synopsis Medicinæ*, 1:259–60.

20. Smellie, *Treatise*, i, iii, v.

21. Smellie, *Treatise*, preface, liv, lv, lxiv, lxxi,
184–89, 372–76; on cases in which Smellie recommended and used instruments, see volume 3. On
the "machine," see Shillace, "Mother Machine."

22. *Man-Midwifery Analysed*, 2–3, 10–11.

23. *Man-Midwifery Analysed*, 3–5, 7–12, 17–18.

24. Baudelocque, *System of Midwifery*, advertisement. On Christian views of medicine in this
era, see Koch, "Experience and the Soul."

25. Seaman, *Midwives Monitor*, iii–ix.

26. Seaman, *Midwives Monitor*, iv–vi, ix–x,
13–14, 18–19, 42–43; 121–22.

27. Taylor, *Great Exemplar*, 31–33. In an
interesting historical twist, the wife of Charles
Francis Adams, who had found Taylor's discourse
on nursing displeasing, would resort to a puppy
when she encountered difficulty nursing. Adams,
diary entry, December 20, 1829, in *Diary of Charles
Francis Adams*, vol. 3; first note accompanying
Adams, diary entry, August 16, 1831, in *Diary of
Charles Francis Adams*, vol. 4.

28. Chamberlain, Mayern, and Culpeper, *Compleat Midwife's Practice Enlarged*, 91.

29. Chamberlain, Mayern, and Culpeper, *Com-
pleat Midwife's Practice Enlarged*, 93; Baudelocque,
System of Midwifery, 302–4; Mather, *Angel of
Bethesda*, 32; Mather, *Elizabeth*, 3–4, 35; Cadogan,
Essay upon Nursing (1748), 23–27.

30. Baudelocque, *System of Midwifery*, 444–49;
Smellie, *Treatise*, 420; Seaman, *Midwives Monitor*,
116; Horton, *Improved System*, 28–29. On barren-
ness and lactation, Horton shares the advice of
"Dr. Ewell."

31. Smellie, *Treatise*, 430–31; Baudelocque,
System of Midwifery, 437–38; Cadogan, *Essay upon
Nursing* (1748), 3–4, 7; Mather, *Elizabeth*, 3–4,
35; Smith, *Letters to Married Women*, 55–61; cf.
Porter, *Flesh in the Age of Reason*, 238–43. See also
Kerber's discussion of Montesquieu's critique of
luxury in *Women of the Republic*, 19.

32. Cadogan, *Essay upon Nursing* (1773); Cadogan, *Essay upon Nursing* (1772). William Buchan
was disappointed that Cadogan's work had gone
out of print, and so he reproduced it in the appendix to his own book, *Advice to Mothers*, 297–352.

33. Morgan, *Laboring Women*, 36–49.

34. Taylor, *Great Exemplar*, 31.

35. Palumbo, "Averting 'Present Commotions.'"
On debates over women, motherhood, virtue,
and politics in the colonial world, see, in particular, Kerber's discussion of Hobbes, Montesquieu,
Rousseau, and Kames in *Women of the Republic*,
16–27.

36. Chamberlain, Mayern, and Culpeper, *Com-
pleat Midwife's Practice Enlarged*, 153–54; Stark,
Hebammenunterricht in Gesprächen, 202–4; Baude-
locque, *System of Midwifery*, 446–53; Smellie,
Treatise, 448; Sharpe, *Midwives Book*, 266–67; cf.
Matthew 7:16–20.

37. See, for example, Elizabeth Rhoads Fisher
to Samuel Fisher, September 10, 1793, and Octo-
ber 17, 1793, Samuel W. Fisher Papers. Historical
Society of Pennsylvania; Mary Smith Cranch to
Abigail Adams, December 24, 1797, and Abigail
Adams to Esther Duncan Black, April 15, 1798, in
Adams Family Correspondence.

38. I have written elsewhere about shared print
and correspondence networks throughout the
mission efforts that accompanied the British
Empire, which necessarily pushes the boundaries
of the "Atlantic world"—as these missionaries
wrote from places in the Indian and the Pacific
Oceans as well and also published reports to
share more widely with potential benefactors. See
Koch, *Course of God's Providence*, 59, 219n8.

39. Christian Friedrich Pressier to Gotthilf
August Francke, December 5, 1733, Missionsarchiv
der Franckeschen Stiftungen 1 B 18:1; Johann
Juncker, *Anmerkungen zu einem Brief von Christian*

Friedrich Pressier, Missionsarchiv der Franckeschen Stiftungen 1 B 18:2. Translation mine. Cf.
Roeber, *Hopes for Better Spouses*, 138–39.

40. See, for example, the description of a small
child, found drowned and alone. The missionaries
reported that "the Mother of the child stood by
without any feeling." *Acht und neunzigste Continuation*, 165–66.

41. Sharpe, *Midwives Book*, 264–65; Culpeper,
Directory for Midwives, 146–47; Taylor, *Great
Exemplar*, 31–33.

42. See, for example, the reflection on nursing
in Samuel W. Fisher, "Biographical Sketch of His
Wife Elizabeth Rhoads Fisher (1770–1796)," 1796,
Eliza Rhoads Fisher Folder #2, Samuel W. Fisher
Collection, Historical Society of Pennsylvania.
Although we only have Samuel's account of the
matter and cannot know if it accurately reflects
Elizabeth's feelings, it does seem that many early
American women found great joy in nursing. See
Norton, *Liberty's Daughters*, 90.

43. Cadogan, *Essay upon Nursing* (1748), 6. For
similar attitudes in the German context, see Stark,
Hebammenunterricht in Gesprächen, 12. Cf. Smith,
Letters to Married Women, 55–61.

44. Taylor, *Great Exemplar*, 34; Kerber, *Women
of the Republic*, 7–12, 31.

BIBLIOGRAPHY

*Acht und neunzigste Continuation des Berichts der
königlich-dänischen Missionarien in Ost-In-
dien*. Halle: Verlegung des Wäysenhauses,
1765.

Adams, Charles Francis. *Diary of Charles Francis
Adams*. Vol. 3, *September 1829–February
1831*. Adams Papers Digital Edition. Massachusetts Historical Society. https://
www.masshist.org/publications/adams
-papers/index.php/volume/ADMS-13
-03.

———. *Diary of Charles Francis Adams*. Vol. 4,
March 1831–December 1832. Adams Papers
Digital Edition. Massachusetts Historical
Society. https://www.masshist.org
/publications/adams-papers/index.php
/volume/ADMS-13-04.

Adams Family Correspondence. Vol. 12, *March
1797–April 1798*. Adams Papers Digital
Edition. Massachusetts Historical

Society. http://www.masshist.org
/publications/adams-papers/index.php
/volume/ADMS-04-12.

Albinson, Cassandra. Catalog entry for Benjamin
West, *The Artist and His Family*, ca. 1772.
In *Paul Mellon's Legacy: A Passion for
British Art: Masterpieces from the Yale
Center for British Art*, by John Baskett.
New Haven, CT: Yale Center for British
Art, 2007. Accessed at https://collections
.britishart.yale.edu/catalog/tms:5040.

Allen, John. *Synopsis Medicinæ; or, A Summary
View of the Whole Practice of Physick*. 3rd
ed. London: Innys, Meadows Manby, and
Cox, 1749.

Arbuthnott, John. "An Argument for Divine
Providence, Taken from the Constant
Regularity Observ'd in the Births of
Both Sexes." *Philosophical Transactions
(1683–1775)* 27 (1710–12): 186–90.

Arndt, Johann. *Paradis-Gärtlein, voller Christlicher
Tugenden: Wie dieselbigen durch andäch-
tige, lehrhafte und trostreiche Gebete in die
Seele zu pflantzen*. Halle: Wäysenhause,
1746.

Baudelocque, Jean-Louis. *A System of Midwifery*.
Translated by John Heath. London:
Parkinson, 1790.

Bloch, Ruth. *Gender and Morality in Anglo-American Culture, 1650–1800*. Berkeley:
University of California Press, 2003.

Buchan, William. *Advice to Mothers, on the Subject
of Their Own Health, and on the Means
of Promoting the Health, Strength, and
Beauty, of Their Offspring*. Philadelphia:
John Bioren, 1804.

Bynum, Caroline Walker. *Jesus as Mother: Studies
in the Spirituality of the High Middle Ages*.
Berkeley: University of California Press,
1982.

Cadogan, William. *An Essay upon Nursing, and
the Management of Children, from Their
Birth to Three Years of Age*. London: J.
Roberts, 1748.

———. *An Essay upon Nursing, and the Management of Children, from Their Birth to Three
Years of Age*. Boston: Cox and Berry, 1772.

———. *An Essay upon Nursing, and the Manage-
ment of Children, from Their Birth to Three
Years of Age*. Philadelphia: William and
Thomas Bradford, 1773.

Chamberlain, Thomas, Theodore Mayern, and Nicholas Culpeper. *The Compleat Midwife's Practice Enlarged*. London: Bentley, Rhodes, Philips, & Taylor, 1698.

Clark, J. C. D. "Providence, Predestination and Progress: Or, Did the Enlightenment Fail?" *Albion: A Quarterly Journal Concerned with British Studies* 35 (2003): 567–69.

Cotton, John. *Milk for Babes: Drawn out of the Breasts of Both Testaments*. London: Coe, 1646.

Culpeper, Nicholas. *A Directory for Midwives*. London, 1693.

Denman, Thomas. *An Introduction to the Practice of Midwifery*. New-York: G. & C. & H. Carvill, 1829.

Deventer, Hendrik van. *The Art of Midwifery Improv'd*. London: Bettesworth, Innys, and Pemberton, 1728.

Doyle, Nora. *Maternal Bodies: Redefining Motherhood in Early America*. Chapel Hill: University of North Carolina Press, 2018.

Fermon, Nicole. "Domesticating Women, Civilizing Men: Rousseau's Political Program." *Sociological Quarterly* 35 (1994): 431–42.

Fissell, Mary. *Vernacular Bodies: The Politics of Reproduction in Early Modern England*. Oxford: Oxford University Press, 2004.

Flemming, Rebecca. "The Pathology of Pregnancy in Galen's Commentaries on the 'Epidemics.'" *Bulletin of the Institute of Classical Studies* 77 (2002): 101–12.

Force, James E. "Hume and the Relation of Science to Religion Among Certain Members of the Royal Society." *Journal of the History of Ideas* 45 (1984): 517–36.

Garrett, Matthew. "The Self-Made Son: Social Competition and the Vanishing Mother in Franklin's *Autobiography*." *ELH* 80 (2013): 519–32.

Hatoum, Sarah. "The Art of Midwifery Improv'd." *New York Academy of Medicine Library Blog*, May 15, 2014. https://nyamcenterforhistory.org/2014/05/15/the-art-of-midwifery-improvd/.

Horton, Howard. *An Improved System of Botanic Medicine*. 3rd ed. Columbus, OH: Howard, 1836.

Jager, Colin. *The Book of God: Secularization and Design in the Romantic Era*. Philadelphia: University of Pennsylvania Press, 2006.

Juster, Susan. "Mystical Pregnancy and Holy Bleeding: Visionary Experience in Early Modern Britain and America." *William and Mary Quarterly* 57 (2000): 249–88.

Kamensky, Jane. *A Revolution in Color: The World of John Singleton Copley*. New York: Norton, 2016.

Kerber, Linda K. *Women of the Republic: Intellect and Ideology in Revolutionary America*. Chapel Hill: University of North Carolina Press, 1980.

Klepp, Susan. "Revolutionary Bodies: Women and the Fertility Transition in the Mid-Atlantic Region, 1760–1820." *Journal of American History* 85 (December 1998): 910–45.

Koch, Philippa. *The Course of God's Providence*. New York: New York University Press, 2021.

———. "Experience and the Soul in Eighteenth-Century Medicine." *Church History: Studies in Christianity and Culture* 85 (2016): 552–86.

Larson, Rebecca. *Daughters of Light: Quaker Women Preaching and Prophesying in the Colonies and Abroad, 1700–1775*. Chapel Hill: University of North Carolina Press, 1999.

Lindman, Janet Moore. "To Have a Gradual Weaning and Be Ready and Willing to Resign All." *Early American Studies* 17 (2019): 498–518.

Man-Midwifery Analysed: And the Tendency of that Practice Detected and Exposed. London: R. Davis, 1764.

Mather, Cotton. *Angel of Bethesda*. Worcester, MA: American Antiquarian Society, 1972.

———. *Elizabeth in Her Holy Retirement*. Boston: Green, 1710.

McManus, Caroline. "The 'Carefull Nourse': Female Piety in Spenser's Legend of Holiness." *Huntington Library Quarterly* 60 (1997): 381–406.

Morgan, Jennifer L. *Laboring Women: Reproduction and Gender in New World Slavery*. Philadelphia: University of Pennsylvania Press, 2004.

Münchhausen, Philipp Adolph von. *Geistliche Kinder-Milch, oder Einfältiger Christen Hauß-Apotheck, daraus das himmlische Manna und die heilsame Artzney der Seelen fürgetragen wird*. Gensch: Franckfurt am Mayn, 1710.

Norton, Mary Beth. *Liberty's Daughters: The Revolutionary Experience of American Women, 1750–1800*. Ithaca: Cornell University Press, 1980.

Palumbo, Anne Cannon. "Averting 'Present Commotions': History as Politics in 'Penn's Treaty.'" *American Art* 9 (1995): 28–55.

Perry, Ruth. "Colonizing the Breast: Sexuality and Maternity in Eighteenth-Century England." *Journal of the History of Sexuality* 2 (1991): 204–34.

Porter, Roy. *Flesh in the Age of Reason*. New York: Norton, 2003.

Prown, Jules David. *Art as Evidence: Writings on Art and Material Culture*. New Haven: Yale University Press, 2001.

Roeber, A. G. *Hopes for Better Spouses: Protestant Marriage and Church Renewal in Early Modern Europe, India, and North America*. Grand Rapids, MI: Eerdmans, 2013.

Rousseau, Jean-Jacques. *Emile; or, On Education*. Translated and edited by Christopher Kelly and Allan Bloom. Collected Writings of Rousseau 13. Hanover: Dartmouth College Press, 2010.

Royster, Paul. Abstract to *Milk for Babes*. Electronic Texts in American Studies 18. DigitalCommons@University of Nebraska, Lincoln. http://digitalcommons.unl.edu/etas/18.

Seaman, Valentine. *The Midwives Monitor, and Mothers Mirror: Being Three Concluding Lectures of a Course of Instruction on Midwifery*. New York: Collins, 1800.

Sharpe, Jane. *The Midwives Book; or, The Whole Art of Midwifry Discovered*. Edited by Elaine Hobby. Oxford: Oxford University Press, 1999.

Shillace, Brandy. "Mother Machine: An 'Uncanny Valley' in the Eighteenth Century." *Appendix* 1, no. 2 (2013). http://theappendix.net/issues/2013/4/mother-machine-an-uncanny-valley-in-the-eighteenth-century.

Smellie, William. *An Abridgement of the Practice of Midwifery: And a Set of Anatomical Tables with Explanations*. Boston: J. Norman, [1786].

———. *A Treatise on the Theory and Practice of Midwifery*. 5th ed. London: Wilson, 1766.

Smith, Hugh. *Letters to Married Women: On Nursing and the Management of Children*. 6th ed. Philadelphia: Carey, 1792.

Stark, Johann Christian. *Hebammenunterricht in Gesprächen*. Jena: Cuno, 1782.

Stevens, Laura M. "Mary's Magnificat in Eighteenth-Century Britain and New England." In *Early Modern Prayer*, edited by William Gibson, Laura Stevens, and Sabine Volk-Birke, 91–107. Cardiff: University of Wales Press, 2017.

Taylor, Jeremy. *The Great Exemplar of Sanctity and Holy Life According to the Christian Institution: Described in the History of the Life and Death of the Ever Blessed Jesus Christ the Saviour of the World*. London: Francis Ash, 1649.

———. *The Life of Our Blessed Saviour Jesus Christ*. Greenfield, MA: Thomas Dickman, 1796.

———. *The Life of Our Blessed Saviour Jesus Christ*. Somerset, PA: J. & T. Patton, 1818.

Wilson, Philip K., ed. *Midwifery Theory and Practice*. New York: Garland, 1996.

CHAPTER 5

Printing England's Plague Past in New England

KATHLEEN MILLER

A book titled *Pathetic History of the Plague in London, in the Year 1665. Whereof Three Thousand Died in One Night; and an Hundred Thousand Taken Sick* was published by J. White in Charlestown, around 1810.[1] The book was a heavily revised and abridged version of Daniel Defoe's *A Journal of the Plague Year*, which was first printed in England in 1722. Despite the limited geography of the Great Plague of London in 1665, which was focused, though not localized, in the early modern London metropolis, the legacy of the outbreak easily transcended borders and time. The prevalence of plague in early modern England meant that texts about the disease proliferated, particularly during the years of frequent epidemics from 1596 to 1665. In the aftermath of these great epidemics, the disease continued to capture the imagination of people living in England, as evidenced by the popularity of texts such as Defoe's *A Journal of the Plague Year*, with its compellingly realistic description of one man's encounter with the horrific plague outbreak in 1665. Plague was not only a subject of interest in England, however. The disease touched numerous countries, and outbreaks of plague in human populations can be traced from 1320 BCE to the present day, with the 2014 outbreak of the disease in the form of pneumonic plague in Madagascar being a twenty-first-century example.[2]

Given plague's infamous history, its presence in myth and literature over time is justified. Understanding of the disease was established and shared through the print culture that emanated from and was inspired by the illness. Books that captured the disease in England were not restricted geographically. Through the seventeenth- and eighteenth-century international book trade, as well as recently established printing practices in New England, settlers in colonial America could interpret the affliction of plague through the reprinting of works originally published in England. This process of reprinting reveals the tastes of readers across the Atlantic. The texts that originated during and later memorialized early modern English plague outbreaks and were reprinted in New England reveal not only an enduring interest in the disease and its iterations in early modern England but also a predilection for works that treated plague as a subject of religious import. Defoe's *A Journal of the Plague Year* takes a prominent position among English plague works reprinted in early America; however, other books emerged, including Thomas Vincent's *Gods Terrible Voice in the City* (1667), William Dyer's *Christs Voice to London* (1666), and John Wilson's *A Song or, Story, for the Lasting Remembrance of Diuers Famous Works, Which God Hath Done in Our Time. With an Addition of Certaine Other Verses (Both Latine and English) to the Same Purpose* (1626).[3] The first section of this chapter addresses Wilson, who was born in England and later moved to New England. Editions of *A Song*, in which Wilson reflected on the English plague outbreaks of 1603 and 1625, were printed in England and New England. The second half of the chapter considers New England editions of the works by Vincent and Dyer, ejected nonconformist ministers who seized the opportunity to return to the pulpit during the Great Plague of London in 1665.[4] Complex interchanges in how plague was understood across the Atlantic, as expressed through New England's early print culture, reveal geographically specific interpretations of medicine and religion as they related to early modern England's plague outbreaks.

When early settlers landed in New England, a process of constant evolution and translation of medical care from England to New England began to emerge. Given the noted lack of university-educated physicians in the New England colonies, new lines of informal medical education developed through apprenticeships.[5] In addition, large numbers of medical practitioners worked outside the limits of established medical training. These included quacks and midwives, as well as the medical care typically provided by women in the domestic space and to friends.[6] So close were the ties between religion and medicine that ministers were often trained and practicing physicians, as well.[7] The diseases that afflicted colonists and the colonized were varied, and many of them were deadly and frightening. It has been posited that disease brought by colonizers played a key role in facilitating colonization, with its especially stark impact on Native populations, a form of what Stephen Greenblatt describes as "unintended but

102 DOCTRINE AND DISEASE

lethal biological warfare," allowing their lands to be overtaken.[8] These same diseases, in tandem with famine and the devastating processes of colonization, meant that life in seventeenth-century colonial America was uncertain and precarious for settlers and often deadly for Native populations.[9] Epidemics were suffered by both colonists and the colonized. Smallpox was a particularly feared disease, and much like plague, it killed up to 20 percent of the population of settlers, while often decimating Native populations.[10] The 1721 outbreak of smallpox in Boston fell a year after the plague outbreak in Marseille, France. Epidemic disease in the age of premodern medicine, prior to the widespread use of vaccinations and antibiotics, was deadly and largely unstoppable once it took hold. Furthermore, whether an epidemic occurred in Europe or colonial America, responses were not relegated to the medical sphere.

Texts from England provided guidelines for the medical theories that would steer medicine in practice in New England. In the American colonies, written medical doctrines, as in England, were read and interpreted by the literate, meaning that despite a lean workforce of formally trained physicians, literate citizens could provide medical care and follow medical theories.[11] Not all of the written material that circulated about diseases, and specifically plague, addressed the disease in primarily medical terms. Plague was interpreted along medical-religious lines throughout early modern England, with emphasis on the natural features of the illness gaining traction as the seventeenth century progressed.[12] Hugh Amory explains in his description of the printing industry in New England from 1638 to 1713 and of the press in Cambridge and its dearth of contributions to medical literature, "The exceptions that are sometimes urged are unconvincing: Is *God's Terrible Voice in the City of London* (1667)—an account of the Great Fire and plague of 1665 by the London minister Thomas Vincent—really 'the first American medical work'?"[13] In contrast, the printed output addressing plague in England, as it evolved throughout the early modern period, saw a decrease in religious interpretations of the disease as the seventeenth century progressed; in 1665, Paul Slack explains in *The Impact of Plague in Tudor and Stuart England*, when the epidemic descended on London, a majority of writing published on plague addressed "the natural causes of plague," "natural remedies," or "the incidence of disease."[14] In contrast and excepting the numerous examples of Defoe's *A Journal of the Plague Year* that were printed, New England presses were more inclined to print religious tracts on the disease. Narratives on plague, both religious and medical, straddled the complex fracture line between opposing understandings of pestilence. A minister might define a

PRINTING ENGLAND'S PLAGUE PAST IN NEW ENGLAND   103

plague epidemic as a biblical judgment, while simultaneously noting the features of the illness that allowed it to be transmitted through apparent contagion. In many documents, from recipe books to plague bills, concoctions to cure the disease were presented alongside prayers for redemption from divine judgment.[15] Wherever plague struck in early modern England, it evoked a complex interplay between religious and medical interpretations of a disease that was in many ways beyond comprehension.

The transatlantic complexion of plague works published in colonial America was reflected by a printing industry that bore direct English ties, in addition to developing its own analogous systems to those in place in England to manage book creation and distribution. England enacted a range of restrictions to limit and censor printing ventures. In 1557, England established a charter, granting the right to manage licensing rights to the Stationers' Company.[16] This system was maintained until 1662, with significant breaks, including that during the period of the English civil wars and into the years that followed.[17] In 1662, the Licensing Act was established, maintaining many aspects of the sixteenth-century charter.[18] A similar regulatory model for printing and distributing texts functioned in New England, overseen by the Massachusetts General Court, followed by the "Governor and Council of the Dominion of New England."[19] Hugh Amory notes that while "New England's censorship differed little from Old England's," it "was more visible, more effective, and culturally more accepted."[20] The printing industry in early New England was shaped, in part, by the pious worldview of the space in which it developed, with the outputs of the presses reflecting the interests not only of the governing figures but also of the population and, no doubt, shaped to some extent by the printers within their control of the local presses. The seventeenth-century printings discussed in this chapter, including the 1680 edition of Wilson's *A Song of Deliverance* and the 1667 and 1668 editions of Vincent's *Gods Terrible Voice in the City*, encompass the two central presses running during the latter half of the seventeenth century in New England, one in Cambridge and the other in Boston.[21]

Books and texts were deemed essential to the process of establishing a presence in colonial America and to erecting corresponding idealized systems of belief. Texts and the ability to read were essential to life in colonial America, forming a pivotal point on which the processes of colonization and imperialism were enacted. Perhaps more importantly, the printed word was central to the effective execution of Puritan religious practices.[22] David D. Hall notes, however, "Not only must the early American book trade be located within the contexts of mercantile capitalism, an imperial state system, and religious reformation, it should also be understood as 'colonial' in the sense of being structurally interrelated with the book trades of western Europe, and especially England," later noting, "American imprints often relied on European authors for their texts and on European presses, paper, and type for their production."[23] Alongside the project of translating and printing texts specifically to communicate with religious converts and potential converts, the tools required to print were conveyed to American soil. The English printer Marmaduke Johnson was brought from England, along with a new printing press, in order to share his expertise in the Massachusetts Bay Colony, as the Reverend John Eliot prepared to print the *Eliot Indian Bible* (1663), the first Bible printed in North America, which was composed in the local language, Massachusett.[24] Working closely with the Christian convert and Nipmuck Indian James Printer, Eliot was largely indebted to Printer's expertise in facilitating the ambitious project, as well as being "aided by three teachers and interpreters, a Montauk Indian from Long Island named Cockenoe and two Massachusett Indians, John Sassamon and Job Nesutan."[25] Similarly, the first known work printed in the Americas was *Breve y mas compendiosa Doctrina Christiana en Lengua Mexicana y Castellana*, a religious text that was produced on a printing press established in sixteenth-century Mexico City by Juan Pablos with the oversight of the Spanish printer Juan Cromberger. The title suggests that the work was published in both Spanish and the Nahuatl language of the local population.[26]

Within early New England's nascent printing industry, plague did not form a subject of overwhelming interest. The numerous versions of Defoe's *A Journal of the Plague Year* were to be expected of a work that reached the book's level of popularity. Among the other works addressing English plague were texts from England reprinted on American presses and appropriated for American audiences, such as Wilson's *A Song of Deliverance for the Lasting Remembrance of Gods Wonderful Works Never to be Forgotten. Containing in it the Wonderful Defeat of the Spanish-Armado, Anno, 1588. The Woful Plague, Anno, 1603. Soon upon the Entrance of King James of Famous Memory, unto the Crown of England. With the Discovery of the Povvder Plot, Anno, 1605. And the Down Fall of Black Fryers, When an Hellish Crew of Papists Met to Hear Drury a Popish Priest, An. 1623. Also the Grievous Plague, Anno, 1625.* (1680).[27] The verse collected in *A Song* captures a series of trials and casts them in a religious light, in which divine judgment and grace provide an overarching framework for interpreting Puritan struggle. In particular, the book narrows in on two plague outbreaks, those in 1603 and 1625.

As a Puritan born in England, with an education obtained at Eton and later in King's College, Cambridge, Wilson was thoroughly established in England before making the journey to colonial America.[28] His preaching made him a popular figure among his Puritan peers though also proved a hinderance at times—Wilson faced challenges of nonconformity on and off—and he eventually made his way to the Massachusetts Bay Colony.[29] Even after his emigration to New England, where he was one of the founders of the First Church of Boston, he made expeditions back to England at points throughout the 1630s.[30] Two extant printings of Wilson's work remain, one printed in 1626 and a later posthumous edition from 1680. Wilson composed the work while still living in England; however, the posthumous edition from the late seventeenth century saw the work packaged in New England for a different audience. Wilson's interpretation of plague in England strikes a complex balance between his inherent understanding of England, which he would leave behind, and the Puritan belief system underpinning his career and eventual emigration to New England.

Wilson's verse captures pivotal events from the late sixteenth century to the first half of the seventeenth century. These include the Spanish Armada, severe pestilential epidemics in 1603 and 1625, the gunpowder plot, the rise and fall of English monarchs throughout the period, and the deadly collapse at Blackfriars. Wilson ties in each plague outbreak with other political upheavals and conflicts weathered in England. The location of each printing, however, imparted subtle distinctions, whether the copy was printed in England or New England. Referring to the conclusion of Wilson's verse introduction to *A Song*, Amy M. E. Morris in *Popular Measures: Poetry and Church Order in Seventeenth-Century Massachusetts* notes that the intention of Wilson's words may be interpreted differently, whether one reads a copy from England or one printed later in New England: "In 1626, the invitation of Wilson's narrator, 'Come Children, hearken and consider well,' was addressed to literal children, but in New England in 1680, the same language would have equally addressed the unconverted adult children, the 'rising generation' of New England."[31] While the text of the two introductions is largely similar, apart from spelling variations, the 1680 edition also offers a slightly different ending to the introductory verse. In the 1626 edition, the final lines of the introductory verse read,

> Come children, harken and consider well,
> Gods Word will teach you best, but works withall
> (Such workes as I shall very plainely tell)

106 DOCTRINE AND DISEASE

Will teach you how with feare on God to call.
Thou Lord, which dost the little ones affect,
Let this poore song thy little ones direct.[32]

In the posthumous edition published in 1680 in Boston, the ending is updated to, "Thou Lord, which dost the little ones affect, / Let this poor Song thy little ones recall."[33] The language, "ones recall," changes the meaning of the passage to an act of looking back in the later edition. It is impossible to determine how authorial or editorial interventions played out between the two printings of Wilson's work, but for the reader, both geography and time provide a changing context for interpreting Wilson's verse.

In addition to the subtle changes or differences in interpretation manifested by the geographical context of the work or time of its printing was the addition of a substantial paratextual apparatus to guide the reader through the process of interpreting the 1680 edition of the work. The 1680 edition of Wilson's poem is prefaced by a letter to the "Christian Reader," signed by Wilson's son, John Wilson.[34] Wilson's son notes the redemptive quality of his father's verse, both for Wilson as an author and for his audience of readers:

What Volums hath he penned for the help of others in their several changes of condition, which if they were all compiled together, would questionless make a large Folio. How was his heart full of good matter? He was another sweet finger of Israel, whoss heavenly Verses passed like to the handkerchief carryed from Paul to help and uphold disconsolate ones, and to heal their wracked Souls, by the effectual pris[ ]nce of Gods holy Spirit. Seeing those are not so visible unto the World, be pleased to peruse these, redivived by this present impression, wherein we may ob[ ]ve what were Gods former mercyes towards his People in great Brittain, his wonderful mercy to King, Peers, and People, and unto our Fathers; when the Spanish Popish Plot was dashed in pieces, and the half Moon of their Navy, (whose horns stood seven miles mile asunder) was shattred into Confusion. Gods Judgements also in the two dreadful plagues (which are mentioned in this Book) and Gods healing hand.[35]

Not only is his father's writing redemptive, but the letter also indicates its curative power. His son refers to Wilson's writing as akin to the "*handkerchief carryed from Paul*," the Apostle, referring to Acts 19:12: "So that from his body were brought unto the sick handkerchiefs or aprons, and the diseases departed

PRINTING ENGLAND'S PLAGUE PAST IN NEW ENGLAND   107

from them, and the evil spirits went out of them" (King James Version). The allusion captures the intersection between unwell souls and bodies, a meeting point where Wilson's verse offers a healing effect. Plague and sickness within this paradigm are indivisible from religious life. The disease is a judgment, and Wilson's writing is a cure for the soul. Toward the conclusion of the letter, Wilson's son notes the dual significance of the text presented to the reader, writing, *"Only let us thankefully remember Gods former mercyes shewed to his people in both Englands, really and unfeignedly repent of whatsoever we have provoked him with."*[36] While Wilson was writing for an English readership in his poem, the addition of the prefacing letter by his son reframes the text for a new audience, noting that the work (and the works of God that the verse describes) may apply to *"both Englands."* Within the letter, and the verse written by his father that the letter frames, plague is positioned as a religious event, one offered as a biblical judgment and resolved by *"Gods healing hand."*[37] While Wilson's son's fleeting reflection on plague in the poem firmly positions it as a religious event, Wilson's verse acknowledges the corporeal and administrative features of the plague epidemics he narrates.

Wilson's description of each plague outbreak follows the contours of political life, as well as the administrative features of early modern English plague outbreaks. His history of the events is informed both by experience—Wilson resided in England during each of the outbreaks he describes, though he offers a more substantial reflection on the 1625 outbreak, which occurred a year before the book's publication, in contrast to that in 1603—and also by the features of a print culture that allowed citizens to track the event. His comparably brief description of the 1603 outbreak touches on the death of Queen Elizabeth I, followed by King James taking the crown—"our hearts were fill'd with laughter, / To see King *James* the Crown possess / So quietly, soon after"—and he situates these events as catalysts for ushering in plague: "But least we should be overjoy'd, / and hope beyond all bounds, / Just then, our Kingdome was annoy'd, / with Plague that all confounds."[38] Wilson goes on to narrate the number of dead from the outbreak, calling on the London bills of mortality to corroborate the gravity of the event:

> In three moneths space to death did pine
> (witnesse the *London*-bill,)
> Thirty four thousand seventy nine,
> yet had not death its fill.

108 DOCTRINE AND DISEASE

> Three thousand three hundred eighty five,
> In one week did depart.[39]

Wilson introduces his extended reflection on the 1625 outbreak by describing a sinful population punished by plague, resulting in the removal of the court to Oxford, the rich fleeing, leaving behind the poor who had no choice but to remain in the city. He describes the sights and sounds of the epidemic—"Nothing was heard but passing-bells," "heaps of dead, / to feed the hungry grave," "Some did the deadly marks sustain, / and some the deadly sore."[40] Wilson turns to the administrative and political features of the epidemic, relating these in conjunction with the religious causes and visible signs of the disease, such as the "deadly marks" that plague left on the body.

Wilson frames his narration of the outbreak of 1625 with the language of an early modern plague outbreak; however, in keeping with his Puritan belief system, he understands these seventeenth-century struggles within a religious framework, calling on 1 Chronicles 21, when David brings three days of plague on Israel:

> "Right so the Jewish Church of old,
> "For *David's* proud presumption,
> "And for their own rebellions bold,
> "fall'n in a quick consumption,
> "Just when the Angel stretcht his hand,
> "*Jerusalem* to stroy,
> "It pleased God no more their Land,
> "with sickness to annoy.[41]

Wilson parallels the moment when the angel prepares to destroy Jerusalem, only stopping when David pleads that so many are suffering for his sins, with the seemingly abrupt end of the outbreak in 1625:

> Now Churches, Streets, shops, houses, men,
> all sure and safe protected.
> The eyes which had not before seen,
> The Cityes desolation,
> Could scarce believe that there had been,
> such deadly visitation.[42]

While Wilson's initial printing of *A Song* was firmly rooted in the England he would eventually leave behind, the reprinting of the work on a New England press demonstrates the continuing appetite among Puritan colonists for religious contextualization of defining moments from life in England.

THE GREAT PLAGUE OF LONDON IN 1665 REPRINTED IN NEW ENGLAND

Settlers found a nostalgia and connection to England in the ability to print that was particularly compelling as they negotiated the challenges of a new land.[43] These presses, furthermore, printed not only original works, such as the *Eliot Indian Bible*, but also works reprinted from London presses, modified for "the colonial market."[44] The reprinting of Vincent's *Gods Terrible Voice in the City* and Dyer's *Christ's Voice to London* in New England reflects an enduring fascination with an England left behind, even at its most chaotic moments. Vincent's work acted as a reflection on and history of the events of the plague in 1665 and the fire of 1666 in London, while Dyer's book collected sermons that the minister delivered at St. Anne and St. Agnes during the visitation of plague in 1665.[45] Both authors were dissenting ministers who preached during the outbreak, contravening restrictions in place to prevent preaching by nonconformist ministers, as outlined in the acts that formed the Clarendon Code. Vincent and Dyer frame the horrific 1665 outbreak of plague in London as a divine judgment. While Vincent and Dyer describe a range of sinful actions that provoked the judgment of plague, in the earliest English printings of Vincent's book, he succinctly ties the ill health of the city to the country's treatment of its ejected ministers, citing the Bartholomew Ejections and the Five Mile Act as inception points for the plague and fire to come: "Here I might speak of the Judgment executed, *August* 24th. 1662. when so many Ministers were put out of their Places, and the judgments executed, *March* 24th. 1665. when so many Ministers were banished five miles from Corporations, the former by way of introduction to the Plague which sometime after did spread in the Land, but chiefly raged in the City ; the latter by way of introduction to the Fire, which quickly after did burn down *London* the greatest Corporation in *England*."[46] Though Vincent's intent was clear in linking the events of the ejections with the outbreak of plague in the earliest English editions of the book, the first editions of the work in New England, which were much abbreviated, would describe the cause of the affliction with less specificity.

The 1667 and 1668 New England copies of *Gods Terrible Voice in the City*, printed in Cambridge by Samuel Green and Marmaduke Johnson, respectively, feature material from the 1667 English printings of *Gods Terrible Voice in the City* that is primarily focused on narrating the histories of the plague and fire, from sections V and VI.[47] The Cambridge copies also reprint the introduction that appeared in the earliest English printings of the work, which begins, "*Shall a Trumpet be blown in the City, and the people not be afraid?*"[48] The 1668 copy published by Johnson also notes the addition of "*The Generall Bill of Mortality*, Shewing the Number of Persons which died in every Parish of all Diseases, and of the Plague, in the Year abovesaid."[49] The Cambridge presses, on which the 1667 and 1668 editions of Vincent's work were printed, produced print matter alongside the presses in Boston—with Boston printing 81 percent of the works still available to us.[50] The location of the presses dictated the type of material being printed. The Cambridge presses were focused on religious works, "practical divinity," and "ecclesiastical and municipal laws," while the Boston presses devoted much of their work to volumes on "history and biography," though their outputs were notably wide-ranging.[51] Green and Johnson, noted on the imprints of the 1667 and 1668 editions printed in Cambridge of *Gods Terrible Voice in the City*, were at odds for a number of years over the rights to print at the Cambridge presses, until joining forces in 1668.[52]

Vincent's apocalyptic vision of the epidemic in *Gods Terrible Voice in the City* was shaped by his position as a nonconformist. The earliest printings of the book in England offered an extended rumination on the events of the outbreak, partly modeled on sermon style and partly fashioned as a history of the events he memorialized. In extant copies of the work printed in seventeenth-century New England, this is not the case. Instead, the texts are dramatically reduced versions of their English counterparts. Though Vincent clearly linked plague to the Bartholomew Ejections, the 1667 and 1668 Cambridge editions of the book are fashioned as histories, with the prefatory material establishing plague more broadly as a judgment for sinful actions before entering into a narration of the epidemic:

> Therefore I shall give a brief Narration of this sad Judgement, and some observations of mine own (who was here in the City from the beginning to the end of it) both to keep alive in my self and others, the memory of the Judgement, that we may be the better prepared for compliance with Gods design in sending the Plague amongst us.
> It was *in the Year of our Lord* 1665 that the Plague began in our City of *London*, after we were warned by the great Plague in *Holland* in the

year 1664, and the beginning of it in some remote parts of our Land the same year ; not to speak any thing whether there was any signification and influence in the *Blazing-Star* not long before, that appeared in the view of *London*, and struck some amazement upon the spirits of many. It was in the moneth of *May* that the Plague was first taken notice of, our Bills of Mortality did let us know but of three which died of the Disease in the whole year before ; but in the beginning of *May* the Bill tells us of nine, which fell by the Plague.[53]

When Vincent's book was "reprinted" in 1770 by T. Green on a New London press, a new introduction was added, derived from section IV in the English version of 1667, titled "The Introduction. *God speaks sometimes to a People by terrible things.*"[54] Furthermore, the 1770 copy reframes the meaning of the outbreak as a consequence of the Bartholomew Ejections, using different introductory material than the Cambridge editions, derived from section IV of the English editions.[55] Though the 1770 edition introduces the history of the outbreak with the earlier starting point of the Bartholomew Ejections, it remains that New England audiences read Vincent's book as a religiously inflected history of the outbreak, in which the author is written into the events of the year.

Though New England versions of *Gods Terrible Voice in the City* focused largely on a narration of the events, delving into the administrative and practical features of living through an epidemic, complete with running tallies from the London bills of mortality and horrifying descriptions of people's bodies succumbing to disease, Vincent also reflected on the seemingly chaotic nature of the illness. Though the bodily impact of the outbreak and religious interpretations underpinning the disease seemed at odds, Vincent reconciled this conflict by noting,

> the plague makes little difference between the righteous and the wicked (except the Lord by a peculiar providence do shelter some under his wing, and compass them with his favor as with a shield, hereby keeping off the darts that are shot so thick about them) yet as there is little difference in the body of the righteous and of others, so this disease makes little discrimination, and not a few, fearing God, are cut off amongst the rest; they die of the same distemper, with the most prophane; they are buried in the same grave, and there sleep together till the morning of the resurrection.[56]

112 DOCTRINE AND DISEASE

While sin may have contributed to the judgment of plague, and the affliction of the disease was ultimately a leveling force even between the godly and sinners, Vincent notes that "Angels convey the souls of the righteous into the heavenly paradise," while "Devils drag the souls of the wicked, after they have received their final doom at the bar of God, into utter darkness, where there is weeping, and wailing, and gnashing of teeth."[57] If medicine and religion made an uncomfortable union in life, this would be divinely resolved after death.

Much like Vincent's *Gods Terrible Voice in the City*, Dyer's *Christs Voice to London* enjoyed popularity in both England and New England. Originally published in England, the work featured three sermons—"*A Call to* Sinners. Or, Christ's Voice to *London*," "The Great Day of His Wrath," and "Watch and Pray"—concluding with a section titled "Considerations of Death: Containing some few Reasons why men fear it ; and opposite Reasons by way of Answer, why they should not fear it."[58] Collected editions of Dyer's writing, printed in England and New England, included the sermons from *Christs Voice to London*. A single sermon from *Christs Voice to London* was printed and circulated in 1768 by Timothy Green in New London as well.[59] The copy only includes the first sermon and was published with the title *Christ's Voice to London: Being the Substance of a Sermon Preach'd in the City, in the Time of the Sad Visitation.*[60] The sermon describes the city's and its inhabitants' sins, including "self-conceitedness," "earthly-mindedness," and "ignorance," offering a location-specific reading of plague as a divine judgment.[61] While the 1666 copy of Dyer's sermons printed in London introduces the first sermon with Revelation 3:20—"*Behold, I stand at the door, and knock; if any man hear my voice, and open the door, I will come in to him, and will sup with him, and he with me*"—copies published in New England attribute the same passage to Revelation 5:2, possibly conflating it with Song of Songs 5:2: "I sleep, but my heart waketh: it is the voice of my beloved that knocketh, saying, Open to me, my sister, my love, my dove, my undefiled: for my head is filled with dew, and my locks with the drops of the night."[62] In the sermon, Dyer alerts his reader that "great cities are places which are usually guilty of great sins," warning that "Jerusalem and other cities were destroyed by God for their sins and wickedness," then turning to London: "O London, repent, that it may not be so with thee. O ye people, rent your hearts and not your garments, and turn to the Lord, who is willing to receive you."[63] As printing expanded throughout New England in the eighteenth century, arriving in New London in 1708, it increased trade of British-originating books and allowed for the greater circulation of books created on "country presses."[64] The New London

PRINTING ENGLAND'S PLAGUE PAST IN NEW ENGLAND 113

press in Connecticut, on which Vincent's and Dyer's abbreviated works were printed in 1768 and 1770, only produced around 3 percent of the print matter that was comparatively produced by the Boston presses in the second quarter of the century.[65] That these plague works were printed in the New London suggests the continuing interest in English plague epidemics among New England audiences, prompting editions printed over a century after they were first circulated in London, England.

CONCLUSION

In the absence of a printer's note in these New England editions, it is impossible to trace how the different editions of Vincent's and Dyer's plague works were devised on early New England soil. While it remains debatable to what extent Dyer's visitation sermons or Vincent's religiously framed narrative or Wilson's instructive verse could reasonably be categorized as medical texts, plague remained an event that, with its horrific destruction of the earthly body, captured minds focused on the redemption of the soul after death. Though plague was not the destructive force in New England that it had been in England, harrowing tales of the bodily struggle wrought by pestilence no doubt resonated among a Puritan population that had endured its own afflictions of famine and diseases like smallpox. In colonial New England, where the borders between religion and medicine were porous and physicians and ministers were often one and the same, it is not surprising that many of the plague works that became fixtures on the early New England printing presses were those that understood plague as a bodily affliction only in tandem with interpreting it as a judgment for sin.

NOTES

1. *Early American Imprints, Series I: Evans, 1639–1800*, no. 28551, offers the date of 1810.

2. The Philistines experienced an outbreak in 1320 BCE, as recorded in the Bible. Department of Communicable Disease Surveillance and Response, "WHO Report," 26.

3. Wilson, *Song* (1626), title page; Vincent, *Gods Terrible Voice* (1667); Dyer, *Christs Voice to London* (1666).

4. For detailed readings of Dyer's and Vincent's works in the context of early modern

plague writing, see Miller, *Literary Culture of Plague*, chapter 4, which addresses some of the same primary and secondary sources that appear in this chapter.

5. Duffy, *From Humors to Medical Science*, 10–12.

6. Duffy, *From Humors to Medical Science*, 16.

7. Herzogenrath, *American Body | Politic*, 118; Watson, *Angelical Conjunction*; for additional perspectives on physician-ministers in early New England, see chapters 3 and 6 in this volume.

8. Duffy, *From Humors to Medical Science*, 2; Greenblatt, "Invisible Bullets," 90.

9. For examinations of the depopulation of Native communities during colonization, see Jones, "Virgin Soils Revisited"; Silva, *Miraculous Plagues*.

10. Duffy, *From Humors to Medical Science*, 6.

11. Duffy gives the example of "ministers and government leaders" contributing to health care (*From Humors to Medical Science*, 11).

12. Slack, *Impact of Plague*, 244.

13. Amory, "Printing and Bookselling," 85.

14. Slack takes into consideration printed matter produced in both 1665 and 1666 (*Impact of Plague*, 244).

15. For additional discussion of recipes on plague bills, see Miller, *Literary Culture of Plague*, 24–34.

16. Hall, introduction to *A History of the Book in America*, 4.

17. Como, "Print, Censorship, and Ideological Escalation," 822–23.

18. Rose, *Authors and Owners*, 31; Hall, introduction to *A History of the Book in America*, 4–5.

19. Amory, "Printing and Bookselling," 83.

20. Amory, "Printing and Bookselling," 83.

21. Amory, "Printing and Bookselling," 83.

22. Hall, introduction to *A History of the Book in America*, 15, 18. For a consideration of the representation of colonial anxieties and print enforcing imperialistic goals, see Cathy Rex's discussion of Massachusetts Bay Colony seals in "Indians and Images."

23. Hall, introduction to *A History of the Book in America*, 7.

24. Rex, "Indians and Images," 77. For a detailed account of the printing history of the *Eliot Indian Bible*, see Winship, *Cambridge Press*, 208–44.

25. Hall, introduction to *A History of the Book in America*, 18–19. Lisa Brooks notes, "Green, Printer, and Johnson were able to produce a full version of the Bible entitled *Mamusse Wunneetupanatamwe Up-Biblum God*, which was distributed in wide-ranging networks of trade. Published in 'huge print runs,' the bible circulated among Native converts (and potential converts) in the Nipmuc, Patucket, and Wampanoag towns to the west and south, and also among curious benefactors and collectors in England" (*Our Beloved Kin*, 88).

26. Stillwell, *Incunabula and Americana*, 140; Oakes, "Publishing and Culture," 101. Oakes suggests that the first book was not published until

six years after the press was installed in 1539, while Stillwell gives the year of the first printing as 1539.

27. Wilson's book was first published in England in 1626.

28. Bremer, "Wilson, John (1591–August 1667)."

29. Bremer, "Wilson, John (1591–August 1667)."

30. Bremer, "Wilson, John (1591–August 1667)."

31. Morris, *Popular Measures*, 200.

32. Wilson, *Song* (1626), last page of introduction.

33. Wilson, *Song* (1680), last page of introduction.

34. Both David D. Hall and Amy M. E. Morris identify the John Wilson signature on the letter prefacing the 1680 edition as that of Wilson's son. Hall, *Ways of Writing*, 26; Morris, *Popular Measures*, 231n26.

35. Wilson (son), "Letter to Christian Reader." The *Oxford English Dictionary* describes the significance of "Israel," when used within biblical allusion, as Wilson's son uses the term, as follows: "In figurative and allusive uses; esp. the chosen people of God, the elect: applied to the Christian church, or to true Christians collectively." "Israel, n."

36. Wilson (son), "Letter to Christian Reader."

37. Wilson (son), "Letter to Christian Reader."

38. Wilson, *Song* (1680), 13.

39. Wilson, *Song* (1680), 14. For the week ending September 1, 1603, *Buried in London* records 3,385 "buried in all, with the places aforesaid," while 3,035 of these deaths were attributed to plague (7).

40. Wilson, *Song* (1680), 31–32.

41. Wilson, *Song* (1680), 34–35.

42. Wilson, *Song* (1680), 35.

43. Amory, "Printing and Bookselling," 88.

44. Amory, "Printing and Bookselling," 86.

45. Leachman, "Dyer, William (1632/3–1696)."

46. Vincent, *Gods Terrible Voice in the City* (1667), 20–21. For a detailed reading of Vincent's interpretation of plague in relation to the Clarendon Code, as he describes it here, see Miller, *Literary Culture of Plague*, 95–96.

47. Vincent, *Gods Terrible Voice* (1667), 24 (sect. V), 46 (sect. VI).

48. Vincent, *Gods Terrible Voice* (1668), A3.

49. Vincent, *Gods Terrible Voice* (1668), title page.

50. I use the plural form of "press," though there is uncertainty as to the number of presses

in Cambridge and Boston when each edition was published: "Technologically, Boston and Cambridge were roughly on a par: from 1639 to 1692, there were one or two presses operating in Cambridge; from 1675 to 1713, one to three presses in Boston; and in New England as a whole down to 1713, there were usually two, and occasionally three or four presses." Amory, "Printing and Bookselling," 85.

51. Amory, "Printing and Bookselling," 85.

52. Amory, "Printing and Bookselling," 90.

53. Vincent, *Gods Terrible Voice* (1668), 4.

54. Vincent, *God's Terrible Voice* (1770), title page, n.p., 3–5; Vincent, *Gods Terrible Voice* (1667), 19–23 (sect. IV). For a discussion of faith in relation to the first section of this passage, see Miller, *Literary Culture of Plague*, 107–8.

55. Vincent, *Gods Terrible Voice* (1667), 20–21.

56. Vincent, *God's Terrible Voice* (1770), 11.

57. Vincent, *God's Terrible Voice* (1770), 12.

58. Dyer, *Christs Voice to London* (1666), 1, 45, 87, 127. For an in-depth reading of Dyer's plague sermons, see Miller, *Literary Culture of Plague*, 109–23.

59. The same printer produced Vincent's *God's Terrible Voice in the City* in New London two years later in 1770. The visitation sermons also appear in larger collections of Dyer's writing, including Dyer, *Christ's Famous Titles* (1698); Dyer, *Christ's Famous Title* (1722).

60. Dyer, *Christ's Voice to London* (1768).

61. Dyer, *Christ's Voice to London* (1768), 6.

62. Dyer, *Christ's Voice to London* (1768); Dyer, *Christ's Famous Title* (1722), 179. For a reading of Revelation and "apocalyptic sentiment" in Dyer, see Miller, *Literary Culture of Plague*, 117–21. For further commentary on the connection between Song of Songs 5:2 and Revelation 3:20, see Beale, *Book of Revelation*, 308; Song of Songs 5:2 (King James Version).

63. Dyer, *Christ's Voice to London* (1768), 33–34.

64. Amory, "Printing and Bookselling," 314–15.

65. Amory, "Printing and Bookselling," 315.

BIBLIOGRAPHY

Amory, Hugh. "Printing and Bookselling in New England, 1638–1713." In *A History of the Book in America*, edited by Hugh Amory and David D. Hall, 1:83–116. Cambridge: Cambridge University Press, 2000.

Beale, G. K. *The Book of Revelation: A Commentary on the Greek Text*. Grand Rapids, MI: Wm. B. Eerdmans; Carlisle: Paternoster Press, 1999.

Bremer, Francis J. "Wilson, John (1591–1667), Clerical Leader of Early Massachusetts." *American National Biography*, February 1, 2000. https://doi.org/10.1093/anb /9780198606697.article.0100988.

Brooks, Lisa. *Our Beloved Kin: A New History of King Philip's War*. New Haven: Yale University Press, 2018.

Buried in London and in the Places Neere Adioyning. London: Iohn Windet, 1603.

Como, David R. "Print, Censorship, and Ideological Escalation in the English Civil War." *Journal of British Studies* 51, no. 4 (2012): 820–57.

Defoe, Daniel. *Pathetic History of the Plague in London, in the Year 1665. Whereof Three Thousand Died in One Night, and an Hundred Thousand Taken Sick. [Eight lines of verse]*. Boston: Printed and sold by J. White, Charlestown, [1810?]. Readex, *Early American Imprints, Series I: Evans, 1630–1800*.

Department of Communicable Disease Surveillance and Response. *WHO Report on Global Surveillance of Epidemic-Prone Infectious Diseases*. Geneva: World Health Organization, February 15, 2000. https:// www.who.int/publications/i/item /WHO-CDS-CSR-ISR-2000.1.

Duffy, John. *From Humors to Medical Science: A History of American Medicine*. 2nd ed. Urbana: University of Illinois Press, 1993.

Dyer, William. *Christ's Famous Titles and A Believer's Golden Chain; Handl'd in Divers Sermons*. Boston: Printed by John Allen for Nicholas Boone, 1722.

———. *Christ's Famous Titles, and A Believer's Golden Chain: Handled in Divers Sermons*. London: Printed for Henry Nelme, 1698.

———. *Christs Voice to London and the Great Day of Gods Wrath*. London: E. Calvert, 1666.

———. *Christ's Voice to London: Being the Substance of a Sermon Preach'd in the City, in the Time of the Sad Visitation*. New

London: Re-printed and Sold by Timothy Green, 1768.

Greenblatt, Stephen. "Invisible Bullets: Renaissance Authority and Its Subversion, *Henry IV* and *Henry V*." In *New Historicism and Renaissance Drama*, edited by Richard Wilson and Richard Dutton, 82–107. New York: Routledge, 2013.

Hall, David D. Introduction to *A History of the Book in America*, edited by Hugh Amory and David D. Hall, 1:1–12. Cambridge: Cambridge University Press, 2000.

———. *Ways of Writing: the Practice and Politics of Text-Making in Seventeenth-Century New England*. Philadelphia: University of Pennsylvania Press, 2008.

Herzogenrath, Bernd. *An American Body | Politic: A Deleuzian Approach*. Hanover: Dartmouth College Press, 2020.

"Israel, n." *Oxford English Dictionary Online*. Oxford: Oxford University Press, April 2023. https://www.oed.com/dictionary/israeli_n.

Jones, David S. "Virgin Soils Revisited." *William and Mary Quarterly* 60, no. 4 (2003): 703–42.

Leachman Caroline L. "Dyer, William (1632/3–1696)." *Oxford Dictionary of National Biography*. Oxford: Oxford University Press, 2004; online ed., 2008. https://doi.org/10.1093/ref:odnb/8354. Accessed August 24, 2021.

Miller, Kathleen. *The Literary Culture of Plague in Early Modern England*. London: Palgrave Macmillan, 2016.

Morris, Amy M. E. *Popular Measures: Poetry and Church Order in Seventeenth-Century Massachusetts*. Newark: University of Delaware Press, 2005.

Oakes, John. "Publishing and Culture: The Alchemy of Ideas." In *The Oxford Handbook of Publishing*, edited by Michael Bhaskar and Angus Phillips, 99–112. Oxford: Oxford University Press, 2019. https://doi.org/10.1093/oxfordhb/9780198794202.013.4.

Rex, Cathy. "Indians and Images: The Massachusetts Bay Colony Seal, James Printer, and the Anxiety of Colonial Identity." *American Quarterly* 63, no. 1 (2011): 61–93.

Rose, Mark. *Authors and Owners: The Invention of Copyright*. Cambridge, MA: Harvard University Press. 1995.

Silva, Cristobal. *Miraculous Plagues: An Epidemiology of Early New England Narrative*. Oxford: Oxford University Press, 2011.

Slack, Paul. *The Impact of Plague in Tudor and Stuart England*. Oxford: Oxford University Press, 1985.

Stillwell, Margaret Bingham. *Incunabula and Americana, 1450–1800: A Key to Bibliographical Study*. New York: Columbia University Press, 1931.

Vincent, Thomas. *Gods Terrible Voice in the City*. London: George Calvert, 1667.

———. *Gods Terrible Voice in the City*. Cambridge, MA: Samuel Green, 1667.

———. *Gods Terrible Voice in the City*. Cambridge, MA: Marmaduke Johnson, 1668.

———. *God's Terrible Voice in the City*. New London: T. Green, 1770.

Watson, Patricia A. *The Angelical Conjunction: The Preacher-Physicians of Colonial New England*. Knoxville, TN: Newfound Press, 1991.

Wilson, John. *A Song of Deliverance for the Lasting Remembrance of Gods Wonderful Works Never to Be Forgotten. Containing in it the Wonderful Defeat of the Spanish-Armado, Anno, 1588. The Woful Plague, Anno, 1603. Soon upon the Entrance of King James of Famous Memory, unto the Crown of England. With the Discovery of the Povvder Plot, Anno, 1605. And Down Fall of Black Fryers, When an Hellish Crew of Papists Met to Hear Drury a Popish Priest, An. 1623. Also the Grievous Plague, Anno, 1625. With Poems Both Latin and English, and the Verses of That Learned Theodore Beza*. Boston, 1680.

———. *A Song or, Story, for the Lasting Remembrance of Diuers Famous Works, Which God Hath Done in Our Time. With an Addition of Certaine Other Verses (Both Latine and English) to the Same Purpose*. London: Printed by R. Young for I. Bartlet, 1626.

Wilson, John (son). "Letter to Christian Reader." In Wilson, *Song of Deliverance*.

Winship, George Parker. *The Cambridge Press, 1638–1692: A Reexamination of the Evidence Concerning The Bay Psalm Book and the Eliot Indian Bible*. Philadelphia: University of Pennsylvania Press, 1945.

CHAPTER 6

Contagious Fasts

Occasional Worship and Medical Practice in
England and Massachusetts Bay Colony

CATHERINE REEDY

Published during the height of the "contagious distemper" that would take
seven hundred lives, Thomas Thacher's *A Fast of Gods Chusing* (1678) offers an
unsettling vision of a public fast gone wrong in the face of one of Boston's worst
smallpox outbreaks.[1] New England bore witness to no fewer than eight such fasts
between Plymouth and Massachusetts Bay Colony during the epidemic, with
Thacher himself serving as preacher and physician throughout the time of high
mortality.[2] A founding member of the Third Church in Boston,[3] Thacher spent
his life moving between the spiritual and physical realms, starting his career as
a minister in Weymouth before moving to Boston to practice medicine after his
wife's death.[4] The end of the year would see both the publication of Thacher's
only other extant work—the broadside *A Brief Rule* (1678), detailing the treatment of smallpox—and his own death, contracted from an unidentified illness
while caring for the sick during the outbreak.[5] Deeply invested in treating the
smallpox at nearly every level, from his medical instructions on eating "thin
water-pottage made only of Indian flour & water" to the devotional guide on
the proper "season" of fasting, Thacher nevertheless only rarely considers the
contagious transmission of the disease within his published pieces. Surprisingly, though, when contagion does appear, it is found not in *Brief Rule*, a text

118 DOCTRINE AND DISEASE

focused primarily on medical discussions, but in *Fast*, which addresses religious thought, as Thacher raises the unnerving suggestion that collective fasts might accomplish the very opposite of their intended function. Remarkably, public prayers might increase rather than decrease "sickness upon those that are well and weakness and death upon the sick" when uttered too formally, like those familiar set prayers in England.[6] Ironically, prayers and practices meant to stop contagion threaten to become that very spreading force itself, morphing into yet another invisibly traveling vector of disease when plagued by "formality," or any faith practice based on ceremony rather than "authentic" worship.[7]

This chapter focuses on the intersections of public health and the public devotional responses to medical crises that were taken to push against "formality," or the set, prewritten forms of prayer found across the Atlantic. Court-ordained days set out for the entire colony, which responded to an ongoing emergency, staged public fasts and prayers for repentance in "days of humiliation" or, conversely, performed paeans to a merciful God in "days of thanksgiving." What some people in the era dubbed the "supernatural" and "natural" causes and cures of disease modified the political script of infection in early colonial life. But I also consider the practices in Boston alongside those across the Atlantic, pushing against the common reading that pits the "formality" of public worship in England against the "timely" rituals in New England. Thacher and other ministers in the colonies certainly marked these differences themselves, contrasting in stark terms their authentic, heart-derived forms of humiliation to what they considered to be the Catholic-like, deadened forms of the Church of England. Reforming ministers set the stakes high, warning of the subsequent punishments of a medico-religious blend where fasts themselves might become "pestiferous infection[s]" of poisoning rather than healing, the ostensible distinction between new and old England vividly medicalized.[8] The nonseparatists' emphasis on *timely* responses to crisis, however, was no radical rejection of the English tradition, despite certain critical differences.[9] In fact, for nearly as long as the Church of England existed, the average parishioner witnessed interruptions to the regular liturgy in the face of crises, when plagues, droughts, the birth of royals, and other major events spurred rituals that staged their own departures from regular space and time, offering an active response to God's ongoing providential interactions with the natural world.[10] The godly colonies drew from this tradition, despite their own sense of exceptional difference, just as they actively performed an anxiety about their proximity to the rituals of England and of Catholics.

CONTAGIOUS FASTS 119

This chapter thus disrupts the common narrative of separated, seemingly monolithic traditions of the visible saints in New England and of the parishioners in a newly restored monarchical England by unpacking their mutually informing religious responses to major epidemics of the seventeenth century: that of the smallpox in Boston and of the bubonic plague in England.[11] Both English and colonial occasion-driven religious responses outline complex interactions among the medical, religious, and political "scripts" of contagion, as described by Colin Jones, that became especially charged in the face of bubonic plague.[12] Understood as a "leveling" force of destruction, consuming rich and poor alike, the plague and its metaphors of unseen, spreading effluvia bled across discourses, crafting an intimate union between "contagion" and an overrun social order. While scholars have analyzed the interrelations between these different "scripts" of the plague's contagion over time in Europe, the interplay between God's smiting hand and advanced medical practices in the colonial fast days has received short shrift, partly because the New Englanders were spared a major visitation of the plague, so far as we can tell, and partly, too, because the days of humiliation are rarely read as medical events.[13]

Still, the lack of attention to the medicalized side of this colonial practice of fasting is surprising, given the otherwise exhaustive analysis of the intersections of religion and medicine in early colonial life, where preacher-physicians merged pulpit and remedy in their inherently hybrid practices.[14] Scholars have more broadly read the days of humiliation and thanksgiving in relation to the ever-present providentialism of the era, finding the ritual fasting and feasting to regulate the collective, political body in an embodied show of humiliation to a smiting God.[15] Moreover, scholars have considered how this providential approach to disease relates to a kind of medically situated historiography, in what Cristobal Silva calls their epidemiological discourse of immunological exceptionalism. There, early settlers rewrote contagion as being part of God's larger plan for the godly in the new world, as "it pleased God" first to eviscerate Native populations and later to visit the backsliding second- and third-generation English occupiers themselves.[16] Offering a narrative of the colonizing English as racially superior and divinely situated in the "wilderness" of the New World, the script of heavenly sent contagion reflects much of the ugliest aspects of English colonization and, insofar as it related to medical knowledge, has been taken to expose a "religious orthodoxy" woefully out of touch with the dangers of transmission.[17]

In this regard, days of humiliation in response to disease, where hungry worshipers prayed privately with their families and collectively at their

120 DOCTRINE AND DISEASE

meetinghouses, seem especially suspect. One often hears of the physical demands of these days, as the hours-long sermons even managed to drain the energy of the spirited John Cotton, who was "too weary now to write" after hours spent fasting and praying in the public humiliation for the 1687 measles outbreak.[18] Not so with the English special services, where the fast is often taken as one part of a tradition-laden ritual comfortably uniting spiritual and physical responses to illness.[19] The occasional services after the restoration of Charles II, in particular, are often described as being a kind of political "throwback," with all the pageantry and custom not necessarily standing at odds with developing scientific thought.[20] The same cannot be said for the days of humiliation in New England. John Blake goes so far as to argue that advanced public health orders could not take root in Massachusetts until the colonists "turned attention away from the invisible world," with more systematic quarantine, isolation, and cleaning regulations arising only as a result of the decreasing number of truly occasional days of worship.[21] Going along with this, Thacher's more medically oriented *Brief Rule* appears to be an interesting blip on the map of an otherwise underdeveloped system of scientific practices, one even opposing his ministerial approach in the *Fast* and almost entirely derivative of the English source, Thomas Sydenham's recently published *Medical Observations* (1676).[22] Thacher, offering both "natural" and "sin-based" accounts of illness in his *Fast* and *Brief Rule*, thus seems to stand in for what has been dubbed the "double-edged" message of these earlier-generation ministers, his account of disease just as paradoxical as the very blend of harming-and-healing that provoked or satisfied God in the sight of humiliated bodies and hearts in prayer.[23]

But how fundamentally distinctive were these epidemic-spurred religious fasts from their English predecessors? Given the renewed scholarly attention to the huge scope of England's special services and to the embodied, recursive devotional practices of the New England Puritans, it seems a more complicated dynamic between developing Anglican and Congregational religious practices is at play.[24] Along those lines, this chapter argues that the medico-religious practices in New England were neither antithetical to the "new science" nor remarkable departures from English practices, although there were some significant alterations. I argue that the joint medical and religious approaches to the smallpox epidemic of 1678–79 broke open the often closed-off accounts of specific collective "sins" and hidden "causes" of contagion such that the colonial practitioners, in their search for causes, began thinking more flexibly about the nature of the time, space, and causes of disease. By outlining both bodies and temporalities at play in *Fast* and *Brief Rule*, Thacher reveals a dynamic world of surprising secrets and forces, one that would continue to mutate in the face of new public health disasters. In the process, the colonists drew from a well-established tradition that understood contagion as something disturbingly on the border between "natural" and "supernatural" in origin and transmission.

THE SEASON OF THE FAST IN NEW ENGLAND

Before turning to the fast's simultaneously contagious and medicinal properties, an account of its role within the colonial days of worship is in order. Given its incredible potential to bring about what Thacher terms the "contrary" effect, why did the fast hold such a central place in both England's and Massachusetts's days of occasional worship? Thacher's instructions for this "extraordinary" public practice were virtually identical to those in a Reformed England: he exhorted worshipers to consume one moderate meal only, to avoid delicacies and other luxuries, from foodstuffs to apparel, and, most critically, to spend the day "consuming" heavenly thoughts in private and collective prayer.[25] What became more urgent for Thacher was the question of the unique temporalities involved with fasting and public prayer. In his assessment, the communal fast itself signaled an altered temporal plane. Repenting populations used the practice, he wrote, as "an extraordinary part or act of Gospel worship wherein for a convenient Season we abstain from the comforts of this life, and upon due examination of our wayes towards God, and consideration of Gods wayes towards us."[26] How to identify this "season" remained his sermon's central question.

Thacher's fast-day sermon would have been the center of such "extraordinary" and searching devotional activities held during the days of humiliation, and it served not one but two major moments of providentially spurred worship. First preached during a public fast in response to the "red Horse" of the wars with Native populations in 1676, the sermon was reprinted in response to the "pale Horse" of the smallpox some few years later, in 1678. Showing Thacher's own "marvelous" and "providential" wisdom, in Increase Mather's words, Thacher's timely sermon considers just that: the *time* of the proper fast in response to public calamity, outlined in remarkably physical terms.[27] How should a worshiper know it is the "proper season" of a fast? This knowledge comes from inside the individual's body, a vividly felt need within the heart and bowels, "when the soul comes with brokenness & contrition of heart, when a holy trembling seizes upon such a man."[28] For Thacher, the question of "when"

122   DOCTRINE AND DISEASE

was as equally pressing as "how," as worshipers struggled to interpret their sinful, inherently broken hearts, becoming all the more vigilant at a sensory level in order to choose the right time for such a day of general lamentation.

Holy tremblings indeed seem to have figured into the colonial experience, given the astounding number of these days of humiliation, in which colonists experienced three times as many fasts as thanksgivings, that other side of the ritual cycle.[29] From William Love's seminal study on the occasional days to recent interpretations on the distinctive temporalities of the practice, many scholars have taken the scale of these fasts to reveal something at the heart of the Puritan devotional experience, in which "the communal *avoidance* of food on fast days contributed to community building."[30] These days of public, as opposed to private, fasting intensified the ritual "preparatory humiliation" that was a regular part of Sabbath worship so colonists might forge a sense of communal humility.[31] Colonists, beginning the day with private and family-led biblical study, would then attend services that would last an entire day, broken into morning and evening sessions of public prayers for repentance, hours-long sermons, and sung psalms. On occasion, the demands were so high that ministers would stand by to replace any weakened or exhausted minister, so that the four-hour stretches of prayers and *ex tempore* sermon-making would remain unbroken.[32] Critically, colonists connected their external shows of penitence—their fasted bodies, simple clothing, and external shows of remorse—with their internal remorse.[33]

The sheer magnitude of the number of these public days of fast draws out a paradox deeply ingrained in reformed religious practice. If concerns over set forms of worship had sent the ritual-shunning, Christmas-less colonists away from England, one wonders what to make of the repetitive quality of these days, with their providential charge and high stakes, as they gradually smoothed into the very seasonal spring fast and autumnal feast so initially dreaded. In part, the colonists dramatized their own out-of-timeness through a system of court-ordered days of grief and thanksgiving. These orders for public fasts and days of thanksgiving can be found across the multivolume *Records of the Governor and Company of the Massachusetts Bay in New England*. One early example from the general courts held in Boston finds an order for public thanksgiving at the start of the records of the Court of Assistants held in Boston on June 5, 1632. Here, the colonists were responding to the ongoing wars between the Holy Roman Empire and Bohemia waged, broadly speaking, between Catholics and Protestants: "The Court, takeing into consideration the greate mercy of God, vouchsafed to the churches of God in Germany and the Pallattinate, etc., hath appointed the 13th day of this present moneth to be kept as a day of publique thanksgiving throughout the serverall plantacions."[34] In part, then, the sense of God's providential action continued through these reissued court actions.

On the other hand, the increasing regularity of these court-appointed fasts and thanksgivings perpetuated a sense of "ritual life," something remarkable given what Alex Ryrie calls the ritual "phobia" of Protestants more generally, as "for a religion so phobic about ritual activity this was the perfect ritual, for fasting of course consists of *abstinence* from activity. It was one of the ways in which Protestantism could re-acquire a ritual life despite itself."[35] Indeed, the seasonally based feast would become, paradoxically, the very set holiday that early Puritans abhorred, just as the fast day of the spring returned, ironically, to the Lenten practices of medieval and early modern England, as later generations of Americans "evoke[d] the celebrations of the colonial and early national eras to give the holiday a sentimental antiquarian atmosphere quite unlike the immediacy it had enjoyed earlier."[36] These days of thanksgiving, usually set in November or December, retained their "occasional" character in part by being issued according to the will of state and local authorities, only finally morphing into the unbroken, annually issued national holiday after Lincoln's proclaimed "Thanksgiving Day" following military victories at Fort Henry in 1862.[37]

Indeed, looking at the records of the Massachusetts General Court in the years surrounding the 1678 smallpox outbreak, one finds examples of both seasonally dictated and occasion-derived calls for fasting and feasting, though all were issued as if responding to God's providence in real time. In the records between 1677 and 1684, for instance, an autumnal thanksgiving was held nearly every year, whether in response to the "success over Indians" in 1677 or, more vaguely, to the "blessings of the year" in 1682.[38] The only years missing such seasonal thanksgivings within that time span, at least from the admittedly spotty court records, were those of the major smallpox outbreak in 1678 and 1679, as days of humiliation and public fasting overran those calendar years. But even as these regular fast and feast days became more or less expected, they remained part of devotional responses to a remarkable number of events, from the "heathens in this wilderness that have risen up against [the New Englanders], and broken in upon many of [their] towns & places as flood" in 1676 to the "manifest pride" of young, degenerate men, wearing "long hair, like weomanes haire . . . made into perewiggs" in 1675.[39] Anticolonial resistance, the so-called heathens rising up in the wilderness, indeed emerged more strongly within the 1670s. Indigenous populations faced not only increasing displacement and dispossession of their territories but also enslavement, as colonizers began routinely shipping Native American prisoners of war to Barbados, Bermuda, and Jamaica during the decade.[40] Occasional worship reencoded these struggles, both between Native populations and within the community, according to their own colonizing narrative of ethical and heavenly superiority.

While such periwig-wearing members of the new generation, donning "superstitious ribbons" and exposing "naked breasts and arms," incited lamentation rather than praise from their disapproving elders, authorities found even this designation—humiliation or thanksgiving—a surprisingly vexing discernment.[41] Ministers argued about whether they would provoke God to greater wrath by setting aside a day of thanksgiving rather than humiliation. The influential ministers Increase Mather and James Allen, for instance, pushed against civic authorities in rejecting the thanksgiving set for the end of King Philip's / Metacom's War, calling instead for yet another day of humiliation; on the flip side, Thacher would join other ministers in vehemently opposing a day set for a public fast for fractious ministers issued in 1671, as the occasion insulted many religious authorities in question.[42] Within these squabbles, one finds a very mutable God and subsequently unpredictable shifting local environment. Their God was easily triggered. Even as the General Court began outlining the "gratious" quality of God during the October 1676 sessions, who had "added an abatement of those epidemical sicknesses" as well as performing other miraculous feats, the court-appointed day of worship switches gears unexpectedly, first "appoint[ing] & set[ting] apart the ninth day of November next to be kept a day of solemne thanksgiving and prayse to God for such his singular & fatherly mercies," as anticipated, and then noting, without further explanation, an almost immediately following day of humiliation. God's familiar blend of "fatherly mercies" and punishments along with the persistent "evill deservings of an unworthy & sinfull people" brought basic categories into considerable flux.[43]

Authorities agonized over the designation of days as if fearful to suggest even momentarily that they were "in the clear," spiritually speaking. One might assume, then, that the experience of mass death from a disease like the smallpox would be more unambiguous in its horrors as a clear indication of God's wrath. This was a community so exposed to sickness and death that the vision of the Lord being "pleased againe to shake his rod over [one's] pore familye [in] visit[ing] one of [their] children with weakness" repeated year after year in family after family.[44] And yet the events of 1677–79 were markedly harrowing. Because the disease could not become endemic within such a sparsely populated region, entire colonial families faced total devastation in the epidemical outbreaks of smallpox, often carried over from transatlantic ships. Of a population of less than six thousand, five to eight hundred would lose their lives.[45] Spreading, confluent sores scaled the bodies of healthy, young adults and newborns alike who came into contact with smallpox. In England, Sydenham described the agonies in vivid detail: "the eyelids become so stretched and swollen, that the patient is unable to see," as if "an inflated and translucent bladder [were] drawn across the eyes."[46]

If God's providential plans for his elect involved such a form of biological warfare, one can easily imagine how this plan was rationalized for Indigenous populations, as some tribes faced total extinction, while others faced equally unimaginable decimations. As David S. Jones succinctly describes it, "As colonists thrived, Indians died."[47] Indeed, Puritan writers of the 1570s and 1580s, looking back at the huge death toll of Native populations from smallpox and other diseases, shifted away from their original providentialist but somewhat more empathic view of the suffering tribes and ultimately rewrote their recent history as being a more stable display of God's preference for the white Europeans over Indigenous peoples. In other words, "the basic fatalism of Puritan minds readily accepted the inevitable demise of Indian populations" to disease, warfare, and a host of other atrocities, as part of their own triumphant, if struggle-filled, history.[48]

If Native death was rationalized in such a manner, New Englanders remained more focused on their own social fears and thereby concentrated much of their writing on the evisceration of the foundational social boundaries that occurred during particularly charged times of providence-guided outbreaks of disease. Some, in fact, referenced the plague in relation to the disrupted social bonds between neighbors and within families; in a diary entry, the schoolmaster and militia captain Joseph Tompson appeals to secondhand accounts of the plague in England, as the destruction in Boston resembled "the time [he] herd of in the plague," when townsmen so feared contagion that bodies were left within their home, unburied, their orphans left comfortless.[49] Out of his lengthy manuscript, in fact, Tompson would go back to identify only the pages of his diary that chronicled the smallpox with a newly penned border listing the year, adding the line "O sorrowful year," during the height of the catastrophe. Nowhere else does he add such a distinctive border, even as he edits and reedits his heartfelt "testimonie" of faith.

126 DOCTRINE AND DISEASE

Thacher's *Fast*, reprinted around the same time as Tompson's purported diary entries, likewise emphasizes the unraveling of the social structure, taken to more apocalyptic levels, and the timeliness of God's interactions with New England in response to the medical crisis. Yet, despite their shared interest in the special quality of the present-tense timing of disease, both pieces were not written in 1678, at that critical moment of God's stretched-out hand. As already mentioned, Increase Mather repurposed Thacher's former wartime fast sermon for the smallpox. In his preface to *Fast*, Mather even indicates that Thacher's text itself was prophetic, moving outside of time to foreshadow that "Lord knew that Boston, yea, that New-England would have cause for many dayes of Humiliation, and therefore stirred up the heart of his Servant, before hand to give instructions and Directions."[50] Tompson, in contrast, potentially worked backward; the diary entries from the pivotal year of both the smallpox and his wife's death appear to be written after the fact, and elsewhere within the text, he rewrites lost entries, describes his retrospective process of revisiting events years later, and continually adds marginal notes, apologies, and excisions all the way until the end of his life (fig. 6.1).[51] In going back either to rewrite his experiences or, at the very least, to identify those dates as belonging to a "sorrowful" and momentous year, Tompson's account of the smallpox mirrors the extraordinary experience of "now-ness" in Mather's preface to Thacher's fast, in the apocalyptic collision of ritual, biblical, and everyday time: "Now there is a pale Horse come, and his Name that sits thereon is Death; Stars are falling, our Heaven, and our Earth are shaking; What will come next, who can say?"[52]

Unlike the abating of skirmishes that might start up again at any moment, the shaking earth and falling stars of Mather's infected world suggest, unequivocally, God's displeasure and the need for communal repentance. Still, agonized ministers and colonists alike claimed interpretive confusion over the causes of this divine wrath, if not the wrath itself. Court-ordered days of humiliation rarely found a single cause for repentance: epidemical sickness, threats at home, threats abroad, and a laundry list of private sins added together very heavily as both New Englanders' corruptions and divine expressions of anger morphed from one to the other. As the smallpox continued to drag on into 1679, the court even went so far as to designate a synod, where church elders convened in Boston to address the looming question of the causes of God's wrath and, by extension, the causes of the smallpox, as they sought to answer what "evils . . . have provoked the Lord" and "what is to be done" to reform these spiritual and physical errors.[53] As Thomas Walley's earlier, election-day sermon would put it,

FIG. 6.1 "O sorowfull year." Tompson identified the year on top of every page during the smallpox epidemic. Notice here that he has accidentally written "1778," perhaps signaling the retrospective identification of this year of sorrow. Tompson, *Journal*, MS Am 929, Houghton Library, Harvard University, Cambridge, MA.

128   DOCTRINE AND DISEASE

ministers and physicians alike often cannot find the source of infectious sin: "oft times the Diseases of Kingdomes, Countries, and Churches are so occult and hid, that the wisest of Physicians cannot finde them out."[54]

Despite this flurry of potential causes of illness, fraught debates over designation and timing, and intense public scrutiny over the particular sins in question, the devotional practices themselves offered surprisingly little variety, even given the *ex tempore*, antistructure structure of the authentic worship in the meetinghouse. The day was filled with private and public devotional activities. Beginning and ending with at-home family instruction and self-analysis, where sinners actively sought, as Thacher emphasized, the "examination of our wayes towards God, and consideration of Gods wayes towards us," the center of the day was the public worship at the meetinghouse, where preaching might last upward of five hours by some accounts.[55] Fasted church members earnestly prayed, silently and aloud, and wrote, at home and in worship, scribbling agonizing entries on the status of their heart's deadened state. Joseph Tompson's diary catalogues each day of "publikque day of prayer" by analyzing his own heart, evidently writing these confessions and soul agonies as part of his fast-day routine.[56] They were time-provoked mediations—responses to the smallpox, the burning down of towns, warfare with the "heathen savages," and "unusuall diseases to be mortall by a Cough"[57]—but they were also remarkably repetitive, returning to the same written formula with little variety across the hundreds of pages of diary entries.

Tompson's manuscript—part diary, part commonplace transcription of devotional materials, part compilation of early colonial poetry—offers critical insights into simultaneously textual and embodied practices of the fast day.[58] Bookended with entries from the eighteenth century, in the "eighty eighth year" of his life, the text registers what Matthew Brown has called the "thick style" of the discontinuous, textual piety that marked Puritan life;[59] as discussed already, this sense of temporal collision and the reencoding of momentous events appears dramatically in the all-important years of the smallpox. But throughout, one finds the textual side of these spiritual-physical practices of humiliation, as Tompson examines his "heart" during a fast and after and rewrites lost pages on the same endless struggle to feel, viscerally, within his organs, the general cause of sorrow. He longs to be "affected" both physically and spiritually. In March 1678, even in the face of the smallpox's devastation, he writes again of the insensibility of his heart, "O Lord I mourne that I cannot mourne," and continually revisits his failures throughout his life, notoriously signing his name to a

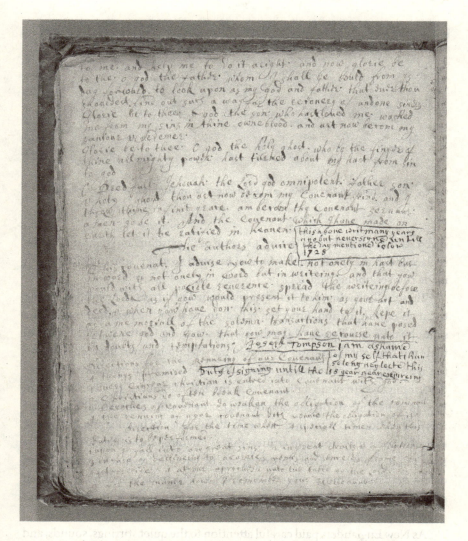

FIG. 6.2   Joseph Tompson's covenant signature. Tompson, *Journal*, MS Am 929, Houghton Library, Harvard University, Cambridge, MA.

proposed covenant some years later, to his grief: "I am ashamed of my self that i hav so long neglected this Duty of signing untill the 88 year near expireing" (fig. 6.2).[60] He also violently crosses out a now-illegible, formerly written phrase that appears above his wedding date at the "start" of the seemingly in-time diary entries. Perhaps in grief, mourning the death of his wife, Tompson cuts off with

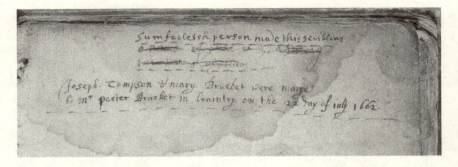

FIG. 6.3   Joseph Tompson, *Journal*, MS Am 929, Houghton Library, Harvard University, Cambridge, MA.

sharp strokes what appears to say, "O name of . . . wisdom and rightious," to be replaced with the small, wobbly lines of his aged writing: "sum fooleish person made this scribbling" (fig. 6.3).

These self-effacing, temporally confounded practices of devotions during the days of humiliation, however, reflect more than the personal quirks of a schoolmaster in Billerica.[61] Like the synod searching for the specific causes of their punishment, Tompson inevitably moves into his own heart to discover the true origin of colony-wide destruction. In one of many examples, after describing the "30 or 40 smitten down the last full moon" in Charlestown in June 1678, he laments that he cannot find the evil within himself that has caused this destruction: "O what in mine heart. What cause of humilation."[62] The fact that Tompson may not have written this at the moment—that he potentially revisited it, rewrote it from loose papers, or wrote it fresh at an unidentified date—only makes more apparent the ways in which the search for the hidden causes of disease never settled into a definitive answer, in both personal and collective practices.

As New Englanders paid careful attention to the quiet stirrings, sounds, and smells in the meetinghouse, their cramping hands actively encoding their devotional struggle, they thus experienced providence as extraordinary, at both a bodily and a temporal level. In moderating their physical consumptions, the fast helped the repentant focus attention on the hidden things inside their bodies and souls, literalizing the goodness of their hearts in the health of their organs. The day of fasting allowed already historiographically minded settlers in the "wilderness" to write and rewrite their physiological-spiritual selves into the bigger-stakes drama of God's harming and healing.

CONTAGIOUS FASTS AND ENGLISH FORMS OF WORSHIP

The manifold occult causes of diseases lurking within individuals give some indication of how a fast might become accidentally contagious. On the one hand, if repenting sinners fasted and prayed for some marginal transgressions but remained unaware of the actual source of their true contaminations, their elemental sources of sin would only continue to multiply. Thomas Walley takes it further in his 1666 sermon, suggesting that minister-physicians themselves might even bear some responsibility. Struggling to uncover the real sources of evil within the heart of God's covenanted, they can inadvertently make the problem worse, as they seek "to cure the Disease that is most visible, [when] some other disease appears that is more dangerous and proves an Impediment to the Cure, so that the sickness increases and becomes mortal."[63] The same kind of instability in the harming-and-healing God and the designated days of worship relates to this secret hotbed of deadly, invisible ailments, where worshipers continually fail to account for the occult or hidden properties dictating their world.

But with greater vigor, ministers offered another explanation for a fast's contagiousness. "Formality" was the tagline encountered in printed sermons, manuscript notes on fast-day services, personal diaries, and shared correspondence, as writers contrasted their antiform forms of authentic worship from the ritualistic liturgies in England and elsewhere.[64] William Adams claims in his manuscript notes for a fast-day smallpox sermon that prior fasts had failed to move God, as individual hearts remained "too cold, dead, formal, lifeless, insipid."[65] In fact, formality would be behind what Thacher and Increase Mather found to be the ironically contagious quality of poorly performed public fasts. Thacher describes such "formality" as provoking contrary effects both within the sinner and within God's response: "Instead of softening it will harden you; instead of mortifying sin, it will quicken it. . . . It will drive the Spirit of God from you, and bring Satan near unto you, and instead of the good you desire, it will bring about the contrary evill."[66] Indeed, the textured language of a "softening" and "hardening" of hearts palpably exposes the dangers of "formality" at an individual level: repenters' formulaic worship will make them physically shut off from feeling, the rigidity of practice mirrored in the harsh boundaries of their organs.

In other words, in order to move God, collective prayer first needed to move the individual. After many days of humiliation failed to stop the smallpox, the General Court of Massachusetts issued another on October 2, 1678, stressing

132 DOCTRINE AND DISEASE

the need for "the said severall colonies . . . to prostrate themselves jointly before God": "That we may be suteably affected with & humbled under all the many tokens of his great anger against us."[67] Notably, the colonists do not suggest that these prostrations will make *God* "suteably affected with" the performance, although clearly they would hope to accomplish that task as well. The work of the communal fast was to suitably affect the sinners themselves.

The focus on the unstable internal heart reveals one of the key differences between the days of humiliation in the colonies and the special services in England. Throughout the plague-time liturgy, parishioners consistently prayed that their show of repentance might move God to "turn" his hand. Like the New Englanders, ministers in England highlighted the double nature of God, as being "the only Lord, who woundeth, and do'st heal again: thou killest, and revivest; bringetst even to hell and bringest back again," and, in effect, hoped that, through congregants' humbled, fasted prayers, they might *turn* God and move themselves out of the ritual time of lamentation and into one of thanksgiving. While still looking to reform worshipers of their clearly contaminating sin, the services, along with the collective prayer, aimed even more at producing a lamentable spectacle for God. In the process, the inner heart rarely appears.

At a more obvious level, too, one finds another, potentially more critical, sense of difference from the humiliations. The English occasional forms were just that: *forms* of worship, the very dreaded specter of idolatrous, image-based Catholic worship haunting the scripts. "Formality" and liturgy seemed hand in hand to many in the colonies. Hugh Peters, an early settler and minister in Boston, addressed just this upon his return to England during the Civil War, as he claimed the corrupted practices in England, from their "Church-censures, Burialls, Christenings, Liturgie, Holy-dayes, Fasts, hallowed Places, Images, Vestures, Gestures, etc.," were identical to those of Irish Catholic rebels, "as unlike as an egge is to an egge."[68] Many returning exiles argued in a similar vein, citing the plaguey nature, literally and figuratively, of ritual worship.

Some scholars have indeed read along with Peters's sense of the fundamental distinction between the colonists' days of humiliation and the elaborations of the English liturgy. Love argues that as "our fathers left behind their prayer books"; they also "shook the dust of centuries off their feet, in renouncing customs which they had loved from childhood," utterly rejecting and substituting the "Jewish ceremonials," "Roman Catholic rituals," and Elizabethan proclamations of enforced, state-ordained worship.[69] Scholars like Martha Finch, who offer a more nuanced account of the connections between colonial and English

CONTAGIOUS FASTS   133

fasts, still nevertheless continue to see the purifying New Englanders as rejecting the "lavish, regularized feast and fast days of the medieval church,"[70] along with the "liturgical calendar and elaborate ceremonies of the Anglican and Roman Churches."[71]

Yet it is critical to keep in mind that neither system of occasional worship and fasting remained static or in isolation, as the dramatic shifts in worship during political upheavals of the Civil War reveal a mutually informing connection between the territories. While New Englanders lamented the formality of their mother country, they still often used their services interactively with those in England, mirroring the fasting English during the outbreak of bubonic plague, during the monthly ritual days of lamentation in the Civil War, and throughout the era. Many even wrote of their simultaneous fasting and prayers as operating as a kind of embodied empathy, in which shared practices connected them at a distance. During the outbreak of war, William Hooke's 1640 sermon *New Englands Teares, for Old Englands Feares* described such a materially felt connection, as he strove to impact listeners in Taunton at a bodily level: "O if you could but see them, your soules would hardly stay within your bodies for running forth to meet them; At last, you would strive to incorporate your selves into them by the closest embraces."[72]

If this occult connection remained only hypothetical, an unrealized and increasingly diminished bond between the suffering English and the bodiless souls, "running forth to meet them," there existed more direct lines of communication between the traditions. In fact, despite their careful differentiation, colonists crafted their days according to the inherited forms of special worship in England, reworking the scripts of plague into the shared rituals prompted by smallpox outbreaks. The embodied temporalities and occult forces that were so fundamentally a part of the days of humiliation rose directly from England's special services, even with the different emphases on moving the self before moving God.

Above all, the replacement liturgies in England, whether those of intercession or thanksgivings, signaled a sense of suspended time. This effect was felt perhaps most fully in the plague liturgy, as it offered the fullest liturgical swap and featured the longest runs in the era, other than the competing monthly wartime fasts. First penned by William Cecil, Archbishop Parker of Canterbury, and Bishop Edmund Grindal in 1563, the "form of common prayer" had been reissued across England's nine thousand parishes numerous times with subtle changes.[73] Along with an order for the public fast on Wednesday, the form

134 DOCTRINE AND DISEASE

replaced the usual liturgy of the Book of Common Prayer with plague-specific readings, collects, or petitionary prayers, call-and-response composite psalms, and the homily exhortation. Issued once plague deaths hit a certain threshold, the revised liturgy would become familiar during especially bad visitations; the average parishioner in London in 1603, for instance, would have seen one of the longest runs of the plague service, set at three times a week for perhaps as long as seventy-eight weeks.[74]

With such few changes, one wonders why authorities did not simply publish the liturgies once and for all within the Book of Common Prayer; indeed, the Book of Common Prayer contained "occasional prayers" at its end, including those for the plague. Instead, authorities performed this temporal suspension at their own cost, both actively creating a sense of disrupted "plague time" and also reencoding everything into a routinized script in a crashing together of disparate temporalities that would prove deeply appealing for the recursive, historiographically minded New Englanders. In this purposeful staging of temporality, one traces that searching temporal collision of the days of humiliation. The suspension of real time for such a "plague time" brought parishioners to a moment of spiritual reflection that "coulde never in health" bring them to the like obedience, according to a 1563 prayer,[75] just as "the dayes are at hand" as "now . . . the pale horse come[s]" and now the "Stars are falling" of the seasonable and temporally suspended smallpox, as described by Increase Mather.[76]

Along with this ruptured sense of time, some people in England reported the same disarmingly contagious effect of the communal fasts that responded to plague. One instance proves telling. In response to another devastating outbreak of the plague in 1636, the radical preacher William Prynne noted a disturbing correlation between plague deaths and the special services for the plague. Under the pseudonym Matthew Brown, the controversial Prynne suggestively tracked the death rate alongside the timing of the Crown-ordered public fasts. In his assessment, God's "plagues and judgments . . . have strangely increased since this fast begun, contrary to all humane reason and probability, whereas it much decreased before, the total number dying of the plague the weeke before the Fast, being but 458 and 58 *Parishes infected*, and the very first weeke of the fast 838 (treble the number the two last greatest plagues) and 67 *Parishes infected*, . . . a cleare evidence that God is much offended with these purgations, and the restraint of preaching on the Fast day."[77] The problem for Prynne was not the use of the fast in and of itself but the "purgations" and "restraint of preaching" that altered the usual form of this special plague liturgy.

CONTAGIOUS FASTS   135

Surprisingly, given Prynne's Puritanical abhorrence of forms, he does not express anxiety about the reliance on such a set and repeated formula of intercession. Instead, Prynne blames his usual villain, Archbishop William Laud, for "geld[ing]" the temporary form of worship by limiting the time spent preaching during the Wednesday Fast. In his words, sermons animate the otherwise deadened form of the humbled body, serving as "the very life and soul of a Fast, as being the only means to humble men for their sinnes, and bring them to repentance," just as fasts without private and public prayers threatened to become a mere Catholic form of "superstition and idolatry."[78] As with the bad fasts in New England, something within the "heart" was deadened.

The changes to the 1636 order of the fast so lamented by Prynne were relatively subtle and understandable given the extreme circumstances. Wanting to reduce both the time spent in dangerously infectious collective gatherings and the burden put on the faithful, the order limited the number of sermons on the fast day, where formerly they had "prescribed two Sermons of one houre long apiece, forenoon and afternoon every fast day."[79] The bishops made further cuts that applied to all the added days of worship, excising a lengthier collect and deleting one line on the dangers of idolatry from a remaining prayer. The pestilential threat of collective gatherings was indeed disturbingly real for parishioners and priests alike. Monarchs routinely set up gallows in front of their plague-time residences, promising immediate execution for any unauthorized, potentially infectious, visitor.[80] The governmental orders, established after the first plague liturgy in 1578, above all regulated the identification of sick bodies and households.[81] Red crosses brandished shut-in homes, slender plague sticks were held at arm's length by the healthy members of an infected household, and officials guarded sealed doorways. William Crashaw even printed a private "helpe of Humiliation and holy Devotion to them that stay at home" in 1625, after Charles I suspended the special services "Out of no dislike of Fasting and Prayer. . . . But out of conscience to his God & care of his Subjects liues," as it became too challenging to identify the "Sick & sore" in the confused heap of "mingled" bodies at prayer.[82]

Considering both the need for collective gatherings and the real and present danger offered by such gatherings, authorities in England still insisted on regular attendance of the services. Even while making obvious exceptions of the sick—for whom "prudent respect" should dictate decisions to assemble "unto the Churche"—the regulations nevertheless increased the time spent in church, as citizens were "to resort, *not onlye* on Sundayes and Holydayes: but *also on*

136 DOCTRINE AND DISEASE

Wednesdayes and Frydayes, during the tyme of these present afflictions."[83] If the rotten smells and pressing, sweating bodies crammed in church remained deadly, the need for a collective performance of repentance remained a serious concern. And the church was above all preferable to other especially toxic locations, "playes, pastimes, idleness, haunting of Taverns," and so forth, those hot zones of simultaneously spiritual and material contaminants.[84] Still, the amenders of the 1636 form, placing a stricter limit on the time spent in church, were perhaps more mindful than Prynne was of what Hamlet might call a "foul and pestilent congregation of vapors" emitted in the shared space of worship. Authorities faced a very challenging balancing act.

But for Prynne, the result of these alterations was utterly disastrous. The prelates had effectively morphed the collective fast from a healing remedy into a literal and figurative contagion. Worse, this contagious form of worship would only continue to draw God's provocation, raining down "plagues upon plagues" in London until "his Majesty shall see these purgations rectified, superstition and idolatry removed, Gods Sabbaths duly sanctified, the suppressed Preachers and preaching of Gods word restored."[85] For this and other polemical writings, Prynne would have the remaining "stumps" of his ears chopped off a year later, and the letters "S.L." (seditious libeler) burnt into the flesh of his cheeks. Importantly, though, Prynne did not suggest that fasts were ineffectual or could not be governed by political figureheads: instead, collective fasts contained within them so much explosive, real power that the form itself had to be just right.

Prynne, along with the minister-physicians in New England, drew from a tradition that defined the fast as an inherently contagious, blended devotional and medical practice. Those in England and New England were acutely aware of the peculiar mix of physical and spiritual effects on display with the fast, and they followed the same guidelines stressed by Thacher with minor variations. In both the plague fasts and days of humiliation, writers forged a sense of moderation by using religious others as straw men. Across the devotional spectrum, Catholics loomed large. Thomas Becon's early and influential account of the fast glosses their Lenten fasts as seasonal holiday making, in which the single meal of the day turned into one of luxurious delicacies, as "al kinde of pleasaunt fishes or whatsoeuer deinties besides could be deuised" would be ravished, to the point that the superstitious papist would "unbuckle and let slacke his girdle a great quantity," devouring meat and sweetmeat in his maw "as the hungry wolf to his pray." On the other side, one found those false-seeming hypocrites who, in fasting for days on end without measure, made so "weake and feable the bodye

CONTAGIOUS FASTS   137

that it be hable to serve neyther God nor our neighbor nor yet our selues and by this meanes utterly quench the use and working of the Spirit."[86] In both cases, the practice fails on a bodily level, throwing Galenic balance out of whack in the grossly stuffed or sapped body in question.

Both territories recognized the real physical demands of the practice, making exceptions for the weak, sick, or elderly. Even the polemical Bostonian Cotton Mather would refrain from fasting during the public order issued in response to the 1721 smallpox due to his "late Illness and the Weakness yet remaining" on him, although, regretfully, "Fasting with Prayer" would be precisely what he "would have done, and as [he] use to do." Still, he insists on his ability to make this public day of repentance one of personal "sacrifice," one "set apart for Humiliations and Supplications."[87] Indeed, this sense of unified humility was the most central component of fasting in both new and old England. Whatever the specifics of the devotional services—however long the public preaching, whether prayers were set or uttered *ex tempore*—the hidden internal stuff of repenters, from the pulpy flesh of their hearts to the hollowed ventricles of their brains, needed to match the visible performance of humility to avoid triggering God's murderous wrath. The risk of hypocrisy fell on either side of the equation for nonseparatist and Anglican alike, between the barely practicing, gluttonous Catholics and the performed humility of extremists. In both cases, the impact was explicitly material. Fasting that went too much to either side threatened to become contagious: a spreading occult force that moved unseen and provoked heavenly rage in a perverse positive feedback loop.

But when performed properly, the fast apparently operated, in part, as a Galenic "contrary," in which unlike forces canceled out like effects. For instance, Crashaw's medicinal "compound" of fasted prayer in response to the 1625 plague combats "the Contagion of our sinnes" that, as a poison, "now justly makest us feare poison in our very meate, drinke, and apparel."[88] Devotional pamphlets published in the wake of the plague often compared themselves to pleasant odors, contrasted with the sulfurous smell of sin ascending into God's nostrils and provoking the smoky exhalations of festering poisons into the air in his wrath. New England, with its overwhelmingly providential approach to illness, drew from an even greater store of particulate-like sin. The physician and renowned author of the *Day of Doom* Michael Wigglesworth describes the spiritual healing of infected souls as following from such purgative medical practices, in which spiritual "meditations / . . . our frail body feeds" by following bloodletting, as spiritual guides: "Empty bad humours out; / First cool and cleanse the

138 DOCTRINE AND DISEASE

Blood: / And then a Cordial will revive / And do the man more good. / So when thou humbled art, / And purged from thy sin: / The Lord himself will comfort thee, / And Cordials sweet give in." Deeply reliant on these metaphors of consumption, Wigglesworth shows the reformed process of fleshly "humiliation" as a "purg[ing]" of the "Bad Humours" of sin, now "cool[e]d," "cleanse[d]," and "empt[ied]" of clogging elements.[89]

The metaphoric conversion of partially digested food, unbalanced humors, and stuffed bodies into sin aligned the empty with the pure. Like the intermediary spirit, standing between the soul and the body, the fasted body was more primed to be "imprinted" with God's mercy, as God's grace flowed through a transfer of wax impressions like those impressed images in brain matter underlying faculty psychology and sensation. Thacher himself described this as a uniquely embodied exchange among God, Christ, Holy Spirit, and sinner, "fashion[ing] the trinity as a conduit for verbal exchange," as Brown puts it.[90] Thacher describes the fasted prayer as a stamped image moving from God's heart materially into the human heart and back up again into heaven, the origins of prayer murkier than ever: "There is not an holy prayer put up unto God, but its Original is God the Father, that prayer of Faith which proceeds from the heart of a Christian, was 1. In the heart of God the Father, and he through the Intercession and Mediation of his Son, sends it down by his holy Spirit into the heart of a poor sinner, and so stamps the Image of it upon the heart of the poor sinner that he believes, and then the Holy-Ghost that stamped it there, takes it from thence, and presents this through Christ unto the Father."[91] If in this circuit God effectively rewards himself through the dispensation of mercy, he still mandates this gift giving to take place within a human heart and through a physically impressed image: a startling note for such an iconoclastic culture.

With the fast-stamped prayer being a material process designed to influence both one's body/spirit/soul and God's heart, would-be repentant sinners needed to follow physical guidelines to shape it. For Becon, the fast's "subdue[ing] the flesh" and "mortify[ing] of her beastelye affectes" unclogs the body of the usual dross of life so that the "spirite might more frely attend on God." A successful fast, then, works on a remarkably medical level, as God's spiritual grace simply cannot easily impress itself into an overfilled, overfueled body, as a man "that commeth out of the Tauern sweating and set of fire with drincking of whot wine and eating of delicious meates, so in like maner is he no fit man either to reade or to hear the word of god that hath a ful gorge and stuffed belly. The more the

CONTAGIOUS FASTS   139

body is filled, the more is the mind dulled and made unapt to receiue any message from God."[92]

The "filled," "dulled," "unapt" mind of Becon's materially inflected rational soul contrasts with the food-emptied, scripture-filled body in William Crashaw's description, in which the fasting "whets and sharpens [our prayers]."[93] Thomas Cartwright takes it further, morphing the invisible prayers of a humiliated subject into knives, as fasting serves as a "Grindstone, to make a poynt of [prayer] that may pierce and . . . cut both the visible and invisible enimies."[94] Weaponized petitions, prayers cut into cutting form from a body on edge, offer equally ambivalent powers, harming others to heal us, spreading invisibly but acting on others materially.

But even here, in this vision of knife-like prayers, one can feel the unnerving mix of paradoxical forces, in which the destructive force of even a properly followed fast suggests the same spreading power of contagious diseases. Astoundingly, the fast's material power appears to arise not despite but along with this ability to turn contagious. Disturbingly close to a God who first "shoots the Arrows of his anger" and then "pour[s] his Spirit from on high" upon his subjects, the fast itself operated as a *pharmakon* in the classical sense.[95] Carrying a hidden blend of harming and healing properties based on "dose" and usage, the fast was another effective drug, a devotional practice straddling the border between poison and cure. The first English terms "poison" and "venom," from Latin *potio*, "drink," and *venenum*, "potions/drugs," likewise did not initially limit the substance to only destructive effects, although, by the early modern period, the terms were used figuratively for a host of deadly, spreading substances, evoking pollution, contamination, sinfulness, and even heresy.

Outside of poison's use as an ambivalent substance, it was also intimately connected with contagion, as writers defined, and redefined, the nature of its spreading force as part of the occult multiplication of *species*, or imprinted images, traveling across space and time. Writers considered poisons' operations to follow from some combination of their "specific form," "total substance," and "occult virtues." To generalize, "specific form" and "total substance" were often used interchangeably to describe the properties of a substance that came from its form as a whole, rather than from a particular mixture of elements. "Occult virtues" are the hidden properties of a substance, as opposed to the elemental properties of the substance's "manifest virtues."[96] As the fast was believed to power prayers to spread at a distance, it necessarily tapped into the rich discourse of the occult forces underlying contagion.

140 DOCTRINE AND DISEASE

In such a moment overwhelmed by epidemic contagion, then, the inherently ambivalent force of the collective fast offered both a powerful and threatening medico-religious effect. It helped further mark the time as special, from the innermost recesses of worshipers outward, while performing the very purgation so yearned for in a community overrun with illness. Thus, worshipers in the colonies and in England found an equally mutated sense of space, as infective hidden forces, swirling atmospherically and inside a sinner's tissue, might be combated with equally traveling, materialized prayers. The fast acted as a poison/potion and, more critically, at a distance.

HIDDEN CAUSES AND THE TREATMENT OF DISEASE

Even as moderate reformers and church officials in England called on the potential danger of an impurely performed fast, they were far less likely than their revolutionary counterparts to cite its contagiousness. What accounts for this difference, given the shared sense of fluctuating temporalities, providential import, and medical power of the practice? Critically, it seems writers in New England were drawn even more than those in England to the rich paradoxes and reversals of the *pharmakon* in their medical and devotional beliefs. Consequently, with so many categories of health and illness in flux, the joint medical-religious practices actually split apart to a greater degree than in England, as the endless search for a hidden cause of sin and contagion left the search for origins to the devotional activities of public fast days.

Wigglesworth's *Meat out of Eater* (1670) exemplifies such sudden, unexpected reversals related to the endless search for one's own sin to explain suffering. A remarkably popular text—so much a part of devotional life that extant copies are worn with use, marginalia, and even hand-sewn stitches—the poetic form offered consoling meditations, meant to be read nonlinearly and repetitively.[97] While earlier, as seen, Wigglesworth relies on the purging and cleansing power of cordial religious practices, sickness suddenly morphs into health, and health into sickness. Splitting the body and the soul, Wigglesworth suggests that God is effectively cruel to be kind: "Our Bodies Sicknesses / Are Physick for the Soul, / Corrected by a skillful hand / That can its force control: / . . . By these he doth prevent / Much hurt that might be got; / Preserves us from Infectious Air / As by an Antidote."[98] Given these unstable categories of health, where "Infectious Air" of epidemic sickness oddly "Preserves us from Infectious Air" of the worse soul sicknesses, it is no surprise that the Wigglesworth reader must "search and try his ways, / To finde out what's amiss" as "His first great Business is" finding out "What sin hath God offended."[99]

This challenging "first great Business" relates to that oddly shifting and vexed concern over identifying days of humiliation or thanksgivings, as seen before, as well as the remarkably bulky list of sins offered as the cause of God's displeasure. In contrast, the English services show little to no confusion over the designation of fasting days of intercession or thanksgiving days of praise. Moreover, the special services almost always listed a single cause for the occasion: the gunpowder plot, famine, the plague, and so on. In fact, colonial worship in this regard reflects other communal orders in England: specifically, those issued by the Parliament and Cromwell. Going through the summary list of these orders from 1533 to 1688, one finds an explosion of days set for "general sinfulness" in the 1650s, with the same burgeoning causes of lamentation. That of the 1653 fast day lists "the growing evidences of his [the Lord's] displeasure against the Land, in the continuance of his sad afflictions upon all ranks of Persons," "the great abuse . . . by our formalities and Fasting unto our selves and not unto God," "the growth of sin of all sorts; particularly, Pride, Uncleannesse, Contempt of Ordinance, Oppression, Violence, Fraudulent dealing," and three more paragraphs on the "general distemper" of the times.[100]

In contrast, the English services remained preeminently concerned with the danger of contagion in their plague services, especially the infectiousness of crowds. While authorities set minor limits to the time spent in public during the fast day of 1636, as seen before, earlier changes to the form went even further, drawing attention to not only the physical dangers of resorting among the sick but also the real contaminating threat of any public place, including the church itself. The added exhortation at the end of the 1603 form, for instance, urges parishioners to follow the governmental orders of isolation, despite its ostensible focus on the divine origins of the pestilence. The exhortation begins with the provocative claim that the plague arises from "a cause not natural but supernatural" and continues to enumerate the "supernatural" causes of the plague, with the usual laundry list of sinners: the gluttonous who "make their belly their God," "the unclean pollution of whoredome," traitors, usurers, swearers.[101] Although the contagiously multiplying molecules of sin have spurred God's wrath—"the stench and brimstone sent of our sins hath ascended up into thy nostrils to provoke thy wrath and procure this plague against us"—the sermon moves into a different register, exposing the plague's decidedly "natural" and political threat. With more than half of the text devoted to defining "contagion,"

142 DOCTRINE AND DISEASE

as opposed to humoral, atmospheric, and divine causes, the sermon places a politically inflected account of contagion front and center, even in the midst of the fasted, "supernatural" remedy of the special service itself.

The service first defines contagion, as opposed to the other "natural" causes, as "not so much any general corruption of the aire, nor any distemperature in the blood, or humors of mens bodies" but as "the contagion that the disease it selfe hath bred, and which one man receiueth from another, the sound from those that are sicke," a cause that immediately leads to the threat of congregation, whereby "men are to learne that one chiefe and ordinary meane of their preseruation in this dangerous time is, the auodying of the contagion that commeth by mingling disorderly among the sound, & the sicke together."[102] After spending extended time on the danger of physical contagion, the preacher ends by warning not of divine but earthly law: "let us be more humble in the day of our affliction, submitting our selues to those good and wholsome orders, and decrees already published for preuenting the further infection of this our calamitie, and making account of all good meanes, and medicinable helpe made knowne unto us for our better preseruation."[103] So, too, would Crashaw's replacement spiritual guide to the 1625 outbreak spend a great deal of ink on following those "good and wholesome orders," both aping the medical plague tractate structure for his spiritual "recipes" of the plague and then returning to a politicized account of the science of contagion.

These distinctions in religious practices, the spiritual salves for epidemics, found counterparts in the various regulations and medical approaches in the face of disease as well. In England, the intense focus on the "natural" cause of the plague meant that little internal searching had to go on. Even if parishioners used the moment as a time for active reflection and private fasts, as they often evidently did, the services at least did not suggest that the causes were in serious dispute, whether natural or supernatural, and whatever the controversy over the practices of shutting in infected households, the "good and wholesome orders" remained centrally part of the natural and supernatural remedies in 1665, the last horrific outbreak of the pestilence that would visit England. The focus of the plague liturgy continued to be the identification of sick and sound bodies, although authorities made subtle, but telling, changes with regard to the supernatural causes. In the aftermath of the Civil War and regicide, a newly restored England heard an enlarged exhortation on those traitors of "these last and perilous days . . . who have dared to lift up their hands also against the Anointed of the Lord; and what wonder that there is wrath gone out from the Lord, and the Plague is begun?"[104] If easily identified English sins helped politicize the contours of the communal sin, so, too, did the subtly altered instructions at the start of the form identify the power of the growing empire. Whereas the earlier forms stressed the need to "excite and stirre up all godly people within this Realm, to pray earnestly and heartily to God to forgive us our sinnes," the altered form of 1665 banks even more on the unified and politically settled performance of lamentation to move, as it stresses how the plague, moving to "more remote parts of this Kingdom," requires "Supplications ... everywhere" throughout the Realm.[105]

CONCLUSION

Though the cause of disease remained ever shifting and ever hidden, New Englanders nevertheless relied on some of the same medical practices designed to treat the spreading corruptions of contagion, as they quarantined infectious ships and regulated the movement of bodies and goods during the outbreaks.[106] Although Thacher considered, briefly, a potential influx of contagion during formalized, deadened fasts, his medical tractate on the treatment of the smallpox does not address the smallpox's contagious qualities. Despite the universal assessment of Thacher's rather slavish use of Sydenham, Thacher parts ways with his medical source in the very same way colonial writers shifted into murkier territory in their spiritual responses to disease. Repurposing a lengthier and more polemical text into a usable broadside during such a charged moment, Thacher swapped the order of sections, cut and clarified definitions and instructions, and emphasized his own humility as a "well-wisher to the sick." The "oatmeal porridge, barely broth, roasted apples, and the like" dished out to Sydenham's English readers became the foodstuffs grown across the Atlantic: "water-pottage made only of Indian flour & water, instead of *Oat-meal*, and boiled apples," served along with a "small Beer only warmed with a Tost."[107] "Indian flour"—or the cornmeal that was a staple of Native cooking, from cakes to fried breads and tortillas—would become appropriated in early colonial cookbooks as part of an early "American" identity, as recipes for the Johnny Cake effaced their debts to Native recipes.[108] Indeed, the use of "Indian flour" speaks to the broader way in which English colonizers appropriated Native peoples' knowledge of remedies, plants, and herbs to address their own anxieties over the local influence of their new environment on their health: a deeply ironic anxiety, given the devastating medical impact they themselves had on Indigenous populations.[109]

144 DOCTRINE AND DISEASE

While drawing on more local ingredients, Thacher perhaps signals through the "Indian" designation a Native expertise, despite the general lack of engagement with Native medical knowledge in this repurposed tract.

More dramatically, Thacher removes Sydenham's language of the mechanistic and occult transfers of the smallpox. References to the "poisonous particles" that "influence one another from a distance" like the "pestiferous body" of the plague all vanish in Thacher's guide.[110] Putting aside the occult origins of disease for the moment, Thacher follows Sydenham's experientially derived practices of moderation, advising physicians to avoid "overmuch hastening Nature beyond its own pace" with overheating or, conversely, "take away that supply" of vital spirits with cooling, purgative practices.[111] The search for invisible causes would occur elsewhere, in the embodied temporalities of the public fast. For now, Thacher need only focus on striking yet another "middle way" of healing, between the excessive filling and draining of bodies in pain. While English services would never dare to forget about the dangers of contagion, colonial healers instead returned to their medico-religious consumptions and deprivations, never settling on a single cause of epidemical punishment in their extraordinary and potentially contagious forms of worship.

NOTES

1. The figure is taken from John Foster's *Almanack*. There, Foster identifies the ship at "Nantasket" purportedly responsible for starting the epidemic. Historians have set the figure at five hundred to eight hundred deaths for Boston's fewer than six thousand inhabitants. See Kass, "Boston's Historic Smallpox Epidemic," 3.

2. Blake, *Public Health*, 4.

3. For more on Thacher's role in the Third Church and its controversies, see Peterson, *Price of Redemption*.

4. For a thorough account of Thacher's life, see Henry R. Viets's introduction to *Brief Rule*. For more on New England's physician-preachers in general, see Patricia A. Watson's seminal *Angelical Conjunction*.

5. Cotton Mather would include this detail in part of his hagiographical biography of Thacher in *Magnalia Christi Americana*, 445–46.

6. Thacher, *Fast of Gods Chusing*, 23.

7. Matthew Brown indeed characterizes Thacher's *Fast* as a piece of conduct literature

that "exemplifies the anxieties around ceremony and efficacy" so fraught with such questions of "formality" in worship (*Pilgrim and the Bee*, 129).

8. The citation is taken from the influential Reformation writer Thomas Becon's *Fruitful Treatise of Fasting*, F6v. In the period, examples abound where English liturgical practices are compared to pestilential infections, especially in the writings of the "separatists" who would arrive in Plymouth. For some examples, see Finch, *Dissenting Bodies*, 140–44.

9. I use "nonseparatist" to describe those settlers in the Massachusetts Bay Colony who looked to "purify" the Church of England from the inside out rather than separate from it, as those colonists in Plymouth. While my focus remains largely on the nonseparatists in Boston, this chapter often considers both separatist and nonseparatist alike.

10. For the authoritative account of the development of the English special services, see especially Mears, "Special Nationwide Worship." For the complete volume of such services, see Mears et al., *National Prayers*, vol. 1.

11. While I focus primarily on the major outbreak of the smallpox in Boston in 1678–79, I consider the plague liturgies in England in relation to outbreaks throughout the seventeenth century as a whole (namely, the liturgies of 1603, 1625, 1636, and 1666 are directly referenced). Attention is likewise paid to the Civil War and Interregnum services.

12. C. Jones, "Plague and Its Metaphors."

13. Martha Finch considers the ritual fasting and feasting in relation to the embodied theologies in New England, especially of the separatists. See in particular her *Dissenting Bodies*, 164–75, and also her "Pinched with Hunger"; for the fast days' alteration of time and space and ritual power, see Hall, *Worlds of Wonder*, 166–212; for more on the discontinuous temporalities and "fundamental tensions of puritan piety," see Brown, *Pilgrim and the Bee*, 107–38 (quote at 122); for the seminal account of the days as a whole, see Love, *Fast and Thanksgiving Days*.

14. See especially Watson, *Angelical Conjunction*; Hall, *Worlds of Wonder*. For more on the providential approaches to medicine, see Harley, "Spiritual Physic"; and Silva, *Miraculous Plagues*.

15. Finch, *Dissenting Bodies*.

16. Silva, *Miraculous Plagues*, 101–7.

17. Blake, *Public Health*, 25.

18. Quoted in Finch, *Dissenting Bodies*, 172.

19. See especially Mears, "Special Nationwide Worship." Her approach is set in contrast to scholars who take the services to be propagandistic, largely performances of political power. Cf. Cooper, "O Lorde Save the Kyng."

20. Lucy-Ann Bates argues that the deep associations of occasional services with "monarchy, custom, and traditional English worship" persisted during the Civil War and Interregnum, as both Parliamentarians and Royalists ordered competing and frequent days of special services (*Nationwide Fast and Thanksgiving Days*).

21. Blake, *Public Health*, 24.

22. Viets describes Thacher as drawing exclusively from Sydenham "without additions" (introduction to *Brief Rule*, xxviii).

23. Hall, *Worlds of Wonder*, 203.

24. In particular, Sarah Rivett's account of the mutually informing discourses of "Puritanism" and empiricism has been influential to this reading, notably her vision of quasi-scientists "discerning, authenticating, collecting, and

recording invisible knowledge of God" (*Science of the Soul*, 23). This chapter in particular takes off from Finch's analysis of embodied, sensory-focused devotional practices in *Dissenting Bodies* and Brown's account of the "alternate time consciousness" of disruptive, recursive, and linear time-scapes in the Puritan experience in *Pilgrim and the Bee*.

25. There were some variations: Becon notably mentioned the secret anointing of the head in the practice of private fasts. See Finch, *Dissenting Bodies*, 171, which in particular cites Nicholas Bowdne's *Holy Exercise of Fasting* (1604) as influencing Thacher's piece.

26. Thacher, *Fast of Gods Chusing*, 4.

27. I. Mather, preface to *Fast of Gods Chusing*, A3r. The language of the "red" (A3r) and "pale" (A4v) horses comes from the Book of Revelation, where the former was typically read as reflecting the apocalyptic intrusion of war and the latter the plague of death.

28. Thacher, *Fast of Gods Chusing*, 9.

29. Finch, *Dissenting Bodies*, 173.

30. Finch, "Pinched with Hunger," 38.

31. For more on "preparatory humiliation" in both everyday and extraordinary worship, see Brown, *Pilgrim and the Bee*, chapter 3.

32. Brown cites Jacob Danckaerts's account from June 1680 of such substitutions that occurred when one minister grew too tired (*Pilgrim and the Bee*, 121).

33. Brown, *Pilgrim and the Bee*, 120–23.

34. Massachusetts Bay Colony, *Records of the Governor*, 1:96.

35. Ryrie, "Fall and Rise," 81. For the shift toward seasonal fasting, see Love, *Fast and Thanksgiving Days*.

36. Baker, *Thanksgiving*, 38.

37. Baker, *Thanksgiving*, 70.

38. Massachusetts Bay Colony, *Records of the Governor*, 5:156, 376.

39. Massachusetts Bay Colony, *Records of the Governor*, 5:130, 59.

40. Fisher, "Why Shall Wee Have Peace," 93.

41. Massachusetts Bay Colony, *Records of the Governor*, 5:59–60.

42. Massachusetts Bay Colony, *Records of the Governor*, 4.2:489–92.

43. Massachusetts Bay Colony, *Records of the Governor*, 5:130–31.

44. Taken from Joseph Tompson, *Journal*, November 9, 1671.

45. Kass, "Boston's Historic Smallpox Epidemic," 3.

46. Sydenham, "Medical Observations," 124.

47. D. Jones, *Rationalizing Epidemics*, 67. For instance, the Pawtucketts of Massachusetts were said to be fully "eradicated" by a disease, either smallpox or the plague, in 1612–13, and nine out of every ten Native Americans were killed between 1617 and 1619. See Robertson, *Rotting Face*, 106. Overall, scholars have estimated that smallpox and the measles wiped out 70 percent or more of Indigenous populations in America, less because of the so-called virgin soil theory of pathology than from the disruption of resources and health in the face of colonization. For more on this, see Ostler, *Surviving Genocide*, 12–13.

48. D. Jones, *Rationalizing Epidemics*, 67.

49. Tompson, *Journal*, June 30, 1678. Many medical texts within the era surprisingly confuse the smallpox and the plague, at times suggesting that one disease might morph into another.

50. I. Mather, preface to *Fast of Gods Chusing*, A3r.

51. Brown describes his process as thereby aiming at "preparatory humiliation" or a "recursive abjection" that was "the ruminator's stasis" (*Pilgrim and the Bee*, 62).

52. I. Mather, preface to *Fast of Gods Chusing*, A4v.

53. Massachusetts Bay Colony, *Records of the Governor*, 5:196.

54. Walley, *Balm in Gilead*, 6.

55. Thacher, *Fast of Gods Chusing*, 3.

56. Tompson, *Journal*, October 1, 1672. Adrian Chastain Weimer describes Tompson's patterned journal entries, outside of the question of the public fast, as reflecting the "recording of affective states" ("Affliction and the Stony Heart," 135).

57. Tompson, *Journal*, September 6, 1675, January 1727/8.

58. Within the journal, I have approximated that 27 percent of the pages are literary (elegies) and miscellaneous transcriptions (mostly of Thomas Shepard's devotional works), with the remainder featuring Tompson's diary entries. Of the approximately 122 pages of diary entries, about half (approximately 55 pages) appear to be transcribed at a later date.

59. Tompson, *Journal*, November 29, 1678; Brown, *Pilgrim and the Bee*, 31–34.

60. Tompson, *Journal*, March 24, 1678, November 29, 1678.

61. For more on Tompson's biography, see Brown, *Pilgrim and the Bee*, 60–62.

62. Tompson, *Journal*, June 30, 1678.

63. Walley, *Balm in Gilead*, 6.

64. For more on the dramatic, shattering tension between the formal instructions of Thacher's fast and his dream of authentic worship, see Brown, *Pilgrim and the Bee*, 128–32.

65. Adams, *Sermons on Fast Days*, 58.

66. Thacher, *Fast of Gods Chusing*, 23.

67. Massachusetts Bay Colony, *Records of the Governor*, 5:195–6.

68. Peters, *True Relation*, 13.

69. Love, *Fast and Thanksgiving*, 27.

70. Finch, "Pinched with Hunger," 38.

71. Finch, *Dissenting Bodies*, 139.

72. Hooke, *New Englands Teares*, 18.

73. The largest substitution occurred in the 1603 liturgy, where a newly written exhortation on the plague's supernatural causes replaced the Elizabethan homily on obedience. Mears et al.'s *National Prayers* offers a clear, and thorough, overview of the specific forms and their changes throughout the era.

74. See especially table 2.1 in Mears, "Special Nationwide Worship," 28–37.

75. Church of England, *Fourme to Be Used in Common Prayer*, D4r.

76. I. Mather, preface to *Fast of Gods Chusing*, A4v.

77. Prynne, *Newes from Ipswich*, A3r.

78. Prynne, *Newes from Ipswich*, A2r.

79. Prynne, *Newes from Ipswich*, A2r.

80. John Stowe describes Queen Elizabeth setting up in Windsor "a new pair of gallows to hang up all such as should come there from London" (*Summarye*, 127). Charles I would also set up a gallows at Woodstock on 14 August 1625, as found in the *Calendar of State Papers*, 84.

81. For more on the development of these hygienic measures, see Wear, *Knowledge and Practice*, especially chapter 7.

82. Crashaw, *Londons Lamentations*, 3.

83. Church of England, *Certaine Prayers*, A3r.

84. Church of England, *Certaine Prayers*, D4r.

85. Prynne, *Newes from Ipswich*, A4v.

86. Becon, *Fruitful Treatise of Fasting*, D3r, D4v.

87. C. Mather, *Diary of Cotton Mather*, 629–30.

88. Crashaw, *Londons Lamentations*, 16.

89. Wigglesworth, *Meat out of the Eater*, Song IV.

90. Brown, *Pilgrim and the Bee*, 132.

91. Thacher, *Fast of Gods Chusing*, 19.

92. Becon, *Fruitful Treatise of Fasting*, I4v.

93. Crashaw, *Londons Lamentations*, 17.

94. Quoted in Ryrie, "Fall and Rise," 80.

95. Adams, *Necessity of the Pouring Out*, 7, A2r.

96. For a good history of "total substance," see Gibbs, "Medical Literature on Poison"; for "total substance" in Galenism, see Nutton, "Galenic Medicine"; for the distinction between "total substance" and "occult properties," see Wear, *Western Medical Tradition*, 261–64, and for Jean Fernel's understanding of diseases of "total substance" that were either "manifest" and "occult," see Richardson, "Generation of Disease."

97. Weimer, "From Human Suffering."

98. Wigglesworth, *Meat out of the Eater*, G3r.

99. Wigglesworth, *Meat out of the Eater*, C3v.

100. See the act of the commission of the general assembly, February 24, 1653, in Mears et al., *National Prayers*, 587–88.

101. Church of England, *Certaine Prayers*, C3v, C3r.

102. Church of England, *Certaine Prayers*, D1v–D1r.

103. Church of England, *Certaine Prayers*, D3v.

104. Church of England, *Form of Common Prayer*, I1r.

105. Church of England, *Form of Common Prayer*, A1r.

106. For instance, Blake, *Public Health*, outlines the orders passed on May 6, 1678, regulating the clothing of the dead, public passing on the street, and the identification of selectmen.

107. Sydenham, "Medical Observations," 138; Thacher, *Brief Rule*, 3.

108. Stavely and Fitzgerald, *America's Founding Food*, 29–35.

109. For an overview of the English approach to Native American medical knowledge and practices, see Robinson, "New Worlds, New Medicine," 94–110.

110. Sydenham, "Medical Observations," Appendix B, 274, 100.

111. Thacher, *Brief Rule*, 2.

BIBLIOGRAPHY

Adams, William. *The Necessity of the Pouring Out of the Spirit*. Boston: Printed by John Foster, 1679.

———. *Sermons on Fast Days*. MS Am 2138, Houghton Library, Harvard University, Cambridge, MA.

Baker, James. *Thanksgiving: The Biography of an American Holiday*. Lebanon: University of New Hampshire Press, 2009.

Bates, Lucy-Ann. "Nationwide Fast and Thanksgiving Days in England, 1640–1660." PhD diss., Durham University, 2012.

Becon, Thomas. *A Fruitful Treatise of Fasting*. London: Ihon Day, 1551.

Blake, John B. *Public Health in the Town of Boston, 1630–1822*. Cambridge, MA: Harvard University Press, 1959.

Brown, Matthew. *The Pilgrim and the Bee: Reading Rituals and Book Culture in Early New England*. Philadelphia: University of Pennsylvania Press, 2007.

Calendar of State Papers, Domestic Series, of the Reign of Charles I: 1625, 1626. London: Longman, Brown, Green, Longmans, & Roberts, 1858.

Church of England. *Certaine Prayers Collected Out of a Forme of Godly Meditations*. London: Robert Barker, 1603.

———. *A Form of Common Prayer, Together with an Order of Fasting*. London: John Bill, 1665.

———. *A Fourme to Be Used in Common Prayer*. London: Richard Iugge and Iohn Cavvood, 1563.

Cooper, John P. D. "'O Lorde Save the Kyng': Tudor Royal Propaganda and the Power of Prayer." In *Authority and Consent in Tudor England: Essays Presented to C. S. L. Davis*, edited by G. W. Bernard and S. J. Gunn, 179–96. Aldershot, UK: Ashgate, 2002.

Crashaw, William. *Londons Lamentations for Her Sinnes*. London: William Stansby, 1625.

Finch, Martha L. *Dissenting Bodies: Corporealities in Early New England*. New York: Columbia University Press, 2010.

———. "Pinched with Hunger, Partaking of Plenty: Fasts and Thanksgivings in Early New England." In *Eating in Eden: Food and American Utopias*, edited by Etta M. Madden and Martha L. Finch, 35–53. Lincoln: University of Nebraska Press, 2006.

Fisher, Linford. "'Why Shall Wee Have Peace to Bee Made Slaves': Indian Surrenderers During and After King Phillip's War." *Ethnohistory* 64, no. 1 (2017): 91–114.

Foster, John. *An Almanack*. Boston: John Foster, 1679.

Gibbs, Frederick. "Medical Literature on Poison." In *Toxicology in the Middle Ages and Renaissance*, edited by Philip Wexler, 159–64. London: Elsevier Science, 2017.

Hall, David D. *Worlds of Wonder, Days of Judgement: Popular Religious Belief in Early New England*. Cambridge, MA: Harvard University Press, 1989.

Harley, David. "Spiritual Physic, Providence, and English Medicine, 1560–1640." In *Medicine and the Reformation*, edited by Ole Peter Grell and Andrew Cunningham, 101–17. London: Routledge, 1993.

Hooke, William. *New Englands Teares, for Old Englands Feares*. London: T. P., 1641.

Jones, Colin. "Plague and Its Metaphors in Early Modern France." *Representations* 53 (1995): 97–127.

Jones, David S. *Rationalizing Epidemics*. Cambridge, MA: Harvard University Press, 2004.

Kass, Amalie. "Boston's Historic Smallpox Epidemic." *Massachusetts Historical Review* 14, no. 1 (2012): 1–51.

Love, William DeLoss. *The Fast and Thanksgiving Days of New England*. Boston: Houghton Mifflin, 1895.

Massachusetts Bay Colony. *Records of the Governor and Company of Massachusetts Bay Colony*. Vol. 1, *1628–1641*. Edited by Nathaniel B. Shurtleff. Boston: William White, 1853.

———. *Records of the Governor and Company of Massachusetts Bay Colony*. Vol. 4, part 2, *1661–1674*. Edited by Nathaniel B. Shurtleff. Boston: William White, 1854.

———. *Records of the Governor and Company of Massachusetts Bay Colony*. Vol. 5, *1674–1686*. Edited by Nathaniel B. Shurtleff. Boston: William White, 1854.

Mather, Cotton. *Diary of Cotton Mather, 1681–1724*. Vol 2. New York: F. Ungar, 1957.

———. *Magnalia Christi Americana*. Vol. 1. Hartford, CT: Silas Andrus, 1820.

Mather, Increase. Preface to Thacher, *Fast of Gods Chusing*, A2r–A4v.

Mears, Natalie. "Special Nationwide Worship and the Book of Common Prayer in England, Wales and Ireland, 1533–1642." In Ryrie and Mears, *Worship and the Parish Church*, 27–55.

Mears, Natalie, Alasdair Raffe, Stephen Taylor, and Philip Williamson, eds. *National Prayers: Special Worship Since the Reformation*. Vol. 1. Rochester, NY: Boydell, 2013.

Nutton, Vivian. "Galenic Medicine." In *Ancient Medicine*, 3rd ed., 185–98. New York: Routledge, 2024.

Oster, Jeffrey. *Surviving Genocide: Native Nations and the United States from the American Revolution to Bleeding Kansas*. New Haven: Yale University Press, 2019.

Peters, Hugh. *A True Relation of the Passages of Gods Providence in a Voyage for Ireland*. London: Luke Norton for Henry Overton, 1642.

Peterson, Mark A. *The Price of Redemption: The Spiritual Economy of Puritan New England*. Stanford: Stanford University Press, 1997.

Prynne, William. *Newes from Ipswich*. London: [s.n.], 1636.

Richardson, Linda Deer. "The Generation of Disease: Occult Causes and Diseases of the Total Substance." In *The Medical Renaissance of the Sixteenth Century*, edited by A. Wear, R. K. Rench, and I. M. Lonie, 175–94. Cambridge: Cambridge University Press, 1985.

Rivett, Sarah. *The Science of the Soul in Colonial New England*. Chapel Hill: Omohundro Institute and University of North Carolina Press, 2011.

Robertson, Roland G. *Rotting Face: Smallpox and the American Indian*. Caldwell, ID: Caxton, 2001.

Robinson, Martha. "New Worlds, New Medicine: Indian Remedies and English Medicine in Early America." *Early American Studies* 3, no. 1 (2005): 94–110.

Ryrie, Alex. "The Fall and Rise of Fasting in the British Reformations." In Ryrie and

Mears, *Worship and the Parish Church*, 69–85.

Ryrie, Alex, and Natalie Mears, eds. *Worship and the Parish Church in Early Modern Britain.* Farnham, UK: Ashgate, 2013.

Silva, Christobal. *Miraculous Plagues: An Epidemiology of Early New England Narrative.* Oxford: Oxford University Press, 2011.

Stavely, Keith, and Kathleen Fitzgerald. *America's Founding Food: The Story of New England Cooking.* Chapel Hill: University of North Carolina Press, 2004.

Stowe, John. *A Summarye of the Chronicles of Englande.* London: Thomas Marshe, 1570.

Sydenham, Thomas. "Medical Observations Concerning the History and Cure of Acute Diseases." In *The Works of Thomas Sydenham*, vol. 1, translated by R. G. Latham. London: Sydenham Society, 1848.

Thacher, Thomas. *A Brief Rule.* Baltimore: Johns Hopkins Press, 1937.

———. *A Fast of Gods Chusing.* Boston: John Foster, 1678.

Tompson, Joseph. *Journal.* MS Am 929. Houghton Library, Harvard University, Cambridge, MA.

Viets, Henry R. Introduction to Thacher, *Brief Rule*, xiii–liv.

Walley, Thomas. *Balm in Gilead to Heal Sions Wounds.* Cambridge, MA: S. Green and M. Johnson, 1669.

Watson, Patricia A. *The Angelical Conjunction: The Preacher-Physicians of Colonial New England.* Knoxville: University of Tennessee Press, 1991.

Wear, Andrew. *Knowledge and Practice in English Medicine, 1550–1680.* Cambridge: Cambridge University Press, 2000.

———. *The Western Medical Tradition 800 BC to AD 1800.* Cambridge: Cambridge University Press, 1995.

Weimer, Adrian Chastain. "Affliction and the Stony Heart in Early New England." In *Puritanism and Emotion in the Early Modern World*, edited by Alec Ryrie and Tom Schwanda, 121–43. New York: Palgrave, 2016.

———. "From Human Suffering to Divine Friendship: 'Meat out of the Eater' and Devotional Reading in Early New England." *Early American Literature* 51 (2016): 3–39.

Wigglesworth, Michael. *Meat Out of the Eater.* Cambridge, MA: S. Green, 1670.

CHAPTER 7

Enslaved Bodies and the White Imagination

(Mis)Perceptions of Dirt Eating on Jamaican Plantations

RANA A. HOGARTH

"The man who could effectually explore the cause and cure of this Disease, so fatal to negroes, and so ruinous to their owners, would deserve a statue."[1] So opened Thomas Dancer's entry on "Malacia Africanorum vel Pica Nigritum the Disease of Dirt Eating among the Negros" in the 1801 edition of the *Medical Assistant; or, Jamaica Practice of Physic.* Dirt eating, a mysterious affliction common in plantation societies of the Atlantic world, was notorious for leaving slaves so debilitated that they could no longer work. More importantly, it could result in death. Competing theories about dirt eating abounded, complicating physicians' attempts to treat and prevent this mysterious disease. Treatises on plantation health, diseases of the tropics, and general descriptions of the Caribbean sounded the alarm over dirt eating's prevalence and exposed frustration over its refractory nature. Bearing this information in mind perhaps excuses Dancer's inclination to hyperbole when describing the misfortune that dirt eating sowed across Jamaican plantations.

With less exaggerated language, Dancer provided a description of dirt eating that closely matched others in its attention to the degree to which the disease enervated its victims. The classic symptoms he mentioned included "pain in the Stomach (whence the French call it the *Mal d' Estomac*), breathlessness on

ENSLAVED BODIES AND THE WHITE IMAGINATION   151

the least motion attended with visible pulsation of the carotids, or the arteries of the neck; they next become bloated."[2] John Williamson, writing nearly ten years after Dancer, noted that the disease was attended with extreme indolence, "from which there is scarcely a possibility of rousing them [slaves] to exertion, laborious breathing, inability to ascend a hill, any attempt to do so evidently accompanied by increased palpitation of the heart."[3] Dr. Collins, author of the 1803 treatise *Practical Rules for the Management and Medical Treatment of Negro Slaves in the Sugar Colonies*, went a step further, noting dirt eating's effects on the plantation economy. "It disables them [slaves] from effective labor for a very considerable time, sometimes for years and often terminates in a dropsy."[4] Failure to curb this disease, then, portended failure to turn a profit.

In the genre of medical texts on plantation management and "negro" diseases, physicians lost no time in drawing links between a healthy slave labor force and economic prosperity. That said, in descriptions of the disease, physicians gave vague, but frightening, assessments of dirt eating's prevalence and destructive powers. John Hunter, a Scottish physician and contemporary of Dancer, briefly addressed dirt eating in his 1788 edition of *Observations on the Diseases of the Army in Jamaica*, noting, "On many estates half the number of deaths, on a moderate computation are owing to this cause."[5] Hunter provided little else in the way of hard numbers on deaths. A simple declaration that scores of slaves died from dirt eating sufficed as proof that the disease was a menace. "I know of no calculation of the general mortality by this Disease," Dancer admitted; however, he added immediately, it "sometimes sweeps off one half or more of the negroes on a plantation."[6] In Jamaica, it was not unusual for plantations to have over one hundred slaves, meaning that Dancer's and Hunter's words reveal that a nontrivial number of slaves were frequently succumbing to this disease.[7]

Contemporary assessments of dirt eating, or pica, as it is now known, suggest that deaths from the condition were unlikely. According to Kenneth Kiple, "It is doubtful that dirt eating swept plantations killing slaves for the very good reason that the use of pica rarely kills anyone."[8] Kiple is correct that pica on its own rarely kills; more than likely, dirt eating might have been a proximate cause of death, one of many existing comorbid conditions that ended a slave's life. However, knowing this does little to explain why dirt eating was so feared in slave societies. Indeed, fixating too much on how many slaves actually died from dirt eating shifts our analytic attention away from why so many white physicians were prone to believe that dirt eating had high mortality. It remains unclear why so many white physicians insisted on spreading this idea of massive mortality from dirt eating in authoritative medical texts. Finally, it is also worth noting that Kiple's modern-day assessment of dirt eating (pica) is different from the dirt eating that white physicians observed during the era of slavery.[9]

Claims about dirt eating's high mortality, though found in published accounts from highly esteemed physicians, amounted to rumors—unverified statements of dubious origins. Rumors about dirt eating, as they existed in this context, owed their longevity, plausibility, and credibility in the collective white imagination to their being repeated in published works by elite white authors. Put another way, men who boasted formal medical training, and experience living and working in slave societies, reported on a mysterious disease linked to mysterious behaviors of Black people that fit with widely held white assumptions about Black people. Bearing this in mind, this chapter incorporates methods of interpreting rumors, as championed by Luise White, as it historicizes the belief in the prevalence of and high mortality associated with dirt eating. Rather than focusing on the validity or "truth" of the accounts, this chapter attends to how and why these accounts were believable in a given context.[10] Considered in this way, these published medical accounts on slave health emerge as useful sources for reconstructing enslaved people's experiences in health and sickness. Their value, however, comes not from what expertise physicians claimed on the topic of slave health but rather from what these sources reveal about the misperceptions and assumptions white physicians held about enslaved people's behaviors and practices. Focusing on physicians' accounts of dirt eating and placing those accounts in conversation with each other reconstitutes the anxieties that physicians experienced when they were called on to oversee and take responsibility for the health of hundreds of slaves on plantations who had little reason to trust them. It also lays the groundwork for educated speculation on why slaves engaged in dirt eating in the first place.

Dirt eating among enslaved Black populations was a socially constructed, socially contingent ailment. Indeed, Kiple does note that dirt eating was also conflated with *mal d'estomac*, another socially constructed disease. Both might have been manifestations of wet beriberi or cardiac beriberi, which often leads to sudden cardiac failure. If we concede that slaves suffered from wet beriberi, then they would have been predisposed to sudden cardiac failure. For slaves suffering from this condition who were forced to perform strenuous labor, death by sudden cardiac failure would have been within the realm of possibility.[11]

White physicians went out of their way to distinguish dirt eating among slaves from other groups of people who also suffered from this condition, so

ENSLAVED BODIES AND THE WHITE IMAGINATION   153

much so that dirt eating among Black populations was also known as *Cachexia Africana* or "African wasting." What physicians described in plantation guidebooks was a racial pathology, not simply an eating disorder brought on by lack of nutrition. That said, another aim of this chapter is to understand how dirt eating among enslaved Black populations in the Americas became tethered to and constituted by ideologies of racial difference. Physicians assumed that the peculiarities of African constitutions, which included a propensity to indolence, pathological nostalgia, suicide, susceptibility to witchcraft or conjuration, and a lack of impulse control, were predisposing factors for the disease. Ironically, none of these traits did much to dissuade whites from viewing Blacks as perfectly suited for hard labor.

The lack of consensus surrounding the etiology of *Cachexia Africana* (dirt eating among Black populations), the failures to prevent it, and the widespread belief that it resulted in loss of labor and death created a circumstance whereby slaves could exploit white anxieties. *Cachexia Africana*, or dirt eating (or what the French knew as *mal d'estomac*), was essentially a pathology of the entire plantation, and slaves were, in their own way, aware of this. Slaves could have hardly ignored the associations whites made between dirt eating, high mortality, and lost profits. Slaves understood that the value that whites attached to their bodies was predicated on their being healthy and able to work. The dependency on healthy slaves coupled with the poorly understood nature of the disease created opportunities for slaves to use the specter of dirt eating to wheedle, trick, and negotiate on the plantation. Were slaves truly suffering from the weakness associated with dirt eating and therefore slow in their labor, or were they malingering? Was dirt eating a disease or a cultural practice? Was slaves' dirt eating due to chronic poor nutrition and ill use, or were they bewitched? Were they cunning or lazy or both? These questions frame this chapter's approach to reconstructing how slaves responded to, and even manipulated, white perceptions about what made a slave healthy versus diseased as means of gaining concessions and having a say in how everyday life on the plantation would proceed.

Reconstructing slaves' possible motives from hundreds of years ago through white medical sources demands caution; white physician-interlocutors were notoriously biased when assessing Black populations. They dismissed enslaved knowledge, wrote off slaves' behaviors as ignorant or primitive, and judged slaves by impossible standards. Indeed, medical accounts of dirt eating often reveal more about a physician's political leanings than about the disease. Thus, these physicians' accounts must be read between the lines to gain access to

154   DOCTRINE AND DISEASE

slaves' actions and motivations. When we read between the lines of these medical accounts, slaves' deception and desperation—their attempts at mitigating slavery's crushing weight—become that much clearer. Somewhere in between, perhaps, exists an explanation for dirt eating. Physicians' writing about dirt eating can also help amplify slaves' agency—that is, their ability to act independently and make decisions—and their ability to wield enough power to manipulate the few whites who staffed Jamaican plantations. The medical historical record is essential in this regard for it is constituted by tense, intimate relationships between enslaved patients, enslaved healers, white physicians, and white overseers. These relationships, which were centered on health, were a two-way street—no matter how subjugated one party was in the encounter. Despite slaves being hemmed in by draconian colonial laws that aimed to erase their autonomy, they remained complex individuals who acquiesced and deceived when they saw fit.[12] This was certainly the case in matters related to their health.

This chapter entertains the possibility of dirt eating as a deliberate act and a desperate measure. It examines the association that physicians made between dirt eating and cultural practice, as well as dirt eating and bewitchment—a topic whites invariably linked to Obeah, an Afro-Caribbean spiritual modality that could heal and harm. Finally, it considers cases in which physicians regarded dirt eating as a bargaining tool—one used to change how a plantation was managed. With this approach to understanding dirt eating, this chapter joins scholarship that highlights the various ways slaves coped with slavery, disrupted labor regimes, and rejected white authority through minor acts of resistance, such as clandestine spiritual practices and truancy.[13] It differs by centering the image of the enslaved dirt eater in the white imagination as the mechanism for challenging white authority.

DIRT EATING IN CULTURE AND PRACTICE

Slavery in Jamaica thrived on a system built on violence, coercion, and fear, a system that pitted slaves against masters, slaves against fellow slaves, and slaves against the white physicians who were contracted to provide care to them. In white physicians' descriptions of slaves' behaviors, habits, and beliefs, the inclination to see calculating noncompliance, ignorance, and backwardness often obscures the reality of what slaves actually knew and did. Slaves in Jamaica certainly engaged in defiant, rebellious acts; they dissembled and fooled whites as ongoing practices that constituted an active culture of resistance that was necessary to survive.[14] Questions arise: Was dirt eating part of this culture of resistance, or was it a manifestation of something else? There were certainly instances when slaves engaged in dirt eating, not out of defiance but out of practicality or out of a desire to maintain cultural ties. The tense relationships between Blacks and whites, the lack of written sources from enslaved populations, and the appalling material conditions of slavery continue to make the process of distinguishing slaves' motivations for eating dirt unclear.

As a desperate act, dirt eating made sense, for it was a way for slaves to supplement nutrients. In reality, the term "dirt eating" is misleading, for slaves more than likely were consuming clay, not loose soil. Clay consumption was possibly a response to nutritional deprivation. It is highly plausible that slaves who were suspected of dirt eating were actually consuming clay and were probably doing it to gain relief from being consistently underfed. As much as physicians reviled the practice and condemned those slaves who engaged in it, a handful recognized the role that poor nourishment played in cases of dirt eating. Modern medicine seems to have validated the belief that slaves ate dirt to make up for nutritional lack. Kiple has, for example, offered compelling evidence on what minerals and vitamins were missing from slaves' diets in the Caribbean and has explained how dirt eating could restore their nutrition.[15]

Cultural factors may have also played a role in the consumption of dirt. As a practice, dirt eating spans the globe, including parts of western and eastern Africa, making it possible that some slaves consumed dirt as a way of continuing a cultural practice. In other words, consuming dirt might have been a way to cope with forced migration and potential cultural erasure, an antidote to the social death that enveloped them in the unfamiliar landscape of the Americas.

It is also possible that dirt eating had medicinal benefit. If we again consider that slaves were probably eating clay, the associations between the practice and palliation emerge in sharp relief. Certain kinds of clay have been known to be effective in soothing stomach upset. Indeed, the over-the-counter antidiarrheal drug Kaopectate was originally composed of pectin and kaolinite, which is a mineral clay.[16] According to the medical geographer John M. Hunter, "Earth has been consumed as a popular medicine to treat certain diseases. *Terra sigillata*, sacred 'sealed' earth from the Greek island of Lemnos that was mixed with goat blood, prepared as small lozenges, dried, and stamped with a seal of a goat figure, is recorded as early as 40 B.C."[17] Medical anthropologists have also confirmed that "geophagia and particularly clay consumption was part of the traditional, culturally prescribed behavior of the society."[18] It would appear that dirt eating

156   DOCTRINE AND DISEASE

could take place for a variety of reasons in a given society, "for religious and magical purposes, for medical purposes, by pregnant and lactating women, as a famine food, or as a regular part of the diet."[19] The long history of the practice, its distribution across continents, and the various purposes mean that dirt eating need not be tied to a specific race of people or viewed solely as a pathology.[20]

Focusing on the kinds of slave populations that were associated with dirt eating also helps situate the practice as palliative as well as restorative. Indeed, anthropologists have shown that dirt eating has practical nutritional benefits under certain circumstances—namely, pregnancy.[21] Twentieth-century research into the practice in western and southern regions of Africa reveals that earth eating is more typical in pregnant women, whose bodies need extra minerals.[22] Thus, the earth consumed by women functions as a kind of prenatal dietary supplement. Data also suggest that dirt eating has a cultural significance among expecting women because the practice can serve as a signal to others in the community of a new pregnancy. In an analysis of modern-day clay production, consumption, and sale in Ghana, Hunter found clear cultural and nutritional motivations behind the practice.[23] Shifting his research eastward to rural villages around Malawi, Hunter claims that "the linkage between clay eating and pregnancy is ubiquitous."[24] According to a physician confederate with whom Hunter spoke, the consumption of clays in Malawi is how one would "know when [they] are pregnant!"[25] It is, however, hard to know how well this practice traveled across Africa over time and how much it evolved.

That said, Hunter's modern research on geophagy in pregnant women, when paired with early historical accounts of the practice, helps sketch out the possible cultural and gendered dimensions of this practice. What Hunter describes bears some similarity to how the Anglo-Jamaican physician James Thomson described dirt eating in his 1820 guidebook on "negro diseases." Thomson concluded that dirt eating was "common practice with negro women when pregnant," and he noted that they consumed what he described as "small cakes of baked earth." According to Thomson, dirt eating helped to manage the "acidity at the stomach" associated with pregnancy. Far from a secretive practice, as some other white observers would claim, dirt eating among pregnant women occurred openly. The women, according to Thomson, "look on it as a privilege of their peculiar situation."[26] Undoubtedly, the circumstances that attended the consumption of earth in Thomson's account and in Hunter's studies varied considerably. As a cultural practice, dirt eating has probably evolved—the circumstances in which people consume dirt today certainly have.

Turning our gaze back to Thomson, questions arise with respect to how he was able to gain such familiarity with the practices of enslaved pregnant women on Jamaican plantations. Thomson was probably an outsider to the community of enslaved pregnant women, so why would these women have trusted and confided in him? Under what circumstances would he have observed them eating dirt? These questions aside, we can reasonably assume that Thomson was a credible witness of some slave behaviors. After all, Thomson had many opportunities to observe enslaved Black populations. After receiving his medical education at the University of Edinburgh, he spent most of his life in Jamaica, practicing on plantations in the countryside. At his death in 1822, he was listed as having died at the Crawle estate in the parish of Saint Thomas in the Vale.[27] By his own accounts, he had extensive experience attending to slaves on plantations—even suggesting that he had dissected both Black and white bodies to gain knowledge on comparative anatomy.[28]

Thomson hardly hid his prejudices toward Black slaves in his published writings, but he was also not so willing to dismiss all slave behaviors as foolish. In classifying dirt eating among pregnant women as a deliberate act, he recognized that it was an appropriate action for quelling acid indigestion so common in pregnancy. He also hinted at the social significance of dirt eating by observing that it was done collectively among women in a similar physiological state. Providing a rationale for why enslaved women consumed earth, however, was not a means of excusing the practice. For all his careful attention to the logic that attended enslaved women's consumption of earth, Thomson declared that the practice "should always be strictly prohibited."[29] He negated the validity of the practice with his professional authority (he pointed out the great risks associated with the practice that he believed trumped any benefits the women might have sought). When Thomson came out against dirt eating, he essentially transformed a social (and cultural) bonding practice carried out by enslaved pregnant women into an aberrant behavior.

That white physicians scrutinized and condemned enslaved people's cultural and social practices is hardly unusual. Dirt eating, like many other slave behaviors, was seen as unfamiliar from the vantage point of white physician interlocutors. In the years leading up to emancipation in Jamaica, slaves' behaviors took on new meaning, as proslavery physicians considered dirt eating proof that Blacks were incapable of cultivation, incapable of looking after themselves. The writings of James Maxwell, a Scottish physician, longtime resident of Jamaica, and staunch critic of dirt eating, reveal as much. Maxwell, like Thomson, apprehended

158   DOCTRINE AND DISEASE

possible cultural and social reasons for dirt eating and recognized that it had been practiced across the globe. "There is not a tribe in Africa who do not indulge in eating an absorbent clay which they call aboo, so do the Egyptians; and in Java it is a species of reddish clay which they bake and sell in the public markets." Citing only cases of nonwhite populations who engaged in dirt eating and dismissing this class of peoples as "barbarians, existing in the lowest stages of savage life," Maxwell's words evinced an approach to normative behavior that was Eurocentric at its core and one that the island's slaves failed to live up to.[30]

Maxwell's views on dirt eating appeared in his 1835 article "Pathological Inquiry into Cachexia Africana as It Is Generally Connected with Dirt Eating." Published in a medical journal for an audience of mostly physicians, Maxwell's article offered both clinical information on dirt eating and documentation of white anxieties about slaves' behaviors before and during a crucial moment of transition in Jamaica's history. Maxwell, it appeared, had little faith in the island's Black population to resist the desire to consume dirt. He lambasted what he described as enslaved women who were "well fed" who "habitually consum[ed] moderate quantities of a species of steatite made up into balls like chocolate, which are baked and sold in the market." He punctuated this sentiment by noting, "Use of this earth is considered by the negroes neither dangerous nor disgraceful; and those who eat it, take it as much to gratify an acquired taste, similar to that of chewing tobacco or opium, as to satisfy any morbid desire."[31] In this way, he cast doubt on dirt eating as a response to the appalling conditions and poor nutrition brought on by slavery, while simultaneously equating the practice to vice and deviance. According to Maxwell, Black populations, when left to their own devices, would eat dirt whether enslaved or free.

Maxwell wrote at a time when gradual emancipation was well under way, and given his own personal investment into slavery, he may have felt particularly aggrieved by what he perceived to be slaves refusing to behave in a civilized manner or acting ungrateful. Maxwell, like Thomson, had extensive experience treating slaves. He was also a slave owner through marriage and attended to slaves on other estates throughout the island. Prior to his arrival in Jamaica in 1816, Maxwell was a licentiate of the Royal College of Surgeons in Edinburgh. He later returned to Edinburgh to attain his MD. There he wrote his medical thesis on yaws, which was viewed by his contemporaries as a loathsome and feared slave disease.[32]

The purposeful use of the phrase "well fed" to describe slaves outed Maxwell as a slavery apologist; in the very least, it worked to erase the possibility that dirt eating was a desperate act brought on by malnutrition. Maxwell's aim was to stigmatize slaves as well as to educate his audience on the dangers of dirt eating. He accomplished both with commentary that dismissed any cultural value in the practice of eating dirt. Instead, he explicitly compared dirt eating to known vices. Thus, in Maxwell's mind, slaves' willingness to consume dirt represented a kind of pathological autonomy—a desire to engage in a practice despite what sickness it might cause and in spite of whites' condemnation of it. Maxwell was appreciably unsure that slaves could be broken of what he perceived to be innately damaging habits even with the advent of gradual emancipation. "Now that freedom is conferred upon the blacks," he opined, "and all the vis inertia of slavery is removed, we may expect to see this African custom in time yield to the humanizing influence of Christianity."[33] Indeed he hoped that through the apprenticeship system, "steps . . . [would be] taken to emancipate them from the mental thraldom [sic] of ignorance."[34]

But before the end of slavery was even a possibility in the eyes of Jamaica's whites, claims that slaves simply could not stop themselves from consuming dirt appeared in accounts of the island from the eighteenth century. Edward Long, like Maxwell, also observed that slaves sold "aboo" at the Spanish Town market. This type of clay, according to Long, was "chiefly found in marley beds" and was of a "smooth, unctuous" nature with a "sweetish taste." Long noted that "Negroes . . . [ate] it in excess"—an action he described as "mortal to them," because dirt eating was known for "obstructing the capillary vessels" and breaking the "texture of the blood entirely," bringing "on a wasting of the flesh, a general depravation of all the organs, and a lingering but certain death." Like others who would write after him, Long considered dirt eating a deliberate action, a consequence of slaves' irresistible compulsion, as he noted it was "exceedingly difficult to wean any from it, who have been addicted to the use of it for any length of time."[35]

OBEAH AND THE WHITE PRACTITIONER

Notwithstanding Maxwell's and Thomson's accounts of the openness with which enslaved women consumed dirt and even sold baked cakes of dirt, many physicians associated dirt eating with secrecy. More often than not, the claims that slaves clandestinely consumed dirt often accompanied explanations for the disease, especially those explanations that saw the disease as a consequence of Obeah. Obeah, as it did then and does now, defies easy classification. It represented a set of practices and worldviews in which the spiritual, supernatural, and natural worlds could be manipulated to harm or heal. Some whites in Jamaica erroneously viewed it as witchcraft, while eventually over time, others dismissed it as backward.[36] During the era of slavery, the conflation of Obeah with evil, dark arts in the eyes of whites was almost certainly erroneous and almost certainly a consequence of the uniform disdain for Black cultural practices by colonial elites. Despite its ties to the spiritual world, the scholars Jerome Handler and Kenneth Bilby assert, "Obeah is not an organized religion."[37] Instead, they define it as a practice that involved the "manipulation of supernatural forces, usually through the use of material objects and recitation of spells."[38] A typical Obeah practitioner could channel their energies to "divination [foretelling, finding lost or stolen goods, ascertaining the cause of illness], healing, and bringing good fortune." Bilby and Handler also note that Obeah could offer protection and cause harm.[39] What would have probably irked white physicians about Obeah practitioners was not merely their claims to supernatural power. Obeah practitioners were highly skilled experts, with deep knowledge of plants—knowledge that white practitioners may very well have lacked. And, just as white physicians expected to be paid for their services, so too did Obeah practitioners, albeit in different ways.[40] In other words, the Obeah practitioner was a clear professional competitor in the plantation medical marketplace. Thus, it is hardly surprising to find that physicians identified Obeah practitioners as responsible for mysterious deaths and illnesses on plantations—especially those associated with dirt eating.

The Obeah practitioner, however, was more than just an existential threat to the white physician. Obeah practitioners had been implicated in slave rebellions in Jamaica and therefore represented a diffuse but palpable threat to white authority on the island. The association of Obeah with insurrection hardened in Jamaica, especially after Tacky's Revolt in 1760. That revolt, which largely caught the minority white population off guard, involved vast networks of slaves across plantations. Its spread and continuation even after the death of its leader, Tacky, nearly spelled ruin for the island. That Obeah practitioners were a part of the revolt and were purported to have emboldened slaves to revolt meant that Obeah went from a backward spiritual practice among the enslaved to a serious offense punishable by death.[41] According to Diana Paton, the criminalization of Obeah "dates from the 1760, 'Act to Remedy the Evils Arising from the Irregular Assembly of Slaves' passed in response to Tacky's Rebellion of the same year."[42] Thus, whites' hostility toward Obeah meant that its practitioners had little choice but to operate in the shadows.

As the eighteenth and nineteenth centuries wore on, whites abandoned witchcraft as a lens for viewing Obeah, but they continued to view it as a potentially dangerous practice linked to fraud and quackery perpetrated against slaves who were too ignorant to know better or too stubborn to relinquish their faith in enslaved healers. Slaves were, according to many white physicians, prone to having their passions manipulated—meaning that physicians saw them as likely to fall prey to scheming Obeah practitioners. In reality, Obeah practitioners, and slaves' willingness to consult with them (instead of white practitioners), underscored the uncomfortable truth that white medical men were not as in control of enslaved people's health as they would have liked to believe. Thus, tethering Obeah to dirt eating's mysterious etiology and refractoriness to treatment gave white physicians a ready-made scapegoat when they ultimately failed to treat the condition. Indeed, Obeah practitioners almost appear as a stock character in discussions on dirt eating in plantation guidebooks and treatises on "negro diseases." They represented a kind of bogeyman, lying in wait to wreak havoc on a plantation's hapless slaves in the white imagination. Indeed, the Obeah practitioner was more than just a competitor; they became a menace to the health of enslaved bonds people.

Dancer, Thomson, and Maxwell are but a few of the physicians who defined Obeah as a deviant art that was associated with dirt eating. Maxwell was perhaps the most explicit in his complaints about Obeah practitioners' knowledge of poisonous plants and their ability to trick others "through extreme dread of their supernatural power."[43] Indeed, Maxwell drew a direct connection between the compulsion to eat dirt and Obeah: "Negro witchcraft is not only used as the means of inducing disease and death through the moral and physical influence of mind and body, but to ward off difficulties and dangers. . . . I have considered it necessary to premise the influence that Obeah has over the Negro mind, as the gloom and despondency exert their powerful agency over the digestive and assimilative organs, and produce that peculiar longing for absorbent earths."[44] Underlying this logic, of course, was the belief that enslaved Black people's passions or mental states, in particular, could be easily manipulated.[45] More to the point, Maxwell highlighted the plight of the white practitioner tasked with treating dirt eaters. White physicians, according to Maxwell, had to be cognizant of the distinctive frailties of the "negro" psyche as well as the strong influence that Obeah practitioners exerted over slaves.

By holding Obeah responsible for cases of dirt eating and then drawing attention to Black people's supposed susceptibility to being manipulated,

162 DOCTRINE AND DISEASE

physicians found an easy and conspicuous way to blame the enslaved patient for their ills. This logic again supports the argument for dirt eating as deliberate resistance. Dancer, who wrote decades before Maxwell, exemplified this dual approach to spreading blame. As he explained Obeah's relationship to cases of dirt eating in his 1801 guidebook, he advised,

> Perhaps, Obeah . . . is a much more frequent cause than any: This at least must be suspected, where there is no apparent ground of complaint;— whatever motives actuate them to eat Dirt, they always do it secretly and clandestinely. . . . They will never acknowledge it. . . . Nothing can extort from them the confession, which shews they are either under the influence of some horrible superstition, or bent on some fell purpose. I consider this Disease then, as sometimes a voluntary one, proceeding from hopeless, though perhaps causeless grief, and a determination to either shun or revenge certain evils, by self-destruction.[46]

Identifying meddlesome Obeah practitioners as likely sources of dirt eating proved one way in which white physicians saw elements of slave resistance in a diseased state. Calling dirt eating "voluntary" certainly worked to ease the burden on the physician should they fail to treat it. More to the point, claiming that slaves were complicit in creating their own misery worked to erode any potential sympathy directed toward them. Instead, Dancer's words presented a different view of slaves—as calculating and manipulative, willing to sacrifice their lives due to emotional distress.

Dancer's view of dirt eating implied not only a concerted effort by slaves to resist but also a repudiation of white physicians' attempts to heal. By keeping dirt eating concealed and denying the practitioner access to knowledge of their behaviors, slaves literally used noncompliance to disrupt the power dynamic between enslaved patient and white physician. Essentially, Dancer constructed an image of a physician who, despite all their efforts, was no match for slaves resigned to resist by bringing about their own demise, through secretive, supernatural, and deliberate means.

The rationale for slaves consuming dirt in secret, or denying the practice when confronted, was not always a simple of matter of the influence of Obeah. Slaves were well aware of the fate that often befell deceased dirt eaters: desecration of the deceased dirt eater's body, including dismemberment and display. Those who did not succumb to the condition but were found to have engaged in

ENSLAVED BODIES AND THE WHITE IMAGINATION 163

it could expect physical punishment, such as whipping. In the second volume of Bryan Edwards's well-known *History, Civil and Commercial, of the British Colonies in the West Indies*, he all but confirmed the unfortunate fate of the slave found out to consume dirt. Edwards complained of "owners and managers who were so ignorant and savage as to attempt the cure by severe punishment; considering dirt eating, not as a disease, but a crime." "The best and only remedy," he continued, was "kind usage and whole some animal food."[47] As an outspoken planter, politician, and enemy of the antislavery movement, Edwards represented planters' approaches to slave management as gentle and enlightened—as a way of pushing back against the realities of the brutal treatment slaves endured. To Edwards, evils associated with slavery, like dirt eating, would simply cease as long as owners treated their slaves well. Edwards, like many planters of his time, cast the inhumanity of slavery on a few rogue planters, rather than the institution itself.

The ignorant owners of Edwards's account would not have been the only group of whites to champion corporal punishment to thwart dirt eating. Physicians understood that dissection was perceived by slaves as a kind of posthumous bodily punishment, and thus these practitioners advocated for the dissection of deceased dirt eaters' bodies. Broadly speaking, physicians were all too eager to access bodies for dissection. Indeed, many physicians were in favor of opening up the bodies of deceased dirt eaters for typical postmortem inspection and as a means to deter slaves from consuming dirt. Though dissection was an instructive practice for physicians, that hardly mattered to enslaved populations that were subjected to seeing the dismembered bodies of slaves accused of high crimes routinely put on public display. Thomson advised, "The other children on the estate should be taught to hold the subject in abhorrence. I recommend that everyone who dies of this practice should be opened, and the body not allowed to be given to the friends for burial, but interred in some spot as a warning to others."[48] As Vincent Brown has argued, the disregard most slave owners showed to the remains of enslaved people's bodies was part of a violent attempt to secure obedience from a restive population of slaves. Rather than relying on sheer brute force, masters accomplished this feat of social control by terrorizing "the spiritual imaginations of the enslaved."[49] Physicians, it seems, were also willing to embrace these methods.

Slaves, then, had good reason to be less than forthcoming about dirt eating. Physicians were especially undeserving of slaves' trust, for their medical interventions blurred the lines between palliation and punishment. Even for those

164 DOCTRINE AND DISEASE

physicians who may have eschewed making an example of deceased dirt eaters, their profession's adherence to dissection would make them complicit in the collective assault against the enslaved dead. Curiously, or perhaps willfully, physicians ignored the habitual depredations that whites made on enslaved people's bodies as a possible reason that fueled slaves' reluctance to offer information about dirt eating when pressed for it. Instead, they saw secrecy and the lack of faith in white medicine to be the fault of Obeah practitioners. According to Maxwell,

> Revenge and jealousy are the passions, which chiefly require the interposition for the Obeah man. When a Negro considers himself injured by another, he secretly applies to a practitioner of witchcraft to remove the impediment, who for a fee, uses his incantations with all the imposing consequence of a conjurer. . . . In every sense of the word, he is rendered both mentally and corporeally invalided, and during this extreme depressed state of the passions, he not unfrequently lays violent hands upon himself. Cases of this kind often occur, and as the patient seldom admits the true cause to his medical attendant, it requires all his acumen and penetration to unravel the complaint.[50]

Wading through Maxwell's racism yields evidence that slaves attempted to manage disputes by seeking out counsel from within their own communities. Indeed, what Maxwell saw as secretive could reasonably have been slaves' rejection of white interference in their affairs. That slaves were less than forthcoming to white outsiders when it came to matters of health and conflict within their communities can be viewed as an inclination to self-government and self-sufficiency—traits Maxwell felt Jamaica's slaves lacked. Thus, Maxwell's passage reveals the varied ways that slaves continued to resist the plantation regime, even during slavery's last days.

The uncooperativeness of the enslaved patient was only the tip of the proverbial iceberg, however, for Maxwell suggested that slaves would collectively convince each other that Obeah was the root cause of their illnesses. Slave patients, wrote Maxwell, "obstinately resist[ed] medical treatment [and] the friends of the patient invariably attribute the cause to Obeah. An Obeah man is sought, who attends with the implements of his art, and generally manages to convince the credulous relatives, that a cockroach or cricket, or scorpion, or piece of glass of bone, is concealed in the affected part, and after the volubile [*sic*] repetition of some abracadabra, he adroitly extracts the object to the amazement of the company, although not always to the relief of the sufferer."[51] The physician, then, was up against an entire community of slaves (including Obeah practitioners) working in tandem to undermine and reject their claims of medical expertise. Obeah, then, existed as a credible threat to slaves' health and physicians' livelihoods. Though Maxwell's choice of words suggested a dismissal of Obeah as mere fraud, he also conceded that Obeah was powerful enough to induce dirt eating. Indeed, by his own logic, Maxwell implied that physicians were up against charlatans (Obeah practitioners) and the gullible slaves who believed in them over white physicians. In this way, Maxwell's diatribe against Obeah revealed that the power and authority that physicians wielded on plantations was more contingent than absolute.

That Maxwell began his 1835 article on dirt eating by lamenting the influence of Obeah suggests that this slave practice was no trivial matter. Maxwell's attack on Obeah, it should be noted, was not unique. His predecessors Dancer and Thomson also saw fit to complain loudly about Obeah in their discussions of dirt eating. A key distinction in Maxwell's description of dirt eating, unlike Dancer's and Thomson's, is that it appeared in the short-lived *Jamaica Physical Journal*, meaning that the intended audience would have been physicians. Dancer's and Thomson's guidebooks, in contrast, would have been intended for medical professionals, as well as overseers, bookkeepers, and other parties interested in plantation management. Maxwell's article, then, can be seen as a way of informing his fellow practitioners of the challenges of managing cases of dirt eating and a call to arms to professional physicians to be vigilant with respect to Obeah's continuing influence over slave health.

As these descriptions of dirt eating reveal, the relationship between physicians, enslaved patients, and enslaved healers was complex to say the least. The existence of enslaved healers, be they midwives or Obeah practitioners, meant that white physicians were not always the first or only practitioners whom slaves saw. Generally, enslaved healers typically served their fellow slaves, though there were cases when whites sought out care from enslaved healers before or instead of calling for a white physician. Enslaved people sought out medical treatment from their own practitioners as a means through which they might protect their bodies from white medical interference and surveillance. In addition, enslaved healers probably chose to keep their means of treatment closely guarded. We can at least assume as much from James Knight's description of typical healthcare practices on Jamaican plantations. "For though every Plantation has one [physician] that constantly attend them every day, yet it is with great difficulty that many of the Negroes are prevailed upon to take their Medicines. The Negro Doctors very seldom discover their Nostrums or method of practice, though some of our Practitioners have now and then got out of them the use and Virtue of many Simples that were unknown to them or to any Phisitian in England."[52]

Transactions of health, if we are to take Knight at his word, presented many opportunities for resistance. Enslaved patients challenged white physicians with noncompliance, while enslaved healers fueled white physicians' professional insecurity with their superior knowledge of local remedies and their unwillingness to share them.

In many circumstances, slave owners, overseers, and even physicians saw enslaved healers as a necessary first line of medical care. In the words of the Scottish physician and resident of St. Kitts Thomas Grainger, slave hospitals on the plantation ought to be staffed by "a nurse," preferably one who was "strong, sensible and sober." Ideally, he continued, "in every plantation some sensible Negroe should be instructed to bleed, give glisters, dress fresh wounds, spread plasters, and dress ulcers."[53] Thus, collaboration with enslaved healers could be expected, provided, of course, that the enslaved healer was willing to practice under the white physicians' terms—an arrangement that would have probably excluded Obeah practitioners.

MANIPULATION AND NEGOTIATION

Although white practitioners believed that slaves were easily influenced by Obeah and suffered from an overall lack of self-control when it came to dirt eating, some were willing to entertain the possibility that dirt eating was an act of resistance. Others still were willing to go further and call it a deliberate and calculated act. In other words, some physicians entertained the idea that slaves were clever enough to use the specter of dirt eating for the purposes of gaining concessions from whites who wielded power on the plantation. The concessions slaves sought—better working conditions, more time to cultivate their garden plots, the removal of a despised overseer—were meant to alleviate, in small measure, the daily traumas of the plantation labor regime.

How slaves were able to negotiate for better conditions often appears as marginalia in physicians' accounts of dirt eating, literal footnotes to their lamentations of how destructive the disease was. What white physicians dismissed as petty or artful and what historians might overlook in written medical accounts of dirt eating provide some of the most compelling evidence of slaves' ingenuity at using their bodies—the very thing that whites depended on and imputed value to—to their advantage. Indeed, if we take physicians at their word when they suggested that slaves' dirt eating was a kind of extortion, then we must also take seriously the notion that slaves were keenly aware of how the basis of white profit making rested on their bodies' fitness for labor.

Slave self-harm or at least the threat of it as a means of resistance is evident in the historical record. Dirt eating, in particular, was understood as a common form of self-harm, though less immediate and less dramatic than suicide. British inhabitants of Jamaica quickly drew connections between dirt eating and suicide among slaves and interpreted dirt eating as a possible response to the misery of enslavement: the violent, permanent removal from home. For example, Knight complained in 1742 of slaves' propensity to consume dirt: "some are so senseless as to imagine the White People have no other intention in bringing them from their Own Country, than to Eat them; and this notion causes them to Pine and take to eating of Dirt, or using other means to make away with themselves."[54] Slaves may have been wrong to assume that their bodies would be literally consumed by white people, but they were not wrong about how their bodies were essential to the creation of white profit. In other words, whites would not consume their bodies; the slave system would. The slow death brought on by consuming earth, then, would at least render slaves incapable of giving whites what they wanted (labor and productivity).

Self-harm, as a means of coping with the sundering of natal and cultural ties that took place during the slave trade, is a recurring theme in writings on dirt eating. Maxwell, whose writings were far removed from the slave trade, noted, "Whole gangs of Negroes had recourse to it [dirt eating], with a determination to kill themselves, firmly believing that after death, they would return to their native homes.—These causes have been long removed, and we must now look for others to account for this fatal propensity."[55] Slaves undoubtedly sacrificed their bodies as a means of depriving whites of the total control they sought over their slaves. Brown has ably demonstrated how slaves used the threat of self-destruction to complicate whites' sense of control in Jamaica. Brown notes that slave owners understood the very real threat of losing an able-bodied slave to suicide, especially among newly imported captive Africans. Indeed, many slaves were not above escaping the brutality and degradation of slavery through

168 DOCTRINE AND DISEASE

self-destruction.[56] And, as Maxwell made clear, self-harm via dirt eating was not limited to Africans desirous of returning to their native lands, nor was it purely a problem brought on by the slave trade.

The finality of suicide was just one way in which slaves denied slave owners access to the profit-making potential associated with their bodies. Slaves assumed no small degree of risk in using their bodies to manipulate slave owners. Some might try to preserve their strength and feign illness to be spared from labor, a point Sharla Fett demonstrates in her scholarship on health and healing in southern plantations in the United States.[57] Indeed, some physicians who practiced in Jamaica entertained the possibility that some slaves took to eating dirt "designedly to produce ill health, as the means of evading work, and becoming hospital patients, or idle invalids in the negroe-houses."[58] However, if caught, such deception typically carried with it corporal punishment, and thus the body they so sought to preserve from work could be subject to a far worse fate. From physicians' accounts, then, it is hard to know with exact certainty if slaves truly pretended dirt eating to gain concessions or actually engaged in the practice because they suffered from nutritional want or sought comfort in the practice.

Dancer's account of dirt eating provides us with perhaps the best evidence of slaves possibly pretending dirt eating as a means of manipulation. In an anecdotal footnote, Dancer recounted, "The negroes on an estate, from dissatisfaction took to eating Dirt, and great numbers of them died. The overseer being discharged, the complaint ceased, but the survivors declared that, if the Overseer had remained, they would all have given themselves up to the same fate."[59] With this example, Dancer showed what he perceived to be the lengths to which slaves would go to express their emotional discontent, but it is also illustrative of slaves' skill at manipulating whites, despite their oppressed status. The dirt eating that Dancer described could have been part of an underlying pathology, but it also could have been a kind of resistance, an articulation of collective defiance and desire for change. In either case, the slaves from Dancer's anecdote worked to deprive owners and overseers of the thing that they valued most, which was their labor.

Though Dancer, like many of his peers, often implicated Obeah as a cause of dirt eating, he did acknowledge that slaves could do much to bring on the disease themselves. "A deficiency of food, and hard labour, though it may contribute to bring on the disease, will not occasion it, where there is not a dissatisfaction or discontent of mind—on the contrary, these are alone or of themselves sufficient

ENSLAVED BODIES AND THE WHITE IMAGINATION 169

to cause it, without any ... hardship."[60] Dancer was willing to give plantation mismanagement only a partial, even secondary role in causing dirt eating. Taking this position certainly lessened whites' role in causing poor health on the plantation and maintained the idea that, overall, Blacks were less rational than whites were: easily led by their passions. However, in his desire to illustrate just how subject to their passions Blacks were, Dancer also revealed slaves' resourceful and resilient nature. As he continued to highlight the ways in which slaves' state of mind drove them to eat dirt, he mentioned that the causes for slaves' dissatisfaction included "a change of master, attorney, overseer, or Driver—the dispossessing them of their ground or habitations—shifting their residence, particularly from the lowlands to the mountains."[61] What Dancer attributed to slaves' discontent could equally have been viewed as disruptions to slaves' sense of justice or routine on the planation. Indeed, Dancer's description also reveals how dirt eating was used to protect against encroachments on slaves' autonomy. To pretend dirt eating or engage in the practice for the purposes of manipulation was to tap into white fears of slave mortality and financial ruin. It was, then, in this context, a possible tool of negotiation and certainly a calculated act.

The circumstances Dancer described in his 1801 guidebook were strikingly similar to another case conveyed years later by a physician who practiced in Dominica. John Imray, a licentiate of the Royal College of Surgeons Edinburgh, offered a similar story of a miraculous cure of dirt eating that took place after the departure of a plantation manager. According to Lennox Honeychurch, Imray joined the cadre of British men, mostly "civil servants and medical officers," who immigrated to Dominica in the nineteenth century to take leadership of the island. Imray was both a physician and botanist, whose research in cultivating specific agricultural products like "Liberian coffee and the lime 'ti citron vert'" reshaped the island's economy.[62]

Like Dancer, Imray viewed cases of dirt eating arising out of "annoyances sometimes of a trivial nature." He went on to explain how he learned from a French planter, "whose veracity every reliance could be placed," that, "on the estate of his family in Martinique, this disease ... was scarcely known, until the negroes, for some reason, formed a strong dislike to the manager. *Mal d'estomac* [dirt eating] then broke out amongst the people, and in one year, thirty died. The manager, at length perceiving the cause, left the estate, and from that period no other case afterwards appeared."[63] Whatever the reasons were for the slaves disliking their new manager, the act of eating dirt, which led to thirty deaths, could hardly have been trivial. Indeed, a cruel or incompetent manager

170 DOCTRINE AND DISEASE

could make life that much more miserable for enslaved populations—a point evidently lost on Imray. Thus, slaves worked collectively to improve their circumstances by exploiting white fears of dirt eating and the potential financial ruin it brought to plantations.

Questions remain, however, about how likely it was that the events Dancer and Imray described were true. The claim of the slaves struck down by dirt eating only to be cured upon the departure of a despised overseer reads almost like an allegory, a tale of warning that rough treatment and abuse of slaves portended tragedy. That Imray's account appeared in the prestigious *Edinburgh Medical and Surgical Journal* raises even more questions. Was Imray's true purpose to demonstrate to his mostly elite white medical professional audience how entirely governed by their emotions Black slaves were? In recounting this story, did Imray consider that the slaves' action was a form of manipulation? Did his readers? Could this case possibly be interpreted as an overdose of dirt; in other words, slaves seeking solace turned to eating dirt (clay) and consumed too much or the wrong kind? Neither Imray nor Dancer commented on how contingent dirt eating was on the type of overseer or manager in place on plantations. While both men conceded that slaves used deception, they made no mention of that when recounting these almost incredible anecdotes. Regardless of the truth of these cases, we can speculate either that slaves used the specter of disease to their advantage or that physicians believed slaves capable of doing so.

CONCLUSION

Data on precisely how many slaves across Jamaica engaged in dirt eating and died from it remain elusive. Deaths from dirt eating were inconsistently recorded. Indeed, some deaths that were attributed to "worms" or "dropsy" could very well have been linked to dirt eating.[64] Rather than a limitation of the historical record, the vagueness around the actual number of slave deaths makes white physicians' preoccupation with this disease all the more arresting. With no consensus as to the exact causes of dirt eating among slaves and no concrete sense of how many slaves died from it, white physicians across Jamaica convinced themselves that the disease presented a palpable threat to the plantation system and even a threat to their professional livelihoods. Dirt eating took on myth-like status as a disease to fear among white practitioners.

We can speculate that dirt eating, with its mysterious etiology and possible ties to Obeah, tested the limits of white physicians' authority on the plantation.

The confidence with which physicians described precise doses and restrictive diets for treating more well-understood diseases was largely absent in discussions of dirt eating or was accompanied by the disclaimer that remedies often failed to save the patient. Instead, physicians across the West Indies resorted to sharing hearsay knowledge about the disease. In Jamaica, they consistently blamed Obeah practitioners for causing the disease and accused slaves of deliberately bringing on the condition to challenge plantation administration. The result is a well-documented record of physicians' preoccupations with an otherwise obscure slave disease that opens up new avenues for understanding the lived experiences of enslaved people. In other words, published medical writings on dirt eating remain valuable, albeit indirect, sources that allow for a cautious reconstruction of previously understudied acts of slave resistance and coping.

NOTES

Rana A. Hogarth has written on this topic in *Medicalizing Blackness*, and some of the primary and secondary sources that appear in this chapter also in appear that book.

1. Dancer, *Medical Assistant*, 170. The second edition, published in 1809, lacks this dramatic introduction for the entry on dirt eating.

2. Dancer, *Medical Assistant*, 175.

3. Williamson, *Medical and Miscellaneous Observations*, 262.

4. Collins, *Practical Rules*, 342.

5. John Hunter, *Observations on the Diseases of the Army*, 313.

6. Dancer, *Medical Assistant*, 170.

7. Edward Kamau Brathwaite cites figures from 1820, suggesting about 20 percent of plantations having over one hundred slaves: "In 1820 there were 5,349 properties in Jamaica. Of these, 1,189 contained over 100 slaves or head of stock or both." He also cites U. B. Philips's assessment that "180 slaves would have been found on an average Jamaican sugar estate." For more, see Brathwaite, *Development of Creole Society*, 121, especially footnote 3.

8. Kiple, *Caribbean Slave*, 99.

9. Dirt eating continues to be a socially constructed disease, whose meanings change depending on context. The recent documentary *Eat White Dirt* (2015) by Adam Forrester and produced by the Willson Center for Humanities and Arts explores dirt eating in contemporary times with an emphasis on the disease as a "southern" practice, though the film acknowledges the practice's global dimensions. Dirt eating as it is construed in the film and the rationales for why professed dirt eaters engage in the practice cannot be superimposed on how and why slaves ate dirt in the past.

10. White, *Speaking with Vampires*, 57.

11. Kiple, *Caribbean Slave*, 96–103.

12. Johnson, "On Agency."

13. Camp, *Closer to Freedom*; Brown, *Reaper's Garden*; Browne, "'Bad Business' of Obeah."

14. Craton, *Testing the Chains*.

15. Kiple, *Caribbean Slave*, 103.

16. Kaopectate is now composed of Bismuth subsalicylate as its active ingredient, after the Food and Drug Administration of the United States (FDA) mandated a change to the formula in 2003.

17. According to Hunter, this practice lasted beyond antiquity in the West: "similar clay lozenges found in Silesia, Sicily, Malta, Portugal, Florence, Constantinople, Armenia and elsewhere were used by European physicians as late as the seventeenth century." John M. Hunter, "Geophagy in Africa," 170–71. Data also suggest that dirt eating occurred among Indigenous groups in the Americas. Reid, "Cultural and Medical Perspectives," 338.

18. Reid, "Cultural and Medical Perspectives," 338.

19. Reid, "Cultural and Medical Perspectives," 338.

20. Reid, "Cultural and Medical Perspectives."

21. The anthropologist Sera Young has confirmed current associations between dirt eating and pregnancy in her scholarship on pica. Young appears as an interviewee in the documentary *Eat White Dirt* (Forrester).

22. John M. Hunter, "Geophagy in Africa," 173–74.

23. John M. Hunter, "Geophagy in Africa," 173–74.

24. John M. Hunter, "Macroterme Geophagy and Pregnancy Clays," 75.

25. John M. Hunter, "Macroterme Geophagy and Pregnancy Clays," 75.

26. Thomson, *Treatise on the Diseases of Negroes*, 46.

27. In *Blackwood's Edinburgh Magazine*, a James Thomson, MD, is listed as having passed on January 5, 1822; his place of residence is given as "Crawle estate in St Thomas in the Vale." See "Births, Marriages, and Deaths," 502.

28. Thomson, *Treatise on the Diseases of Negroes*, 3.

29. Thomson, *Treatise on the Diseases of Negroes*, 46.

30. Maxwell, "Pathological Inquiry into Cachexia Africana," 416.

31. Maxwell, "Pathological Inquiry into Cachexia Africana," 416.

32. Maxwell's MD thesis, "Observations on Yaws and Its Influence in Originating Leprosy," won a gold medal from the University of Edinburgh in 1839, and upon completing his degree, Maxwell returned to Jamaica, where he continued to practice. For more, see Hogarth, *Medicalizing Blackness*; and Stewart, "James Maxwell," 112.

33. Maxwell, "Pathological Inquiry into Cachexia Africana," 412.

34. Maxwell, "Pathological Inquiry into Cachexia Africana," 412. The passage is also cited in Hogarth, *Medicalizing Blackness*, 214n38.

35. Long, *History of Jamaica*, 851–52.

36. Handler, "Slave Medicine and Obeah."

37. Handler and Bilby, "Obeah," 153. See also Handler, "Slave Medicine and Obeah."

38. Handler and Bilby, "Obeah," 153.

39. Handler and Bilby, "Obeah," 154.

40. Handler and Bilby, "Obeah," 154.

41. Hogarth, *Medicalizing Blackness*, 87; Paton, "Obeah Acts," 4.

42. Paton, "Obeah Acts," 4.

43. Maxwell, "Pathological Inquiry into Cachexia Africana," 411.

44. Maxwell, "Pathological Inquiry into Cachexia Africana," 412. Hogarth, *Medicalizing Blackness*, chapter 3.

45. I have found no references to whites being susceptible to Obeah in Maxwell's, Thomson's, or Dancer's writings on dirt eating. It is unclear if these physicians truly believed that there was a racialized difference in susceptibility between Blacks and whites or if they simply did not bother to consider or compare cases; ailments in white people were suspected of being brought on through psychological rather than somatic factors.

46. Dancer, *Medical Assistant*, 176.

47. Edwards, *History, Civil and Commercial*, 167.

48. Thomson, *Treatise on the Disease of Negroes*, 46.

49. Brown, *Reaper's Garden*, 131.

50. Maxwell, "Pathological Inquiry into Cachexia Africana," 411. Parts of this passage are also quoted in Hogarth, *Medicalizing Blackness*, chapter 3.

51. Maxwell, "Pathological Inquiry into Cachexia Africana," 411–12; Hogarth, *Medicalizing Blackness*, chapter 3.

52. Knight, "Of the Inhabitants, Masters, Servants, and Negroes," 496.

53. Grainger, *Essay*, 91–92.

54. Knight, "Of the Inhabitants, Masters, Servants, and Negroes," 485.

55. Maxwell, "Pathological Inquiry into Cachexia Africana," 413.

56. Brown, *Reaper's Garden*, 132.

57. Fett, *Working Cures*, 171.

58. Mason, "On *Atrophia a Ventriculo*," 291. Mason is one of the few physicians to explicitly draw connections between dirt eating and purposefully avoiding work. He is also one of the physicians of this era to omit any discussion of Obeah.

59. Dancer, *Medical Assistant*, 175.

60. Dancer, *Medical Assistant*, 175.

61. Dancer, *Medical Assistant*, 175.

62. Honeychurch, *Dominica Story*, 145–46.

63. Imray, "Observations on the Mal d'Estomac," 305.

64. A handful of scholars cite statistics that allege dirt eating caused nearly 50 percent of deaths among slaves in Jamaica in 1687. Abrahams and Parsons, "Geophagy in the Tropics," 65. This

statistic is particularly arresting and difficult to verify given the inconsistent and vague way causes of death were listed among slaves. Abrahams and Parson attribute this statistic to a 1987 article by McNeill, "History of Medicine."

BIBLIOGRAPHY

Abrahams, Peter W., and Julia A. Parsons. "Geophagy in the Tropics: A Literature Review." *Geographical Journal* 162 (March 1996): 63–72.

"Births, Marriages, and Deaths." *Blackwood's Edinburgh Magazine* 11 (April 1822): 501–2.

Brathwaite, Edward Kamau. *The Development of Creole Society in Jamaica, 1770–1820.* Oxford, UK: Clarendon, 1971.

Brown, Vincent. *The Reaper's Garden: Death and Power in the World of Atlantic Slavery.* Cambridge, MA: Harvard University Press, 2008.

Browne, Randy M. "The 'Bad Business' of Obeah: Power, Authority, and the Politics of Slave Culture in the British Caribbean." *William and Mary Quarterly* 68, no. 3 (2011): 451–80.

Camp, Stephanie. *Closer to Freedom: Enslaved Women and Everyday Resistance in the Plantation South.* Chapel Hill: University of North Carolina Press, 2004.

Collins, Dr. *Practical Rules for the Management and Medical Treatment of Negro Slaves in the Sugar Colonies by a Professional Planter.* London: J. Barfield for Vernor and Hood, 1803.

Craton, Michael. *Testing the Chains: Resistance to Slavery in the British West Indies.* Ithaca: Cornell University Press, 1982.

Dancer, Thomas. *Medical Assistant; or, Jamaica Practice of Physic.* Kingston, Jamaica: Alexander Aikman, 1801.

Edwards, Bryan. *The History, Civil and Commercial, of the British Colonies in the West Indies.* Vol. 2. 3rd ed. London: John Stockdale, 1801.

Fett, Sharla. *Working Cures: Healing, Health, and Power on Southern Slave Plantations.* Chapel Hill: University of North Carolina Press. 2002.

Forrester, Adam, dir. *Eat White Dirt.* Produced by the Willson Center for Humanities and Arts. 2015. https://www.youtube.com /watch?v=kbsdKInA6dk.

Grainger, James. *An Essay on the More Common West India Diseases: And the Remedies, Which That Country Itself Produces: To Which Are Added Some Hints on the Management & of Negroes.* 2nd ed. Edinburgh: Mundell and Son, 1802.

Handler, Jerome. "Slave Medicine and Obeah in Barbados, circa 1650–1834." *New West Indian Guide* 74 (2000): 57–90.

Handler, Jerome, and Kenneth M. Bilby. "Obeah: Healing and Protection in West Indian Slave Life." *Journal of Caribbean History* 38, no. 2 (2004): 153–83.

Hogarth, Rana. *Medicalizing Blackness: Making Racial Difference in the Atlantic World, 1780–1840.* Chapel Hill: University of North Carolina, Press, 2017.

Honeychurch, Lennox. *The Dominica Story: History of the Island.* London: Macmillan Education, 1995.

Hunter, John. *Observations on the Diseases of the Army in Jamaica; and on the Best Means of Preserving the Health of Europeans, in that Climate.* London: G. Nicol, 1788.

Hunter, John M. "Geophagy in Africa and the United States: A Culture Nutrition Hypothesis." *Geographical Review* 63, no. 2 (1973): 170–95.

———. "Macroterme Geophagy and Pregnancy Clays in Southern Africa." *Journal of Cultural Geography* 14, no. 1 (1993): 69–92.

Imray, John. "Observations on the Mal d'Estomac." *Edinburgh Medical and Surgical Journal* 59, no. 155 (1843): 304–21.

Johnson, Walter. "On Agency." *Journal of Social History* 37 (2003): 113–24.

Kiple, Kenneth. *The Caribbean Slave: A Biological History.* Cambridge: Cambridge University Press, 1984.

Knight, James. "Of the Inhabitants, Masters, Servants, and Negroes; Their Number, Strength and Manner of Living; as Also an Account of the Negroes, Who Were Many Years in Rebellion, and Settled in the Mountains, Together with the Treaty Made with Them in 1738, upon Which They Submitted, and Became Free

Subjects of Great Britain." In *The Natural, Moral, and Political History of Jamaica, and the Territories Thereon Depending: From the First Discovery of the Island by Christopher Columbus to the Year 1746*, edited by Jack P. Greene and Taylor Stoermer, 470–510. Charlottesville: University of Virginia Press, 2021.

Long, Edward. *History of Jamaica*. Vol. 3. London: T. Lowndes, 1774.

Mason, David. "On *Atrophia a Ventriculo* (Mal d'Estomac,) or Dirt-Eating." *Edinburgh Medical and Surgical Journal* 39, no. 115 (1833): 289–96.

Maxwell, James. "Pathological Inquiry into Cachexia Africana as It Is Generally Connected with Dirt Eating." *Jamaica Physical Journal*, November–December 1835, 409–35.

McNeill, K. "A History of Medicine and Surgery in Jamaica." *Journal of the Medical Association of Jamaica* 1 (1987): 7–12.

Paton, Diana. "Obeah Acts: Producing and Policing the Boundaries of Religion in the Caribbean." *Small Axe* 28 (2009): 1–18.

Reid, Russell M. "Cultural and Medical Perspectives on Geophagia." *Medical Anthropology* 13, no. 4 (1992): 337–51.

Stewart, D. B. "James Maxwell (1795–1862): A Good Scottish-Jamaica Doctor." *West Indian Medical Journal* 43 (1994): 112–16.

Thomson, James. *A Treatise on the Diseases of Negroes, as They Occur in the Island of Jamaica: With Observations on the Country Remedies*. London: Alex Aikman, 1820.

White, Luise. *Speaking with Vampires: Rumor and History in Colonial Africa*. Berkeley: University of California Press, 2000.

Williamson, John. *Medical and Miscellaneous Observations Relative to the West India Islands*. Vol. 2. Edinburgh: A. Smellie, 1817.

Afterword

REBECCA TOTARO

The chapters in this volume offer fascinating examinations of the complex problems and exciting opportunities that surfaced as Europeans expanded their Atlantic trade routes and encountered both new diseases and the medical and religious practices of Africans, Indigenous peoples, and others whose beliefs were not always easily accommodated, let alone understood. This exposure to new peoples, places, ideas, and technologies brought with it fears, exposed blind spots, and held the promise of radical, positive discovery. The same is the case again today, in our internationally interconnected world. Grappling with the COVID-19 pandemic, we, too, experienced profound fears, realized blind spots, and benefited, in some cases, from innovative approaches to old problems. The thoughtful and rigorously interdisciplinary chapters in this volume thus serve doubly to highlight the challenges emerging at the crossroads of medicine and religion in the early modern Atlantic world and to shine a light on present-day clashes over the ownership of best practices related to illness and health.

The distance between our medical and religious beliefs did not always feel quite so vast. Prehistoric groups (and existing remote communities) with amply shared oral histories communicated (and still communicate) their beliefs with one another through time-honored rituals, reinforcing regularly and locally the ties binding religious and medical beliefs.[1] The internal integrity within and integration of religious and medical beliefs was the norm for centuries among medieval Europeans and Indigenous peoples alike. These time-honored rituals and practices were placed under special stress, however, not only by increases in exploration and "new" territory settlement efforts but also by the rise of European humanism, challenges to the Catholic Church, the increasing proliferation of dissent within

176 DOCTRINE AND DISEASE

Protestantism, and corresponding increases in literacy and in easily disseminated printed texts. For example, as Crawford Gribben explains, with England as his focus and quoting N. H. Keeble, "the 1660s" brought "a sequence of terrible calamities" (56) that called authority over spiritual and physical health into question, such that "writing about health and healing became an important, if relatively understudied, part of the 'literary culture of nonconformity'" (59). Even among Puritans, Gribben shows, consistent denominational adherence to a set of religious and medical beliefs and practices was nearly impossible, with communities often stretched across not just nations but oceans and with the shifting securities of colonial ventures and pandemic disease adding to the challenges. Ties to traditional ways of being and coherence within communities were eroding.

This erosion of beliefs and practices is part of the dynamic historical context examined in this volume—one that demands rigorous interdisciplinary and archival research practices from those scholars who undertake the challenge. Early modernist scholars were until recently experts principally in their own narrowly prescribed disciplines, often unable to identify, understand, or give due to the many converging contextual fields that a study such as the one at hand demands. The scholars contributing to this volume, in contrast, are practitioners able not only to conduct the layered thinking, research, and writing necessary to understand the confluences and conflicts related to medicine, religion, and culture but also to convey these findings with high use value for us now, aware as we are of the need to continue this important interdisciplinary work, in the academy and beyond. The contributors' diverse areas of expertise span the fields of Iberian Atlantic history (Matthew James Crawford); Spain, Latin America, and gender studies (Allyson M. Poska); religion, history, and anthropology (Crawford Gribben); the history of religion in America, with a focus on colonial America and the Atlantic world (Philippa Koch); early modern plague writing and gender (Kathleen Miller); transatlantic medicine, politics, and religion (Catherine Reedy); and medical and scientific constructions of race during the era of slavery (Rana A. Hogarth). As their contributions show, the rigor with which they perform their expertise extends in two directions: to the labor-intensive detail of archival manuscript review that painstakingly sifts words in script and in translation and to the continent-crossing contexts of the big-picture content of this volume. This volume is thus both fascinating, due to its depth and range, and a rare gift, demanding so much from its practitioners that few scholars ever hazard to undertake it.

AFTERWORD   177

In the balance of this afterword, my goal is to illuminate just one of many lenses through which to appreciate and use this volume as a scholarly aid, as a reflection on our recent pandemic period, and as a guide to future intersections of religion and medicine. A recent pandemic and coming threats from climate change are forcing us to grapple with basic questions of survival that the early moderns whose works feature in this volume also faced. Under new pressures, to what degree are our resources stable? How long and with what quality might we and our loved ones live? In the interim, where do we place our energies and with whom do we partner for survival? As the chapters in this volume also attest, encounters with radical otherness and the corresponding potential for profound change produce fear, expose our blind spots, and open unforeseen paths for opportunity and growth.

FEAR

This volume's chapters by Matthew James Crawford, Rana A. Hogarth, and Philippa Koch expose the pronounced fears related to the intersections of medicine, religion, culture, and power that in the period treated in this volume were emerging regularly and with repercussions often beyond the vision of their instigators and perpetuators. Crawford examines how Jesuit missionaries in Peru appropriated Indigenous medical products in part by erasing knowledge of the potentially fear-producing contexts of their use in Indigenous spiritual practice. Similarly, Hogarth finds that the eighteenth-century white physicians who diagnosed pica (dirt eating) among Jamaican slaves treated it only in the context of the moral failing of those who exhibited its symptoms. This relegation of its consideration to enslaved populations served to underscore their radical otherness in the eyes of those who benefited from the slave trade. With respect to the codification of birth and nursing practices in seventeenth- and eighteenth-century midwifery manuals, Koch similarly exposes a desire to diminish the suffering of others in preference for tidy explanations that advance the agendas of those in power. The midwifery manuals she examines fundamentally diminish the complexity of birth and nursing practices to impose on them a Western Christian religious framework of morality.

Taking a closer look at Crawford's chapter instructively paints some of the side effects resulting from overcorrecting for fear. Early on, Crawford details what will be one of his main claims in this regard:

178 DOCTRINE AND DISEASE

> By looking more closely at Jesuit efforts to collect, extract and re-present knowledge of medicinal plants from Indigenous peoples in Peru from the sixteenth to the eighteenth centuries, this chapter argues that the writings of Jesuit missionaries about medicinal plants contributed to the broader and longer process of the secularization of nature. In the context of Spanish colonial frontiers, the spiritual meanings attributed to medicinal plants by Indigenous healers were considered erroneous, if not heretical, and, in some contexts, dangerous. As a result, Jesuit missionaries sought to strip knowledge of medicinal plants of the connotations of Indigenous religions and aimed to extract only the most pragmatic and naturalistic knowledge of these plants and their medicinal uses. (20)

The fear of Peruvian conflations of culture, religion, and medicine and the association Jesuits had made in some cases between Peruvian healers and "the Devil" sanctioned Jesuit efforts to strip the medicinal products of prior contexts (27). What the Jesuits were unable to anticipate is that Protestants would later use the same tactic to strip the Jesuit contexts from the same products: "As [Andrés] Prieto and others have observed, the Jesuits were largely written out of the history of science for a long time. In part, this situation was a result of a historiographical tradition originating in the Protestant lands of northern Europe that were suspicious of, if not hostile toward, the Catholic Church and its institutions" (34). Then, as now, encounters with new diseases and with the medical and religious practices of those whose religious beliefs are not always easily accommodated will excite fear and the desire to neutralize that fear, often with unintended consequences.

The fear-based responses to encounters with new diseases and/or new medicinal treatments discussed in the chapters by Crawford, Hogarth, and Koch show efforts, respectively, to streamline and then generalize products to remove any uncomfortable taint of prior use; to isolate a practice and label it as so heinously other as to shut down further discussion of its still more feared causes (in the case of dirt eating, those being malnutrition and/or resistance); and to press into the service of Christian values the common but messy, painful, and dangerous lived experience of motherhood. These efforts to tidy up the human condition would, in hindsight, seem doomed to fail, but clearly their practitioners were as committed to them as many people in the COVID-19 pandemic were committed to theirs.

BLIND SPOTS

Some responses to new or otherwise threatening situations are not born of fear so much as of what we might call metaphorical blind spots or, perhaps more accurately, achromatic vision. These two conditions I define by way of Duncan Sabien's explanation in his essay "The Metaphor You Want is 'Color Blindness,' Not 'Blind Spot'":

> We often use "blind spot" as a metaphor to gesture toward things we are unaware of, while also being at least somewhat unaware *of our unawareness*—we know that something fishy is going on, but we can't quite get our eyes on it, e.g., "I think I might have a blind spot when it comes to status dynamics." The thing about status dynamics, though, is that they aren't in *one spot*. There isn't a whole world that is being fully and accurately perceived, except for one blank space that's being glossed over. Instead, what's usually going on (at least in my experience) is that the person can see *everything*, but there's some crucial component of the picture that they are [entirely] unable to process or comprehend.[2]

The "crucial component" missed might be colors in a certain spectrum, for example, which would alter the whole picture enough to make progress impossible despite "see[ing] *everything*." Responding to a novel threat—pandemic or otherwise—humans will always face challenges to their perception of it, at least initially. Resilience demands that we recognize the likelihood that we should not be looking for the blind spot to correct, the singular patient zero, for example. We will as often need a new paradigm from which to assess the threat, and this paradigm may simply be out of reach, which then will demand devising other strategies.

Two of the chapters in this volume treat actions, the practice of which is symptomatic of Sabien's metaphorical vision problems. In chapter 6, Catherine Reedy productively wonders about the seemingly hypocritical fasting practices of Massachusetts Bay Colony:

> If concerns over set forms of worship had sent the ritual-shunning, Christmas-less colonists away from England, one wonders what to make of the repetitive quality of these days, with their providential charge and high stakes, as they gradually smoothed into the very seasonal spring

180 DOCTRINE AND DISEASE

fast and autumnal feast so initially dreaded. . . . On the other hand, the increasing regularity of these court-appointed fasts and thanksgivings perpetuated a sense of "ritual life," something remarkable given what Alex Ryrie calls the ritual "phobia" of Protestants more generally, as "for a religion so phobic about ritual activity this was the perfect ritual, for fasting of course consists of *abstinence* from activity. It was one of the ways in which Protestantism could re-acquire a ritual life despite itself."[3]

Reedy's examination of the Massachusetts Bay Colony's use of fasting in the management of smallpox outbreaks and other emergent crises highlights the "despite [ourselves]" nature of many human practices related to disease management. In the face of novel or extreme threats—as in adopting life in a colony far from one's birthplace or in knowing that bubonic plague has visited one's own city—we adopt comfortable practices without entirely believing in them and/or without having the time or energy, already expended toward survival, to find viable alternatives.

In the face of new threats, it is understandable that we would cling to known practices that are already part of our shared cultural, religious, or medical inheritances. In chapter 5 in this volume, Kathleen Miller provides another layered example of this phenomenon. New England colonists appropriated English thinking and practices related to bubonic plague to help them process their experiences with smallpox, finding within them a meaningful medical and religious framework that functioned to close the gap in time and place from their kin back in England. In their eagerness to read plague works to understand a disease with very different causes and symptoms, we see what we might consider a willing unawareness of the difference between the diseases and thus an acceptance of achromatic vision more comfortable to endure than actual change in beliefs and practices. In Sabian's words, "The person can see *everything*, but there's some crucial component of the picture that they are unable to process or comprehend." In this case, the colonists were unable medically to distinguish between the two diseases—one "crucial component" they lacked being bubonic plague's bacterial versus smallpox's viral transmission. Using the early modern Galenic medicine most common at the time as well as religion to understand both diseases provided the colonists with the shades of gray that monochromatically, and comfortingly, aligned them.

In the case presented by Reedy, it is especially striking that a people fleeing from rather than hoping to stay connected to a particular set of religious practices should turn around and, in a most critical time of need, double down in those very practices that had been vehemently abandoned. She asks again, "why did the fast hold such a central place in both England's and Massachusetts's days of occasional worship?" (121). Part of her answer, as can be applied to the phenomenon that Miller observes, is that the two territories inherited medical practices rooted in the same tradition of Galenic medicine. Those medical beliefs predated Protestantism and even Catholicism by centuries and were the shared inheritance—and shared source of comfort—for both.

OPPORTUNITY

The intersections between medicine and religion considered in this volume result in mixed or negative outcomes more often than they result in positive ones. Allyson M. Poska's chapter 2 stands as a near exception, with its example of an existing framework of faith used to improve health in the face of a novel threat. Poska finds, "the Spanish Crown initiated the first truly global health campaign" to manage smallpox by working through its Catholic Church network in overseas territories and by "opening of vaccination rooms in hospitals across Spain" and in Spanish-held territories (41). The Crown and church, she explains, practiced "what Yves-Marie Berce has called a 'theology of hygiene'" (49), with the following impacts:

> Most of the ecclesiastical hierarchy, from bishops to parish priests to missionary friars, eagerly complied. Bishops enjoined their clergy to extoll the virtues of vaccination and encouraged their parishioners to submit themselves and their charges to the procedure. They put on spectacles, gave sermons, opened their coffers, and used their influence to gently persuade parents about the efficacy of the vaccine. At a critical moment, the church's participation fulfilled an array of political, social, and spiritual goals. Promoting vaccination reinforced the church's relationship with the Crown, provided a new way to fulfill pastoral responsibilities, and reasserted its authority over the bodies and souls of parishioners throughout the Spanish Empire. (51)

This is a scenario in which overall health improved because faith, government, and science came together consistently, on multiple levels and over time, to advance health care. The willingness of those in the Church's care to embrace

182 DOCTRINE AND DISEASE

change was, moreover, managed in a largely transparent fashion: the scientific, governmental, and religious communities shared knowledge, disseminated that knowledge consistently to their shared populations, and were responsive to the lived, on-the-ground needs of those whom they served both in Spain and in the Spanish colonies.

The situation Poska describes in nineteenth-century Spain tracks with what Gary Gunderson and Teresa Cutts saw during COVID-19: "faith communities [acting] as a social immune system." "Already present, [faith communities] were ready for the unthinkable and not as isolated cells," they explain, "but connected to broader faith networks. Acting like fibroblasts do in physical injuries, the immune response created a locally relevant connective tissue.... Faith assets, like an immune system, are interconnected in unpredictably effective ways, mobilizing resources, information and more. Science can travel across such connections in the form of testing, counsel, vaccines and direct access to medical care."[4] When we think about our future of pandemics among the many symptoms accompanying climate change, science and government would do well to embrace their faith communities in this way. Leuconoe Grazia Sisti and colleagues agree, explaining recently in "The Role of Religions in the COVID-19 Pandemic: A Narrative Review," "Health systems and health policy should become more sensitive to religious and cultural issues, for example, by training the health workforce and structuring cultural and religious-sensitive health pathways. In turn, religious organizations can act as intermediaries to reach out to communities that may have difficulties in accessing health services or are resistant to implementing evidence-based measures."[5] Poska shows that the Spanish government did just this, mobilizing the church and then allowing local communities to share information and roll out a vaccination campaign that would be flexible enough to acknowledge uniquely local needs.

What Sisti and colleagues conclude from their work finds exemplification in one salient example from the COVID-19 pandemic that illustrates why even greater sensitivity to complexities across hardened boundaries matters. The Spanish government was able to succeed with its campaign in the 1800s in part, as Poska admits, because "to a significant degree, the church and its clergy functioned as an arm of the Spanish monarchy, which then employed the church and its resources to advance its own political and social goals" (42). The United States and other democracies do not already have such alignment, nor do they desire it. They also have track records that can make trust in them a challenge. Among the reasons for vaccine hesitancy in the United States, for example, was the federal government origin of and payment for the COVID-19 vaccine. As Joel D. Howell explains, "African Americans' hesitancy to take the vaccine comes in part from an awareness of the medical system's long-standing structural racism. One of the most visible ways racism was made manifest was in multiple instances of physicians carrying out unethical experiments using African Americans. Two of the most well-known examples of such experimentation are the infamous experiments done by J. Marion Sims and the experiments done in and around Tuskegee, Alabama."[6] For these and other reasons, the need to repackage the COVID-19 vaccine to remove the taint of this rightly fearful context was clear. The scientific community and federal government chose to invest with care in, rather than abandon, those communities by taking a series of actions, working with states to reach out to Black churches, barber shops, and beauty parlors and to other groups trusted by the populations that did not trust either scientists or the government. The aim was to show that transparent, respectful, locally integrated communication can make a difference.

According to studies of those efforts, the results were worth all investment. DaKysha Moore and colleagues, for example, report, "As trusted leaders in their communities, Black pastors are in a unique position to promote equitable community outreach for COVID-19 vaccination in Black communities. In this study, pastors played an integral role in increasing access to relevant and accurate COVID-19 vaccine information and reducing structural barriers to vaccine access in Black communities in South Carolina experiencing low vaccination rates. Future public health efforts should support and invest in local Black congregations to establish a sustainable infrastructure to disseminate COVID-19-related information and to provide resources needed for COVID-19 outreach."[7] The researchers N. Kenji Taylor and colleagues found similar barber shop outreach of high value in viably disseminating lifesaving health information:

> In our study, many barbers were already engaged in health outreach in Black communities and were even more committed to partnering with the public health and health service delivery system as public health extenders, despite the challenges they faced as a result of COVID-19. Barber-administered health education and promotion along with direct linkage to health systems should be a focus in designing interventions to prevent the spread of COVID-19 and future variants. Future research should examine how to best implement barbershop-based COVID-19

184 DOCTRINE AND DISEASE

public health interventions, while supporting them to safely keep their doors open to the Black community, including providing the necessary PPE [personal protective equipment]. Furthermore, studies may also evaluate the essential nature of barbering as it relates to the health impacts of limited barbering in black communities as has been suggested by our research during the COVID-19 pandemic.[8]

Moore and colleagues' and Taylor and colleagues' examinations show what can happen when barriers of fear and achromatic vision are acknowledged and respectfully navigated in order to build bridges to close the gaps between us.

CONCLUSION

The contributors to this volume did not intend to uncover trends in early modern reactions to change from which we should learn, but they have. This is in part because the proverbial lessons we fail to learn are ones we will repeat. It is also because the chapters do, per Miller's introductory description, "demonstrate that ... the delivery of medical care was contingent on geographical context and the religious and spiritual beliefs of the people who lived there" (5). This volume's valuable thick descriptions of lived experience are thus of great value to us now, featuring important lessons about human behavior that we keep having to relearn. With prescriptive and precautionary accounts of transatlantic encounters, this volume underscores the fact that if we are to navigate our own futures well, we will need as much hindsight as possible, even if it can never be 20/20, and we will need an increasingly resilient social immune system that is at once interconnected globally *and* rooted in local communities that know they are respected and supported.

NOTES

1. On Indigenous spirituality and medicine, see Fleming and Ledogar, "Resilience and Indigenous Spirituality"; Oliver, "Role of Traditional Medicine Practice"; Brady, "WHO Defines Health?"; and Brady, "Culture in Treatment." See also Spiro, Curnen, and Wandel, *Facing Death.*

2. Sabien, "Metaphor."

3. Reedy here cites Ryrie, "Fall and Rise," 128, and further notes, "For the shift towards seasonal fasting, see Love, *Fast and Thanksgiving Days.*"

Reedy also cites here Massachusetts Bay Colony, *Records of the Governor,* vol. 1.

4. Gunderson and Cutts, "Faith Communities," 154–55.

5. Sisti et al., "Role of Religions," 16.

6. Howell, "Understanding Black Distrust of Medicine."

7. Moore et al., "Role of Black Pastors," 7–8. See also Taylor et al., "Pandemic Through the Lens"; Bugos, "Initiative Leverages Barbershops"; and Antlfinger, "Black Community Has New Option."

8. Taylor et al., "Pandemic Through the Lens," 664.

BIBLIOGRAPHY

Antlfinger, Carrie. "Black Community Has New Option for Health Care: The Church." Associated Press, June 17, 2021. https://apnews.com/article/race-and-ethnicity-coronavirus-pandemic-health-religion-2d92637b5e86dbb939a37aef17fa5a8d.

Brady, M. "Culture in Treatment, Culture as Treatment." *Social Science and Medicine* 41, no. 11 (1995): 1487–98.

———. "WHO Defines Health? Implications of Differing Definitions on Discourse and Practice in Aboriginal Health." In *Aboriginal Health: Social and Cultural Transitions*, edited by Gary Robinson, 187–92. Darwin: NTU Press, 1995.

Bugos, Claire. "Initiative Leverages Barbershops to Increase Vaccination Among Black Americans." *Very Well Health*, June 15, 2021. https://www.verywellhealth.com/initiative-leverages-barbershops-to-increase-vaccination-among-black-americans-5188686.

Fleming, John, and Robert J. Ledogar. "Resilience and Indigenous Spirituality: A Literature Review." *Pimatisiwin* 6, no. 2 (2008): 47–64.

Gunderson, Gary, and Teresa Cutts. "Faith Communities as a Social Immune System: Recommendations for COVID-19 Response and Recovery." *Journal of Creative Communications* 16, no. 2 (2021): 153–67.

Howell, Joel D. "Understanding Black Distrust of Medicine." *Findings* (Michigan School of Health Magazine), May 14, 2021. https://sph.umich.edu/findings/spring-2021/black-distrust-of-medicine-from-sims-to-tuskegee-and-its-impact-on-vaccine-hesitancy.html.

Love, William DeLoss. *The Fast and Thanksgiving Days of New England*. Boston: Houghton, Mifflin, 1895.

Massachusetts Bay Colony. *Records of the Governor and Company of Massachusetts Bay Colony*. Vol. 1, *1628–1641*. Edited by Nathaniel B. Shurtleff. Boston: William White, 1853.

Moore, DaKysha, Lisa N. Mansfield, Elijah O. Onsomu, and Nicole Caviness-Ashe. "The Role of Black Pastors in Disseminating COVID-19 Vaccination Information to Black Communities in South Carolina." *International Journal of Environmental Research and Public Health* 19, no. 15 (2022): 1–10.

Oliver, Stefanie J. "The Role of Traditional Medicine Practice in Primary Health Care Within Aboriginal Australia: A Review of the Literature." *Journal of Ethnobiology and Ethnomedicine* 9, no. 46 (2013).

Ryrie, Alex. "The Fall and Rise of Fasting in the British Reformations." In *Worship and the Parish Church in Early Modern Britain*, edited by Alex Ryrie and Natalie Mears, 89–108. Farnham, UK: Ashgate, 2013.

Sabien, Duncan. "The Metaphor You Want is 'Color Blindness,' Not 'Blind Spot.'" *Less Wrong*, February 13, 2022. https://www.lesswrong.com/posts/7Pq9KwZhG6vejmYpo/the-metaphor-you-want-is-color-blindness-not-blind-spot.

Sisti, Leuconoe Grazia, Danilo Buonsenso, Umberto Moscato, Gianfranco Costanzo, and Walter Malorni, "The Role of Religions in the COVID-19 Pandemic: A Narrative Review." *International Journal of Environmental Research and Public Health* 20, no. 3 (2023): 1–20.

Spiro, Howard M., Mary G. McCrea Curnen, and Lee Palmer Wandel, eds. *Facing Death: Where Culture, Religion, and Medicine Meet*. New Haven: Yale University Press, 1996.

Taylor, N. Kenji, Melvin Faulks, Cati G. Brown-Johnson, Lisa G. Rosas, Jonathan G. Shaw, Erika A. Saliba-Gustafsson, and Steven M. Asch. "Pandemic Through the Lens of Black Barbershops: COVID-19's Impact and Barbers' Potential Role as Public Health Extenders." *Journal of Immigrant and Minority Health* 25, no. 3 (2023): 660–65.

CONTRIBUTORS

MATTHEW JAMES CRAWFORD is an associate professor in the Department of History at Kent State University. He is a specialist in the history of science, medicine, and knowledge in the early modern Spanish Atlantic world. He is author of *The Andean Wonder Drug: Cinchona Bark and Imperial Science in the Spanish Atlantic World, 1630–1800* and coeditor of *Drugs on the Page: Pharmacopoeias in the Early Modern Atlantic World.*

CRAWFORD GRIBBEN is a professor of early modern British history at Queen's University Belfast. He is the author of several books on Puritan literary cultures, including *John Owen and English Puritanism: Experience of Defeat* and *An Introduction to John Owen,* and the coeditor of titles including *The T&T Clark Handbook on John Owen.* His current projects include writing a book titled *John Owen's Social Network: Friends, Rivals, and the Literary Culture of Nonconformity* and coediting Owen's unpublished sermons for a critical edition, titled *The Sermons of John Owen: Notes from the Congregation, 1667–1683,* with Martyn Cowan and Zachary McCulley. He coedits the monograph series Christianities in the Trans-Atlantic World.

RANA A. HOGARTH is an associate professor in the Department of History and Sociology of Science at the University of Pennsylvania. researches the creation of ideas about racial difference in the Anglophone Americas as they emerged through the language of medicine and its allied fields. She is the author of *Medicalizing Blackness: Making Racial Difference in the Atlantic World, 1780–1840,* which examines how white physicians defined Blackness in slave societies of the American Atlantic. Her research has appeared in *Social History of Medicine, American Quarterly,* and *American Journal of Public Health* and in the edited volume *Medicine and Healing in the Age of Slavery.*

PHILIPPA KOCH is an associate professor of religious studies at Missouri State University. Her research and teaching center on religion, health, and society in North America and the global context. Her recent publications include "Records of Relinquishment: Caregiving and Emotion in the Philanthropy Archive," an article that appeared in the *Public Historian* in May 2024, as well as her first book, *The Course of God's Providence: Religion, Health, and the Body in Early America*. She is currently working on her next book, *Religion and Medicine in America*.

KATHLEEN MILLER is a visiting scholar at Queen's University Belfast. After receiving her PhD in English literature and book history from Trinity College Dublin, she published *The Literary Culture of Plague in Early Modern England* and coedited *Dublin: Renaissance City of Literature*. She is completing her second monograph, on women's plague writing in early modern England, based on research completed during the Marie Skłodowska-Curie Postdoctoral Fellowship she held at the University of Toronto and Queen's University Belfast.

ALLYSON M. POSKA is a professor of history emerita at the University of Mary Washington in Fredericksburg, Virginia, and the author of four books: *Gendered Crossings: Women and Migration in the Spanish Empire*, winner of the 2017 best book prize from the Society for the Study of Early Modern Women; *Women and Authority in Early Modern Spain: The Peasants of Galicia*, winner of the 2006 Roland H. Bainton Prize for best book in early modern history or theology; *Women and Gender in the Western Past* (two volumes, coauthored with Katherine French); and *Regulating the People: The Catholic Reformation in Seventeenth-Century Spain*. She coedited *The Ashgate Research Companion to Women and Gender in Early Modern Europe* (with Jane Couchman and Katherine McIver). She was coeditor of *Early Modern Women: An Interdisciplinary Journal* (with Bernadette Andrea and Julie Campbell). Her current project examines the role of race and gender in the spread of smallpox vaccination in the Spanish Empire.

CATHERINE REEDY is a visiting assistant professor of English at Lake Forest College, where her teaching and research interests include English Renaissance drama, medical and religious practices, and narratives of revenge and disease. Her work has been published or is forthcoming in *Early Modern Literary Studies*, *Historicizing the Embodied Imagination in Early Modern English Literature*, and the Map of Early Modern London digital resource. She received her doctorate from Harvard University, where she studied revenge, poison, and the plague. When not avoiding all three of those forces in her own life, she is at work on a book-length study on contagion and performance, tentatively titled *Pestilent Congregations: Drama and Devotion in the Early Modern Theater*.

REBECCA TOTARO is associate dean of curriculum and assessment and a professor of English in the College of Arts and Sciences at Florida Gulf Coast University. A book series editor for Kent State University Press and reviews editor for *Kritikon Litterarum*, she has served as an invited to speaker on bubonic plague at Shakespeare's Globe Theatre and at the Folger Shakespeare Library, where she held a fellowship. Her sixth book on early modern literature and culture is *Care and Contagion in Shakespeare's Changing World*, co-edited with Darryl Chalk and forthcoming from Arden Shakespeare.

INDEX

aboo (clay eaten in Africa), 157–59
Acosta, Bernadino de, "La vacuna o patriotismo lanzaroteño," 47–48
Acosta, José de, 21–22, 25, 28
  De procuranda Indorum., 21
  Historia del Nuevo Mundo, 31
  Historia natural y moral de las Indias, 19, 21, 24, 28
Act of Uniformity (1662), 58
'Act to Remedy the Evils Arising from the Irregular Assembly of Slaves' 1760, 160
Adams, William, 131
African wasting. *See* dirt eating
Allen, James, 124
Allen, John, *Synopsis Medicinæ*, 83
America, colonial, medicine and religion in, 4–5, 74–99
Anagnostou, Sabine, 29, 30
Annesley, Samuel, 64
Argentina, vaccination in, 53n59
Argerich, Cosme, 44
Arndt, Johann, 76
Arriaga, Pablo José de, 26–28
  The Extirpation of Idolatry, 26–27
Asty, John, 69
Atlantic world, early modern, 175
  medicine and religion in, 4–5, 8, 74–99
Aymara (Indigenous people), 28

Bajamar, Marquis of, 42
Balmis y Berenguer, Francisco Xavier de, 41, 46–47
Barbados, 123
Bartholomew Ejections, 109, 111
Baudelocque, Jean-Louis, 85, 87, 89–90
  A System of Midwifery, 86, 86
Baxter, Richard, 64–65
  Short Instructions for the Sick, 65
Becon, Thomas, 136, 138
Berce, Yves-Marie, 181
Bergosa y Jordan, Antonio, 42–43, 48
Bermuda, 123
Bloch, Ruth, 81
Bohemia, 122
Book of Common Prayer, 58, 62
  plague-specific readings and, 134

Bradstreet, Anne, 1, 3
  "A Dialogue Between Old England and New, Concerning Their Present Troubles, Anno 1642," 1–2, 4
  Several Poems Compiled with Great Variety of Wit and Learning. . . ., 1
  The Tenth Muse, Lately Sprung Up in America, 1
Brazil, smallpox in, 13n27
breastfeeding, 81, 177
  in 17th century, 89–90
  in 18th century, 88–90
  Christianity and, 80–82, 88–89, 95n13
  Mary, mother of Jesus and, 76, 77, 78, 88–89
  medical interest and, 90
  moral interpretation of, 5, 88–94
  providential interpretations of, 5
  See also nursing; wet nursing
Brown, Matthew. See Prynne, William
Brown, Vincent, 163
bubonic plague, 57, 62, 180
  See also plague
Buenos Aires, vaccination in, 44
Bynum, Caroline Walker, 76

Cachexia African (African wasting). *See* dirt eating
Cadogan, William, 91, 93
  Essay on Nursing, 94
Caldera de Heredia, Gaspar, 16, 18
  De pulvere febrifugo Occidentalis Indiae (On the febrifugal powder of the West Indies), 16, 18
  medicinal plants and, 16–18
Calvinist theology, 65
Canary Islands
  Royal Philanthropic Expedition and, 41
  vaccination in, 41
Cañizares-Esguerra, Jorge, 31–32
Caribbean, 150
  smallpox in, 13n27
Carrafa, Juan, 44
Casa-Cagigal, Marquis of, 46, 48
Catholic Church, 19, 34, 42, 175
  parish priests help with vaccination, 44–46
  religious missions, 5
  smallpox and, 7, 181

192 INDEX

Catholic Church (*continued*)
    Spanish Empire and, 5, 12
    vaccination and, 5, 7, 10, 12, 40–55, 181
    See also Jesuit missionaries; Jesuits; Society
        of Jesus
Catholics, 4–5, 122
Cecil, William, 133
Chamberlen, Peter, 60
Charles I, 60, 135
Charles II, 59–60, 69, 120
Charles III, 42
Charles IV, 40, 42
    cowpox vaccine, 41
    vaccination and, 48
childbirth, 5, 177
    18th century discussions of, 88
    in the Atlantic world, 74–99
    Caesarian operations, 84
    in early America, 74–99
    medicine and, 74–99
    morality and, 5, 82–88
    nature and, 82–88
    politics and, 74–99
    providence and, 5, 83, 88
    reason and, 82–88
    religious beliefs and, 5, 10, 74–99
Christianity
    maternity as redemption, 74, 76–82, 88–94
    medicine and, 86, 94
    nursing mother and, 91
    in Spanish America, 27
Church of England, 56, 58–59, 118
Civil War, English, 1, 79, 132–33, 141
Clarendon Code, 58, 64, 109
clay eating. *See* dirt eating
Cobo, Bernabé, 21–24, 25
    Historia del Nuevo Mundo, 21–24, 29–30
Cockenoe, 104
Collins, Dr., *Practical Rules for the Management
    and Medical Treatment of Negro Slaves in
    the Sugar Colonies*, 151
Colombia, 40
Compleat Midwife, The (1698), 89
Concordat of 1753, 42
Convent Carmen, 23
Conventicle Act (1664), 58
Copley, John Singleton, *The Nativity*, 77, 78
Coppe, Abiezer, 60
Corporation Act (1661), 58
Cotton, John, 120
Council of the Indies, 42, 44

Court of Assistants, Boston, 122
Covid-19, 12, 175, 178, 182
    vaccination and, 181–83
cowpox, smallpox and, 40–41
Crab, Roger, 60–61
    *The English Hermite, or, Wonder of This Age:
        Being a Relation of the Life of Roger Crab .
        . . (1655)*, 60
Crashaw, William, 135, 137, 141
Crawford, Mathew James, 9, 11–12, 16–39, 176–78
creoles
    in Europe, 31–32
    in Spanish American, 31–32
Cristobal, Silva, *Miraculous Plagues: An Epidemi-
    ology of Early New England Narrative*, 7
Crocker, Rebecca, 33
Cromberger, Juan, 104
Cromwell, Oliver, 66
Cromwell, Richard, 66
Cuba, vaccination in, 41, 43, 49
Culpeper, Nicholas, 93
    Directory for Midwives, 93
Cutts, Terry, 182

Dancer, Thomas, 165–66
    dirt eating, 150–51, 161–62, 169–70
    *"Malacia Africanorum vel Pica Nigritum the
        Disease of Dirt Eating among the Negros,"*
        150
    Obeah and, 161–62
de la Calancha, Antonio, *Corónica moralizada del
    Orden de San Augustin*, 27
de los Desamparados, Lorenzo Justiniano, 50
Defoe, Daniel, *A Journal of the Plague Year*,
    100–101, 104
Descartes, René, 4
Díaz, Manuel, 45
Diemerbrock, Isbrand de, 89
Dioscorides, 28–29
dirt eating, 169–70, 171n17, 178
    in Africa, 156
    in the Americans, 152
    enslaved populations and, 150–74, 177
    in Ghana, 156
    in Greece, 155
    in history, 156
    on Jamaican plantations, 150–74
    malnutrition and, 152, 155, 159
    medicinal effects of, 155
    misperceptions of, 150–74
    pregnancy and, 156

INDEX 193

punishment of, 162–63, 168
secrecy and, 162–64
as self harm, 167–68
White physicians and, 11, 150–74, 177
disaster, meanings of
John Owen and, 56–73
plague and, 56–73
See also providentialism
disease
in Atlantic world, 5
causes of, 128, 140–43
colonization and, 13n23
contagiousness of, 117–49
enslaved populations and, 5
epidemic, 8
fear of new, 178
Indigenous people and, 36n58
Native populations and, 119
providence and, 125
religious meaning of, 8, 10, 58
spiritual life and, 5, 11
treatment of, 140–43
See also dirt eating; plague; smallpox
dissenters. *See* English Dissenters
Dolittle, Thomas, 64
Doña Isabel, 41
Duffy, John, *From Humors to Medical Science: A History of American Medicine*, 7
Dyer, William, 101, 109, 112–13
"A Call to Sinners. Or Christ's Voice to London," 112
Christ's Voice to London (1666), 101, 112
"The Great Day of His Wrath," 112
"Watch and Pray," 112

Edinburgh Medical and Surgical Journal, 170
Edwards, Bryan, *History, Civil and Commercial, of the British Colonies in the West Indies*, 162
Edwards, Thomas, *Gangreana*, 59
Eliot, John, *Eliot Indian Bible*, 104, 109
Elizabeth I, Queen, 107
Elmer, Peter, 59
England, 9
colonizers' appropriation of Native knowledge of plants, 143
medical practice in, 117–49
occasional worship and, 117–49
plague and, 6–7, 9, 100–16
special services in, 132, 140
English Civil War. *See* Civil War, English
English Dissenters, 10, 56, 62, 66

calamities as punishment, 61–65
John Owen and, 61–65
preachers took up medicine, 59–60
English nonconformity. *See* Nonconformists, English
English Reformation, 68, 78
English Revolution, 59
Enlightenment, 63, 75
"moral motherhood" and, 81
enslaved populations, 162, 164
dirt eating and, 150–74, 177
disease and, 5
Jamaican plantations and, 5, 8, 150–74
self-harm and, 167
spiritual life and, 5
suicide and, 168
White imagination and, 150–74
"Enthusiastick Owenistical Spirit," 57
epidemics, 119
Native Americans and, 6
See also bubonic plague; measles; plague; smallpox
Espada y Fernández de Landa, José Díaz de, 43
España, Gabriel de, 18
European humanism, 175
Europeans
Africans' medical and religious practices, 175
Indigenous peoples and, 175
new diseases and, 175
Eve, 91
childbirth and, 76
punishment of, 80
Ewalt, Margaret, 17, 19

fast days, 141
Colonists and, 122
contagiousness of, 131
Court-ordained, 118
public fast, 134
fasting, 121–22, 137
beliefs about, 117–18, 131
in colonies, 119, 121
contagiousness of, 121, 131
in England, 117–49
Galenic "contrary" and, 137
in Massachusetts, 180
in New England, 117–49
public prayer and, 121
fear, 177–81
novel threats and, 179–81
Ferdinand VI, 42

194   INDEX

Fett, Sharla, 168
Fifth Monarchists, 60
Finch, Martha, 132
Five Mile Act (1665), 58, 109
Fleck, Elaine Cristina Deckmann, 20
Fleetwood, Charles, 63–64, 69
Flores, José, 44, 50
Foster, John, 1
Friedrich, Markus, 19

Galen, 28
General Court of Massachusetts, 131
geophagy. *See* dirt eating
Goffe, William, 57, 62, 64
González del Campillo, Manuel IgnacioII, 43, 49
Governor and Council of the Dominion of New
    England, 103
Grainger, Thomas, 165
granadilla (passionflower), Christian references
    and, 30
Great Fire of London, 56, 101
Great Plague of London, 56, 61, 100–101
    English texts about reprinted in New
        England, 109–13
Greatrakes, Valentine, 61
Green, Samuel, 109
Green, Timothy, 112
Greenblatt, Stephen, 101–2
    "Invisible Bullets: Renaissance Authority and
        Its Subversion, *Henry IV* and *Henry V*," 7
Gribben, Crawford, 10, 12, 56–73, 176
Grindal, Edmund, 133
Guadalajara, 49
Guarani (Indigenous people), 26
    in Paraguay, 23
Guevara Vasconcelos, Manuel de, 48
Gunderson, Gary, 182
gunpowder plot, 105

Hall, David D., 103–4
Hannah (bible), 76
Harriot, Thomas, 7
Harriot, Thomas, *A Brief and True Report of the
    New Found Land of Virginia* (1588), 7
Harris, Steven J., 19
Hartlib circle, 62
Harvey, William, 89
Heath, John, 86
Hobbes, Thomas, 60
Hogarth, Rana A., 8, 10–11, 150–74, 176–78
Holy Roman Empire, 122

Hooke, William, *New Englands Tears for Old
    England*, 133
Hospitaller of the Order of San Juan de Dios, 50
Howell, Joel D., 183
Hunter, John, 151, 156
    *Observations on the Diseases of the Army in
        Jamaica*, 151
Hunter, John M., 155

illness. *See* disease
Imray, John, 169–70
"Indians of Ica Valley," 24
Indigenous botanical healing knowledge, 28–29
    Jesuit missionaries and, 9–10
Indigenous healers, 19
    Jesuit missionaries and, 5, 11, 26–27
    in Peru, 11–12, 26, 178
    seen as sorcerers, 27
Indigenous healing knowledge
    Jesuit missionaries and, 16–39
    Peru and, 8–9, 16–39
Indigenous people
    knowledge of plants, 22, 24
    languages of, 24
    medicines and spirituality, 3
    of Peru, 25
Indigenous religions, 27

Jamaica, 9, 123, 164
    (mis)perceptions of dirt eating and, 150–74
    emancipation and, 157
    enslaved population and, 150–74
    plantations and, 5, 8, 150–74, 171n7
Jamaica Physical Journal, 165
James, succession of, 68
Janeway, James, 64
Jenner, Edward, *Inquiry into the Causes and Effects
    of the Variolae Vaccine*, 40
Jesuit College of San Pablo in Lima, Peru, 32
Jesuit missionaries, 19–20, 32
    botanical knowledge, 31, 34
    botanical knowledge, indigenous, 19, 23–24,
        29–30, 178
    Christian framework for medicine, 31
    Christianization of Indigenous peoples,
        19–20, 30–32
    creole patriotism, 31–32
    discovery of *chinona bark*, 18
    disease in Indigenous people, 31, 36n58
    in early modern Peru, 16–39
    expulsion from Spanish Empire, 25

INDEX 195

healing and, 27
Indigenous healers and, 5, 11, 26–27
indigenous healing knowledge and, 16–39
Indigenous medicine and, 9–10, 16–39, 177
Indigenous religions and, 178
materia medica and, 30
medical histories and, 21
missions and motives of, 30–32
nature and, 12, 16–39, 178
New World, 32
science and, 32, 34
Spanish American, 19
Jesuit texts
"Materia medica misionera,," 22
medicinal plants and, 5, 22, 37n72
Jesuits (Society of Jesus), 19, 32
See also Jesuit missionaries
Johnson, Marmaduke, 104, 109–10
Jones, Colin, 119
Jones, David S, 125
"Virgin Soils Revisited," 6
Josselin, Ralph, 62
Juana Inés de la Cruz, Sor, 3–4
"Primero sueño," or "First I Dream," 3
Juncker, Johann, 93
Juntas de Vacuna. See vaccination boards

Keeble, N. H., 176
King, Edmund, 69
King Philip's War, 124
Kiple, Kenneth, 151–52, 155
Knight, James, 165, 167
Koch, Philippa, 10, 74–99, 176–78

lactation. See breastfeeding
Laud, William, 135
Letter to a Friend Concerning Some of Dr Owens
     Principles and Practices, A, 56–57, 69
Lindman, Janet Moore, 77
Little Ice Age, 58
Locke, John, 81
Long, Edward, 159
Love, William, 122
Lutes, Jean Marie, "Negotiating Theology and
     Gynecology: Anne Bradstreet's Repre-
     sentation of the Female Body,' 3

mal d'estomac. See dirt eating
Manton, Thomas, 64
Manuel de Amayz, Lorenzo, 50
Mapuche tribe, 28

María Semper, José, 47
Marimón, Juan, 47
Mary, mother of Jesus, 76, 80
     breastfeeding and, 76, 77, 78, 88–89
     childbirth and, 76, 78
     motherhood as redemption, 10, 89
     Protestant art and, 77
     Protestant beliefs and, 78
Massachusetts Bay Colony, 7, 104
     fasting practices in, 179–80
     medical practice in, 117–49
     occasional worship and, 117–49
     smallpox outbreaks in, 117
Massachusetts General Court, 103, 123
maternal bodies. See childbirth
maternity
     medical practitioners and, 75
     redemption and, 74
     religion and, 75
     See also childbirth; motherhood
Mather, Cotton, 76, 90, 137
Mather, Increase, 57–58, 121, 124, 134
     preface to Thacher's A Fast of G d's Chusing,
        126
     Thacher's sermon and, 126
Mattes, Mark Alan, 8
Maxwell, James
     dirt eating and, 157–59, 161, 164–65, 167–68
     Obeah and, 161, 164–65
     "Pathological Inquiry into Cachexia Africana as
        It Is Generally Connected with Dirt Eating."
        (1835), 158
     racist views of, 158–59, 164
     Royal College of Surgeons in Edinburgh, 158
measles, 146n47
     outbreak of 1687, 120
Medical Assistant; or, Jamaica Practice of Physic, 150
medicine
     in Christian framework, 29–30
     in England, 117–49
     English medical texts in New England, 101
     epidemic disease in the Atlantic world, 6
     fear of new treatments, 178
     in New England, 117–49
     religion and, 4–6, 9, 101, 177, 180
     See also Indigenous healing knowledge
medicine, Galenic, 180
     fasting and, 180
Memling, Hans, Virgin and Child, 77
Metacom's War. See King Philip's War
Mexico, smallpox in, 13n27

196 INDEX

midwifery, 83–84, 87
  manuals for, 10, 177
  scientific practice of, 88
midwives, 87–88, 92–93
  gender and, 85, 87
  New England colonies, 101
Miller, Kathleen, 1, 11, 12, 100–116, 176, 180, 184
missionary life, illness and, 31
Mohegan (Native American tribe), 6
Monardes, Nicolas, 16–17, 35n5
Montenegro, Pedro, 25, 28–29, 31
  Hospital General in Madrid, 22
  Society of Jesus and, 22
  Spanish America and, 23
Montenegro, Pedro, writing by
  "Materia medica misionera," 22–23, 31
  "Prologue to the Reader" in Materia medica
    misionera, 26
Moore, DaKysha, 183
morality, 177
  childbirth and, 5, 82–88
motherhood, 94
  Enlightenment thought and, 81
  Evangelical thought and, 81
  religion and, 10, 79–82, 88–89 (*see also* Mary,
    mother of Jesus)
Múzquiz y Aldunate, Rafael de, 47

National Library of Madrid, 23
Native Americans, 92
  diseases and, 101, 146n47
  medicines and spirituality, 3
  prisoners of war, 123
  rationalization of deaths of, 125
  smallpox and, 7, 101, 146n47
  See also Mohegan people
Nesutan, Job, 104
New England, religious tracts about plague in,
  101–2
New England, colonial, 9, 126, 133, 136
  diseases in, 101
  English texts about the plague and, 100–116
  fasting in, 121–40
  medicine in, 3, 101, 141
  printing industry in, 101–3, 112
  smallpox and, 7
New Granada, smallpox and, 40
New Granada, Viceroy of, 46
New London press, Connecticut, 113
New Spain (Mexico), vaccination in, 41
Newson, Linda, 33

Nonconformists, English, 10, 58–61
North American colonies, 59
Norton, John, 57
nursing. *See* breastfeeding

Obeah, 161
  Afro-Caribbean spiritual practice, 154, 160
  criminalization of, 160
  dirt eating and, 159, 161–62, 164, 168–70
  indigenous knowledge of plants and, 160
  influence on slaves health, 165
  seen as witchcraft by some whites, 160
  White practitioners and, 159–66
Obeah practitioners, 161
  enslaved healers and, 165
  in Jamaica, 12
  seen as competitors by physicians, 12
  slave rebellions and, 160
  Tacky's Revolt and, 160
occasional days, 122
occasional worship, 123
  in England, 117–49
  fasting and, 133
  in New England, 117–49
Osma, Pedro de, 35n5
Owen, John, 56–73
  anonymous attack on, 56
  Calvinist theology, 65
  death of, 69
  deaths of his children, 62–63
  disaster, religious meaning of, 10, 56–73
  English Dissenters and, 61–65
  English protestantism and, 69
  influence in New England, 57
  plague and, 56–73
  preaching of, 68
  Protestant Christianity and, 66
  providentialism, 10, 56–73
  Religious Nonconformity and, 58–61
  theodicy and, 66
Owen, John, works by
  A Brief Instruction in the Worship of G d, 56,
    66–67
  Of Schism, 63
Owen, Judith, 62–63
Owen, Mary (spouse), 63–64
Owen, Matthew, 62–64

Pablos, Juan, *Breve y mas compendiosa Doctrina
    Christiana en Lengua Mexicana y Castel-
    lana*, 104

INDEX   197

Paraguay, 26, 36n58
    Guarani (Indigenous people) in, 23
    Jesuit missionaries in, 20–21
parish priests
    Juntas Subalternas, 51
    vaccination effort and, 44–46, 53n59
pase regio, 42
Paton, Diana, 160
Pawtuckets (Native American tribe), 146n47
Peru, 19, 30, 36n60, 50
    early modern (1590–1710), 16–39
    Indigenous healers, 11–12, 26, 178
    Indigenous healing knowledge, 8–9, 16–39
    indigenous healing knowledge and, 8–9,
        16–39
    indigenous people in, 25
    Jesuit college in Lima, 21
    Jesuit missionaries in, 5, 11, 12, 16–39, 177
    smallpox and, 40
    smallpox in, 13n27
    vaccination in, 41
Peru, Viceroy of, 24
pestilence. See disease; plague
Peters, Hugh, 132
Philadelphian Society, 60
Philosophical Transactions, 62, 69
physician-ministers, in New England, 12
pica. See dirt eating
Pietist movement, 76
plague, 6, 57
    advanced medical practices and, 119
    in bible (King David brings plagues on
        Israel), 108
    in England, 3, 5, 100, 125
    fasts and days of humiliation, 136
    in France, 102
    John Owen and, 56–73
    meanings of disaster and, 56–73
    New England and, 100–101
    as punishment for sin, 11, 109, 111–13, 119
    Puritans and, 113
    religion and, 5, 107–8
    See also bubonic plague
plague texts, English, 8
    reprinted in New England, 11, 100–116
Plymouth, MA, smallpox outbreaks in, 117
Poletto, Roberto, 20
Pope Benedict XIV, 42
Pordage, John, 60
Poska, Allyson M., 10, 40–55, 176, 181–82
preachers-turned-doctors, 59–61, 119

Presbyterians, 59
Prieto, Andrés, 17, 19, 30, 33–34
    study of "Jesuit science" in South America,
        33
Printer, James, 104
printing presses
    in Boston, 103
    in Cambridge, 103
Protectorial Parliament, 66
Protestant Reformation, 68, 76
Protestantism, 5, 66
    dissent and, 176
Protestants, 122, 178
providence
    childbirth and, 5, 83, 88
    disease, 125
    Owen, John, 10, 56–73
    plague and, 125
providentialism
    John Owen and, 10, 56–73
    Native American disease and, 125
    plague and, 57, 125
    Puritans and, 57
Prynne, William, 135–36
    link between plague deaths and special
        services, 134
Puebla (New Spain), 43
Puerto Rico, Royal Philanthropic Expedition
    and, 41
Puritanism, 5, 59, 63
    medicine and religion indivisible, 3, 103
Puritans, 1, 4, 176
    belief system and, 105
    fatalism and, 125
    medicine and religion related, 2
    New England and, 120
    piety and, 128
    plague and, 6, 57
    providentialism and, 57

Quakers, 77
Quechua (Indigenous people), 28

Ramírez, Vicente, 47
Real Patronato, 42
Records of the Governor and Company of the
    Massachusetts Bay in New England, 122
Reedy, Catherine, 10–12, 117–49, 176, 179–80
religion
    Atlantic world and, 4
    danger of contagion in services, 141

198 INDEX

religion (*continued*)
    medical beliefs and, 175
    medicine and, 2–5, 8, 74–99
    See also providence; providentialism
Restoration, 57–58, 61, 66
Restoration England, 58–61
    religious nonconformity in, 58–61
Rogers, John, 60
    Disputatio medica inauguralis, 60–61
Romay, Dr. Tomás, proponent of vaccination in
    Cuba, 43
Rosillo y Mereulo, Andrés, 48
Rousseau, Jean-Jacques, 81
Royal College of Surgeons Edinburgh, 169
Royal Philanthropic Expedition, 42
    Canary Islands and, 41
    Puerto Rico, 41
    sermons and, 46–49
    smallpox and, 41
    Spanish Empire, 41
    spectacle and, 46–49
    vaccination and, 41, 46–49
    Venezuelan coast, 41
Royal Society, 59, 63
Royal Society of London for Improving
    Knowledge, 82

Sabien, Duncan, 180
    "The Metaphor You Want Is 'Color Blind-
    ness,'" 179
Salas, Juan de, 20–21
Salem, Massachusetts, 1
Salvany y Lleopart, José, 41, 44, 47, 50
Sánchez de León, Don Francisco, 50
Sarah (bible), 76
Sassamon, John, 104
Scientific Revolution, 19, 63, 69
Seaman, Valentine, 87–88
Second Dutch War, 56, 62
Senier, Siobhan, 6
    "Traditionally, Disability Was Not Seen as
    Such," 6
Sharpe, Jane, 93
    Midwives Book (1671), 92–93
Sisti, Leuconoe Grazia, 182
    "The Role of Religions in the Covid-19
    Pandemic: A Narrative Review" (Sisti et
    al), 182
Slack, Paul, 102
smallpox, 6, 40
    in Boston, 11, 101, 117, 144n11
    in Canary Islands, 45

    in Chile, 40
    epidemic of 1677–1679, 125
    in Massachusetts, 123, 146n47
    medical and religious approaches to, 120
    Native Americans and, 101, 146n47
    in New England, 3, 5, 11
    in New Spain (Mexico) and, 40
    religion and, 5, 11
    Royal Philanthropic Expedition and, 41
    Spanish colonization and, 13n27
    viral transmission of, 180
smallpox vaccination, 40–55
    Catholic Church and, 40–55
    in Spanish Empire, 40–55
    See also vaccination
Smellie, William, 83–85
    *A Treatise on the Theory and Practice of Mid-
    wifery*, 84
Smith, Nigel, 59
Society of Jesus. *See* Jesuits
Solomon, 94
Spain, vaccination and, 51n1
Spanish America, 34
    Jesuit missionaries and, 30
    nature in, 30
    shortage of healers and, 28
Spanish Armada, 105
Spanish colonists, Indigenous use of plants and, 178
Spanish colonists, Indigenous use of plants and, 23
Spanish Crown, 42
    Catholic Church and, 43, 51
    papacy and, 42
    smallpox vaccination and, 41, 181
    vaccination and, 41, 43, 49, 51
Spanish Empire, 8–9, 40
    collapse of, 51
    medical and scientific discovery in, 8
    Royal Philanthropic Expedition and, 41
    smallpox vaccination and, 5, 7, 9–10, 40–55
    vaccine distribution by Catholic Church, 5
Spanish government
    church and, 182
    smallpox epidemic and, 182
Spanish New World, 9
    smallpox in, 13n27
Spanish Viceroyalty of Peru, 20
Stubbe, Henry, 59–60
Sydenham, Thomas, 125, 143–44
    Medical Observations (1676), 120

Tacky's Revolt, 160
Taylor, Jeremy, 78, 80, 88, 94
    motherhood, religion and, 79–82, 88–89

INDEX 199

Taylor, Jeremy, works by
    The Great Exemplar of Sanctity and Holy Life
      According to the Christian Institution, 78
    "Of Nursing Children in Imitation of the
      Blessed Virgin Mother," 79
Taylor, N. Kenji, 183
Thacher, Thomas, 117–18, 128, 143–44
    fast-day sermon, 121
    Third Church in Boston, 117
Thacher, Thomas, works by
    A Brief Rule, 117, 120–21
    A Fast of God's Chusing, 117–18, 120–21, 126
"Thanksgiving Day" proclaimed by Lincoln, 123
Thomson, James, 156–57, 159, 161, 163
    guidebook on "Negro diseases," 156
    guidebooks and, 165
Thornton, John, 63
Tompson, Joseph, 126–27, 130
    diaries of, 128, *129*
    Journal, 127, *130*
    smallpox and, 126
Toon, Peter, 63
Totaro, Rebecca, 175–84
Trans-Atlantic World conference, Trinity
    College, Dublin (2013), 4
Tuskegee, Alabama, 183
Tyrell, Thomas, 64

University of Edinburgh, 157
University of Oxford, 56

vaccination, 40–55
    administration of, 49–50
    in the Americas, 50
    Catholic Church and, 40–55
    Indian curanderos and, 50
    parish priests and, 44–46
    role of bishops in, 49–50
    Royal Philanthropic Expedition and, 41,
      46–49
    smallpox and, 40–55
    Spanish Empire and, 45
Vaccination Boards, 51
van Deventer, Hendik, *Art of Midwifery Improv'd,*
    82–83
Vatican, vaccination and, 42
Venezuela, 40
    Royal Philanthropic Expedition and, 41
Verdugo y Albiturría, Bishop, 46, 50
Viana, Domingo, 48
Vincent, Thomas, 64, 101, 109, 110–12
    God's Terrible in the City (1667), 101, 103, 109–12
    printings of works, 109–11, 113

Wally, Thomas, 126–27, 131
Walwyn, William, 60
Webster, Charles, 59
Wednesday Fast, 135
West, Benjamin
    The Artist and His Family, 77, 79
    Penn's Treaty with the Indians (painting), 92
wet nursing, 92–93
Whalley, Edward, 57, 62, 64
White, J., *Pathetic History of the Plague in London,*
    in the Year 1665. . . ., 100
White physicians, 154
    Black populations and, 153
    dirt eating and, 11, 150–74, 177
    Obeah and, 161–62
    slavery and, 154
Wigglesworth, Michael
    Day of Doom, 137
    Meat out of Eater, 140
Williamson, John, 150–51
Wilson, John, 106
    Blackfriars, 105
    English monarchs, 105
    English plague and, 107–8
    founder of First Church of Boston, 105
    in Massachusetts Bay Colony, 105
    plague and religion, 108
    son John's preface, 107
    works printed in England and New England,
      101, 105–6
Wilson, John, works by
    A Song of Deliverance for the Lasting Remem-
      brance of Gods Wonderful Works Never to
      Be Forgotten. . . ., 104, 109
    A Song or, Story, for the Lasting Remembrance
      of Diuers Famous Works, Which God Hath
      Done in Our Time. . . ., 101, 103
women
    18th century America and Atlantic World, 94
    African, 91
    in colonial sites in British Empire. (*see*
      motherhood)
    in early American republic, 94
women's bodies
    18th century America and Atlantic World, 74
    in religion and in science, 82

Yersinia pestis (plague). *See* plague

Zacetecas (New Spain), 46–47